Claire Denis

D1611146

Published in our
centenary year
≈ **2004** ≈
MANCHESTER
UNIVERSITY
PRESS

FRENCH FILM DIRECTORS

Claire Denis

MARTINE BEUGNET

Manchester University Press
MANCHESTER AND NEW YORK

distributed exclusively in the USA by Palgrave

The right of Martine Beugnet to be identified as the author of this work
has been asserted by her in accordance with the Copyright, Designs and
Patents Act 1988.

Published by Manchester University Press
Oxford Road, Manchester M13 9NR, UK
and Room 400, 175 Fifth Avenue, New York, NY 10010, USA
www.manchesteruniversitypress.co.uk

Distributed exclusively in the USA by
Palgrave, 175 Fifth Avenue, New York, NY 10010, USA

Distributed exclusively in Canada by
UBC Press, University of British Columbia, 2029 West Mall, Vancouver,
BC, Canada V6T 1Z2

British Library Cataloguing-in-Publication Data
A catalogue record for this book is available from the British Library

Library of Congress Cataloging-in-Publication Data applied for

ISBN 0 7190 6480 5 *hardback*
 0 7190 6481 3 *paperback*

First published 2004

13 12 11 10 09 08 07 06 05 04   10 9 8 7 6 5 4 3 2 1

Typeset in Scala with Meta display
by Koinonia, Manchester
Printed in Great Britain
by Bell & Bain Ltd., Glasgow

Contents

List of plates

Series editors' foreword

To an anglophone audience, the combination of the words 'French' and 'cinema' evokes a particular kind of film: elegant and wordy, sexy but serious – an image as dependent on national stereotypes as is that of the crudely commercial Hollywood blockbuster, which is not to say that either image is without foundation. Over the past two decades, this generalised sense of a significant relationship between French identity and film has been explored in scholarly books and articles, and has entered the curriculum at university level and, in Britain, at A level. The study of film as an art-form and (to a lesser extent) as industry, has become a popular and widespread element of French Studies, and French cinema has acquired an important place within Film Studies. Meanwhile, the growth in multi-screen and 'art-house' cinemas, together with the development of the video industry, has led to the greater availability of foreign-language films to an English-speaking audience. Responding to these developments, this series is designed for students and teachers seeking information and accessible but rigorous critical study of French cinema, and for the enthusiastic filmgoer who wants to know more.

The adoption of a director-based approach raises questions about *auteurism*. A series that categorises films not according to period or to genre (for example), but to the person who directed them, runs the risk of espousing a romantic view of film as the product of solitary inspiration. On this model, the critic's role might seem to be that of discovering continuities, revealing a necessarily coherent set of themes and motifs which correspond to the particular genius of the individual. This is not our aim: the *auteur* perspective on film, itself most clearly articulated in France in the early 1950s, will be interrogated in certain volumes of the series, and, throughout, the director will be treated as one highly significant element in a complex process of film production and reception which includes socio-economic and political determinants, the work of a large and highly skilled team of artists and technicians, the mechanisms of production and distribution, and the complex and multiply determined responses of spectators.

The work of some of the directors in the series is already known outside France, that of others is less so – the aim is both to provide informative and original English-language studies of established figures, and to extend the range of French directors known to anglophone students of cinema. We intend the series to contribute to the promotion of the informal and formal study of French films, and to the pleasure of those who watch them.

DIANA HOLMES
ROBERT INGRAM

Acknowledgements

I would like to thank the following: La Bibliothèque du Film; Le Forum des Images; La Fondation Cartier; Arena Films. I am grateful to the Arts and Humanities Research Board for the Research Leave Award, and to the Carnegie Fund and Edinburgh University's Research Fund for the grants that enabled me to carry out this work. Thanks also to editor Olivier Barlet for granting permission to use material published in my book *Sexualité, marginalité, contrôle – Cinéma français contemporain*, published by L'Harmattan. Thanks to Jane Sillars, co-author of the article, and to the editors of *Studies in French Cinema*, for granting me permission to use material published as part of an article on *Beau travail*. Thanks to Geneviève and Olivier of the *Inrockuptibles*; thanks to Eero Porko, Peter Rimmer and Marie Campbell; and thanks to Diana Holmes – for her precious help – and Robert Ingram, editors of the series.

Introduction

Claire Denis' first film, *Chocolat* (1988) was a deceptively gentle family chronicle set in colonial Africa. Selected for the Cannes Festival, it was hailed by the critics and festival audiences as a remarkable first feature. In 2001, part of the same Cannes Festival public booed and left the theatre during the screening of the controversial *Trouble Every Day* (2001), a lyrical and gory account of vampirism in today's Paris. In between, Denis has shot several shorts (*Keep It For Yourself*, 1991, *La Robe à cerceau*, 1992, *Nice, Very Nice*, 1995), documentaries (*Man No Run*, 1989, *Jacques Rivette, Le Veilleur/The Sentinel*, 1990, *Contre l'oubli/Against Oblivion*, 1992) and video-art films (*Duo*, 1995, *A propos d'une déclaration/Declaration of Love*, 1995), as well as a series of fiction films made for the cinema and for television. In contrast with the relatively lush production of *Chocolat*, her second feature, *S'en fout la mort* (*No Fear, No Die*, 1990), is a dark drama set in the French underworld of cockfighting, and stylistically close to the documentary. It was followed by *US Go Home* (1994) a bittersweet coming-of-age film set in the mid-1960s. Released the same year, *J'ai pas sommeil* (*I Can't Sleep*, 1993) plays on the conventions of the *noir* genre to unravel a complex tale of serial murders set in nocturnal Paris. Shot in Marseille, the next feature, *Nénette et Boni* (1996), explores the link between sensuality and emotions through the unorthodox depiction of a brother–sister relationship. In 2000, Denis produced the critically acclaimed *Beau travail* (*Good Work*), a highly stylised work about the French Foreign Legion filmed in Djibouti. Denis came back to Paris to shoot *Trouble Every Day*, which was followed by *Vendredi soir* (*Friday Night*). Premiered at the Venice Festival 2002, *Vendredi soir*, Denis' second book adaptation after *Beau travail*, depicts the brief encounter of two strangers in a Paris brought to a standstill by a transport strike.

Based on these succinct descriptions, Denis' filmography may appear protean. The filmmaker herself claims to have no preconceived, coherent vision of her 'trajectory'. When asked, in Sébastien Lifshitz's filmed documentary, *Claire Denis, La Vagabonde* (1995),[1] to define the overall direction of her work, she answered: 'Ce qui est troublant, c'est que j'ai une vision floue de cette perspective ... Hors les films, pas de sens'.[2] Denis' filmmaking eschews conventions and pastiche, but it nevertheless draws on a diversity of genres. It also features a wide array of locations and atmospheres, and constructs a highly diverse set of characters and story lines. Yet, beyond this apparent versatility, a remarkable aesthetic and thematic consistency marks the development of her work, and underpins her emergence, since the late 1980s, as one of the most important directors of contemporary independent cinema.

Denis' stories are tales of foreignness – a foreignness that is simultaneously physical and mental, geographical and existential. In its narrative, stylistic and aesthetic aspects, her filmmaking strives to find the cinematic form best suited to evoke the often unspoken feeling of exile and sense of want[3] that besets contemporary individual consciousness. She focuses on ordinary people, men and women, black and white, homosexuals and heterosexuals, whom displacement and difference have set apart, relegated to the outskirts of society and to the margins of representation.[4] Her cinema eschews

1 Significantly, Lifshitz chose a title that recalls that of a documentary on Jean Genet, underground cult figure of the French literary and art worlds, whose work is an important reference for Denis: *Jean Genet, Le Vagabond*, Michel Dumoulin, 1992.

2 'The troubling thing is that I don't have a clear vision of a trajectory ... Outside of the films themselves, there is no sense.' (Unless stated otherwise, the translations of extracts of interviews and articles in French are mine.)

3 French writers often talk of the contemporary *malaise* to evoke the lack of direction and of guiding ideals that marks contemporary Western societies. Traditionally, one's identity, as well as the meaning of one's existence, was based on a religious, or on an ideological, pre-existing model. While it opens up the possibility for more diverse systems of values, the disappearance of such beliefs also left a void, an anxiety about the future, and weakened the individual's sense of identity and belonging.

4 'I always consider that to make a film – all that energy, all that money – is to put the camera in the direction of the people I want to see and not the people I watch

the expository mode to probe the more hidden implications of the multiform experience of exclusion, and in particular the internalisation of discriminatory discourses. The foreignness at the heart of Denis' films thus needs to be understood in the widest sense of the term. In its most immediate meaning, it is the experience of being displaced, the desire or fear of becoming integrated, assimilated or marginalised in a foreign land. But it is also an inner feeling of fragmentation and meaninglessness that may, in the extreme, express itself through the hatred of the Other, through self-hatred or through the loss of any sense of identity. In effect, there are few filmmakers whose body of work encapsulates better than Denis' the deep-seated malaise that inhabits the collective psyche of our postcolonial world.

Denis' filmmaking never ceases to question definitions and value systems based on binary oppositions, where the Other[5] is reduced to what 'I/we are not', where foreignness and differences are stigmatised and fetishised[6] so as to reinforce, by contrast, our feeling of belonging to a unified, coherent community. On the contrary, in her films, the perception of the Other is always complex and ambiguous. As the foreign body, neither fully defined nor fully understood, otherness may trigger fear or rejection. But the unknown is also that which spurs curiosity and creates desire. Beyond the investigation of cross-cultural and cross-racial tensions, the foreignness that imbues her filmmaking thus functions equally as an opening, an invitation to

---

on TV.' Claire Denis in interview with Jonathan Romney, *The Guardian NFT interview*, www.filmunlimited.co.uk, 2000.

5 The terms Other and Otherness are essential notions in postcolonial and gender studies and play a crucial part in an analysis of Denis' work. They designate an entity (not only a human, but also a geographical or a cultural reality for instance) that represents that which I cannot 'recognise' or comprehend fully. The Other can thus become synonymous with desire or with fear, and in traditional/binary discourses, including in cinematic form, the Other has been cast primarily as that which threatens my identity, that which I must strive to assimilate or destroy.

6 In the process of transforming Otherness into a fetish, difference (racial, sexual, cultural, social, etc.) ceases to be one element of definition amongst others, to become the only element that is taken into account: one person amongst other persons becomes a White amongst Blacks for exemple. As such, Otherness is fetishised, privileged over any common ground that exists between myself and an individual or a community designated as the Other.

explore uncharted territories of human experience and of cinema. The experience of exile and the encounter with the unfamiliar become intrinsic parts of the *mise en scène*[7] of desire and a necessary premise to a narrative, formal and sensual experimentation. From up close or far away, the foreign territory, in its geographic or human form, is at one and the same time fascinating, mysterious and threatening. As such, it takes up its role as the source of the fiction and as the driving force behind the narrative – the Other that generates, and reciprocates, an integral confusion of fear and desire – and emerges as a crucial, constitutive element of cinematic pleasure. Denis' body of work includes films that may appear opposed in their principal concerns: films that present an acutely critical vision of a contemporary world poisoned by latent currents of discrimination, unfairness and hatred, and films that use cinema as a means to explore the sources of desire and sensual awakening. The one principle that underlies her approach throughout, however, corresponds to the ambiguous status of the Other: the principle of the unknown as an irreducible part of human reality and a necessary companion to movement and to desire. 'All my films function as a movement toward an unknown Other and toward the unknown in relation to other people' (Romney 2000). Ultimately, the foreignness that imbues Denis' films' elliptical narratives and enigmatic characters and creates the atmosphere specific to her cinematic world is the foreignness that besets and inhabits each of us. It is, in Julia Kristeva's words:

> Symptôme qui rend précisément le 'nous' problématique, peut-être impossible, l'étranger commence lorsque surgit la conscience de ma différence et s'achève lorsque nous nous reconnaissons tous étrangers, rebelles aux liens et aux communautés.[8] (Kristeva 1988: 9)

Denis' filmmaking plays not only on our attraction to the foreign and the mysterious, but also on our fascination for that which is out of bounds and unlawful. Even as they portray the most ordinary places and situations, her films draw on the effect of defamiliarisation that

7 The *mise en scène* is the organisation (composition, lighting, choreography of the movements in front of the camera, etc.) of all the elements (from the setting to the human figure and the props) to be filmed.
8 'A symptom that renders the "we" problematic, maybe impossible, foreignness starts when the consciousness of my difference emerges, and finishes when we all recognise ourselves as strangers, refractory to bonds and to communities.'

cinema can create so powerfully. No matter how banal it may initially appear, the real has a hidden face, occasionally threatening, and always intriguing.

This book will attempt to outline the multi-faceted, poetic vision of the contemporary world that emerges through Denis' filmmaking to date, and to bring to light its main thematic, temporal, spatial and stylistic implications. The analysis will focus primarily on her fictional feature films, which form the main body of her work and have generally become easily accessible in video or DVD format. It will also include brief discussions of her documentary and short films. Less readily available for viewing, these works nevertheless form an important aspect of her filmmaking, and help to identify determinant cinematic and artistic references.

The book will develop from the general to the specific. The opening chapter, 'Foreignness and the aesthetics of the unsaid', summarises the principal aspects of the director's biographical and professional background, with reference to the wider historical context, and to French cinema production in general. It proceeds with an outline of the director's thematic and aesthetic approach, and highlights the recurrent features of her work. The following chapters provide detailed analysis of each of her feature films. The works are grouped in thematic rather than chronological order so as to bring forth the issues that appear central in Denis' approach as a whole. Chapter 2, 'Screening exile' (*Chocolat, Man No Run, S'en fout la mort, Contre l'oubli, J'ai pas sommeil, Beau travail*) will focus on the representation of cultural tensions, and the issues of colonialism, identity and difference. Chapter 3 (*Duo, A propos d'une déclaration, US Go Home, Nénette et Boni, Trouble Every Day, Vendredi soir*), will concentrate on (sexual) transgression as exploration, and on the 'correspondences' – the sensual and symbolic analogies – at work in Denis' filmmaking.

Throughout, the study will stress the link between Denis' work and a tradition of counter-culture, both cinematic and literary. As such, the analysis of the films will highlight the director's renewed fascination for the concepts of the sublime and the abject, and of difference and desire's irreducible bond. It will also illustrate her attachment to the elaboration of a poetic vision detached from the hegemony of causality and explanation, her drive to create a cinema that explores the fluid, uncertain relationship between time and narration, identity and truth.

References

Denis, Claire (2000), Lifetime series, www.ammi.org/calendar/SeriesArchives, accessed 12 January 2003.
Kristeva, Julia (1988), *Étrangers à nous-mêmes*, Paris, Gallimard.
Lifshitz, Sébastien (1995), *Claire Denis, la Vagabonde*, 48 minute documentary, colour, Prod. La Fémis.

Foreignness and the aesthetics of the unsaid

Cinema, stories and histories

One crucial source to Denis' initial approach to cinema is a seminal convergence of History and personal history. Explicitly present in her first feature, *Chocolat*, the director's early experiences made her sensitive to certain issues and spurred her interest in themes that she continued to explore in subsequent films: oppression and misappropriation, exile and racism, alienation and transgression. Thus, from an early encounter with 'an established order that, already in my childhood, appeared unfair' (Lifshitz 1995),[1] grew a questioning of the ethics of belonging and appropriation:

> En France, je ne me sens pas du tout chez moi. Peut-être parce que je n'ai pas grandi en France. Mais en Afrique, je me sentais étrangère parce qu'on comprend assez bien, quand on est un petit enfant blanc, qu'on est pas de cette terre-là.[2] (Denorme and Douin 2001: 21)
> Je trouvai moral – je ne peux pas dire autrement – d'expliquer ma place par rapport à l'Afrique, ma place symbolique.[3] (Lifshitz 1995)

Claire Denis was born in 1948, the daughter of an administrator of the French colonial services. She spent her childhood in West Africa with her parents and her younger sister, moving country wherever her father's post required the family to settle. She thus lived on

---

1 'un ordre qui, déjà dans mon enfance, me paraissait injuste'.
2 'I do not feel at all at home in France. Maybe because I did not grow up here. But in Africa, I felt foreign because when you are a white child you understand pretty well that you are not from this land.'
3 'I found it moral – I cannot say otherwise – to explain my place in relation to Africa, my symbolic place.'

colonial soil during the last ten years of the French rule, as the movements of independence gathered momentum. This feeling of the end
of an era is clearly present in *Chocolat*, voiced in particular by one of
the characters, the French administrator of the settlement, who
readily admits that the colonial presence is merely continuing on
borrowed time. Denis grew up a foreigner, and a representative,
albeit, as a young girl, a marginal one, of an oppressive colonial power.
Yet, her 'coming back' to France, at 14, was a return to a country
where she belonged by nationality, but which she did not know at all.
She settled with her mother and sister in one of Paris's newly built
suburbs, similar to the ones depicted in *US Go Home*: an unfinished
zone where the expanding urban space met the remains of a
vanishing countryside. The director often stressed in her interviews
how these early experiences made her consciously and unconsciously
receptive to certain debates – to the social and cultural conflicts that
destabilise conventional notions of belonging and national identity,
the traditional beliefs in progress and in universal common good: 'J'ai
eu envie de parler de la fin de la colonisation. Parce que c'est quelque-
chose que j'ai connu, où les choses se *delete* (sic) un petit peu, où les
certitudes s'en vont' (Lifshitz 1995).[4]

Denis' films stand out from the main trends of contemporary
French cinema where the treatment of similar issues has tended to be
either heavily didactic, or, more frequently, adapted and rendered
more palatable through the deforming lens of nostalgia. Indeed, a
constant reference to the historical background appears necessary not
only to comprehend the complex, often indirect way in which the
director's films, even when set in contemporary times, relate to a past
that is inextricably enmeshed with the present, but also to place her
work in the context of the French film production as a whole.

The period and circumstances of Denis' childhood are linked to a
series of events that not only precipitated a massive political change,
but also actualised a profound shift in the fundaments of Western
systems of thought. The advent of the wars of independence and
decolonisation undermined the very basis of the universalist ideal of
historical progression of which modern France in particular had been
a champion. By the same token, it also brought into question the

---

4 'I wanted to talk about the end of the colonial period. Because it is a period I
lived through, where things began to delete, where certitudes disappeared'.

whole structure of binary oppositions on which much of Western identity had been constructed.

> In France, 'crisis' seems to be the most popular term used to describe this predicament, although *malaise* must run it a close second ... Pluralism challenges uniformity, relativism challenges truth, hierarchies have been flattened, assimilation has broken down, the margins are at the centre, a sense of history has given way to an undifferentiated present. Faith in the future and progress has dissolved into a multitude of anxieties about self and the world. (Silverman 1999: 4–5)

The disappearance of the colonial empires, and the realisation, albeit partial, of what had been involved in the process of colonisation, contributed to further the demise of the traditional 'grand narratives'[5] of human progress. The concept of historical progression had arguably already been rendered obsolete by the revelation of the horror of the Holocaust (how could this unspeakable event be compatible with the concept of a progression of humanity in time?). The decolonisation process further questioned the status of a Western culture that had so far posited itself as the superior model, and made itself the source and the centre of a universal 'civilising' project. The former colonies did not simply reject this model, but fought for their political independence and for the affirmation of their own identities.

Historically, the occidental world has tended to define itself and to legitimise its supremacy and aggressive imperialism through a discourse[6] of difference primarily based on binary oppositions: Christian versus heathen, male versus female, black versus white, poor versus rich, etc. The colonies had become a crucial part of this process. The very project of imperial conquest rested on the concept of a superior model that should be exported and duplicated, and like other colonial powers, France cast itself as the civilised norm. At the same time, the

---

5 The term 'grand narrative' was coined by Jean-François Lyotard to designate a narrative that claims to be universal, to explain the historical process and include all other narratives. The grand narrative of colonialism for instance, based on enlightenment ideals such as reason and the notion of universal knowledge, posits universal progress as its legitimation and goal. One characteristic of postmodernity is to question such grand narratives (Christianity, Enlightenment, Colonialism, Marxism, Capitalism, etc.).

6 Here, the term discourse is used in a sense that connects it to ideology: as a system of exposition (verbal, visual, written and so on) destined to promote a set of ideas.

'differences' between *métropole*[7] and colonies were exploited and exacerbated, and helped to reinforce the feelings of national (and racial) unity and superiority. In its portrayal of the perverse, lingering effects of the colonial ethos on the psyche of the colonisers and of the colonized, Denis' work, like much of the output originated in the postcolonial debate, is indebted to the writings of the psychoanalyst Frantz Fanon. Fanon was one of the first to investigate in any depth the impact of the internalising process of inferiority that widely affected those who lived in former colonies or had come from these territories to establish themselves in France. Importantly, the psycho-analyst also underlined the likely persistence of this process on the oppressed as well as on the oppressing nations long after the decolonisation.

Cinema contributed greatly to the elaboration of a fantasised empire. During the colonial era, a flurry of films exalted feelings of adventure and exoticism and played a crucial role in the development of a fascination for faraway lands and the foreign Other and their transformation into spectacles (Ezra 2000). Cinema's ability to construct an apparently 'authentic' vision of reality, and its essentially visual quality, turned it into a privileged vector for a discourse of difference. As former colonies regained their independence, often through a bloody process of armed struggle and civil war, the French national identity was forced to redefine itself in completely new terms. Yet, and this partly underpins the significance of the kind of work produced by Denis and a handful of other directors, the coming to terms with decolonisation, the process of 'mourning' and of potential reconciliation which should have accompanied the elabora-tion of a new sense of identity in the former colonies and *métropole*, was obstructed by denial and censorship. Unsurprisingly, taken the impact of film on mass audiences and its past link with the colonising project, this collective forgetting or blindness (at first, a deliberate, then an internalised process of denial) particularly affected cinema. The few directors who chose to address the issue did so in an indirect

---

7 Interestingly, this term, used to designate both a capital city and a state that rules over a colonial empire, derives from the ancient Greek terms for city and for *mother*. In keeping with such terminology, the inhabitants of the colonies were often described as 'children'.

fashion, or were mercilessly censored.[8] 'Colonial wars were doomed topics (*sujets maudits*). French people did not want to be confronted with their past, and amnesia dominated French screens and French history generally until the 1970s.' (Sherzer 1996: 7). Indeed, even in the face of the contemporary conflicts inherited from it, large parts of the history of the colonisation and of the de-colonisation still remain overlooked, and have almost never been evoked on screen.

After this period of virtual invisibility, the colonial theme came back into fashion in the 1970s with the detailed historical reconstitutions of the *rétro* trend, and became one of the topics treated by the large-budget productions of heritage cinema (Austin 1996: 28–42). As part of the *rétro* or heritage genre, a number of films attempted to portray the colonial past with a degree of criticism: 'With regard to representation of the natives in the films of the 1980s and 1990s, in comparison with those of the 1930s, the casting has changed. It is no longer conceivable to have an Arab or an African played by a white actor. Nor is it any longer acceptable to have non-white characters playing roles of inept, ridiculous or childish individuals' (Sherzer 1996: 9). But even then, the nostalgia of the former imperial grandeur tends to overshadow potential feelings of collective guilt, and if some of the exploitative aspects of the colonial rule are depicted, greater attention is often granted to the suffering of the defeated colonials (Austin 1996: 151). The dominant approach was to continue to exploit the former colonies' potential as exotic backdrop for the adventures and conflicts of primarily white heroes, thus operating the kind of symbolic reappropriation of the lost territories that Denis sternly refutes:

> Quand j'étais jeune et que je lisais *La Ferme africaine* de Karen Blixen, je m'étouffais de rage. Cette nostalgie pour la terre, cette terre, cette culture, cette ferme ... Ce sentiment d'amour était infâme, parce qu'ils ne lui appartenaient pas ... Si je l'aime, je me l'approprie, et je n'en ai pas le droit.[9] (Lifshitz 1995)

---

8 See for instance Alain Resnais and Chris Marker's *Les Statues meurent aussi* (1952), Paul Carpita's *Rendez-vous sur les quais* (1953), Jean Rouch's *Les Maîtres fous* (1954), mentioned in the discussion on *Trouble Every Day*, Jean-Luc Godard's *Le Petit soldat* (1960), discussed in relation to *Beau travail*.

9 'When I was young, and I was reading *Out of Africa*, by Karen Blixen, I used to choke with rage. This nostalgia for the land, that land, that culture, that farm ... That expression of love was infamous because none of this belonged to her ... By loving it, I appropriate it and I have no right to do so.'

The nostalgic mood and the renewed fashion for the exotic also signalled a distinctive change in the nature of contemporary discourses of exclusion within the former imperialist countries themselves. Whereas the principle of assimilation (to a Western model) that legitimised the colonial project was based on a seemingly 'progressive' idea of a universal good, the postcolonial discourse of discrimination is essentially 'regressive'. Its driving principle is that of a return to a former state of affairs, before the emergence of multi-ethnic societies in the West, before a (fantasised)[10] unified nation was challenged by the lasting presence of the Other on its soil. Many of Denis' characters – Jocelyn and Dah in *S'en fout la mort*, Daïga and Théo in *J'ai pas sommeil*, for instance – encounter such forms of 'New Racisms' (Silverman 1999).

Latent discourses thus mutate but continue to inhabit our spoken and written languages, to influence our strategies of representation, and to inflect the grammar and aesthetics of our cinemas: the way things and people are filmed keep on shaping and informing the vision that is proposed to the spectator. In the 1970s, feminist film theory demonstrated its effect on the representation of gender. The techniques at play in the representation of race in film also came under scrutiny, with their insistence on difference and emphatic presentation of the racial Other as exotic spectacle. Elizabeth Ezra has underlined how cinema combined, very early on, entertainment and a seemingly ethnographic approach: in precisely plotted and composed scenes, the 'colonial subject' was, from the start, shown as an exotic 'type' (Ezra 2000). Such procedures persist in the cinema of the postcolonial era, combined with subtle strategies of opposition: one of the techniques of the heritage cinema of empire consists in using 'native' people as ('colourful') setting and backdrop against which the destiny of the (white) heroes unfolds. Such conventions, and the implicit discourse that they carry, are constantly in question in Claire Denis' films, in her stylistic as well as thematic choices. As we will see, as a historical production, her first feature is in some aspects close to a heritage-type of cinema. Yet even *Chocolat* is usually set apart, associated with the different approach of a '*Féminin colonial*' (see Chapter 2) that eschews factual and spectacular reconstructions

10 Like any other Western nation, throughout its history, France has been a human melting pot. The nostalgia for a 'pure', original France is nothing more than a delusion.

to present an un-heroic past devoid of embellishments and justifications.

In none of Denis' subsequent films are faraway locations and a historical mode combined. To paraphrase Lola Young, after *Chocolat*, Denis' exploration of cross-racial and cross-cultural tensions leaves the depiction of a 'then' and 'out there' to concentrate mainly on the portrayal of a contemporary 'over here' (Young 1996: 21). The kind of nostalgic overtones that still inhabit the partly autobiographical world of *Chocolat* reappear in *Beau travail*, but subsumed by a profound sense of *malaise* and doubt. In this, her directing trajectory appears to parallel the emergence of an alternative vision first imposed by a *beur* cinema (*beur* means Arab in retro slang) and of a *'cinéma black'*, and also reflected in much of the new realism of the 1990s. While the countries that were former colonies continued to produce their own cinema and to propose new cinematic representations of their colonial past, in the 1980s, a number of directors had begun to depict life in a multiethnic France. Black and *beur* cinemas focused in particular on the 'second generation' (young French people born in France of parents who were originally immigrants) growing up in one of the *cités*, the housing estates established in the 1960s and 1970s in the suburbs of large cities. The *cinéma de banlieue* (literally, the 'cinema of the suburbs', a denomination that includes much of *beur* and black cinema) tends to depict life amongst largely disenfranchised communities, charting the effect of a *fracture sociale* (the widening economic and 'social gap' that splits French society into classes) partly inherited from the country's colonial past and initiated in the aftermath of decolonisation. In the 1990s, French cinema seemed to continue its mutation with a renewed focus on social issues: a new realist trend was putting on screen stories of ordinary people and their daily problems shot in unexceptional locations. Denis' main thematic concerns seem related to these trends, yet the similarities are limited. Denis' films do not yield to the expository ambitions and didactic messages that have characterised a large part of the *cinéma de banlieue* for instance. Even though many of her central characters are immigrants or belong to ethnic minorities, they rarely resemble the staple, well-defined characters created by the typical films of the *cinéma de banlieue*. Most strikingly, it is the combination of a highly stylised approach applied to a complex thematic texture and provocative subjects that creates the distinctive quality of Denis' films. *Beau travail* and *Vendredi soir* are arguably the most accomplished examples of a filmmaking that privileges the visual and the rhythmic (that is, the way the images are edited together but also the structure of the soundtrack, ambient or musical) over scripted dialogue and plot. *Trouble Every Day* is probably the most daring in its choice of subject and its play on the tradition of horror cinema. This renewed formal quest and the favouring of taboo topics set her work apart from the documentary and MTV-inspired *cinéma de banlieue* or from the deceptively raw style of the New Realism of the 1990s. Denis' specific approach, as well as her set of cinematic, artistic and literary sources brings her closer to a contemporary French 'cinema of abjection' (Beugnet 2003) represented by the atypical films of directors such as Bruno Dumont, Gaspar Noé, Philippe Grandieux or Catherine Breillat. In common with the work of some of these filmmakers, Denis' filmmaking draws from a complex tradition of underground culture that extends across art forms and national borders, from France to the USA and from literature to music, and includes authors such as Baudelaire, Lautréamont, Bataille, Fanon, Himes, Genet, and Fassbinder. As we will see, Denis' preferences point to those writers, filmmakers and artists whose production belongs to the art of the outcast and the subversive, to the social, cultural, racial and sexual margins.

Denis' is a cinema of observation, but one that reconstructs its own reality, focusing and lingering on the darker zones, the cracks that belie the existence of a coherent, unified reality. Whether the trajectories of her characters are considered from the point of view of exclusion, desire or transgression, her filmmaking appears sustained by 'ce désir qui les constitue de traverser quelque chose pour aller voir au delà' (Denorme and Douin 2002: 20) ('the desire to cross in order to see beyond').

A contemporary *cinéma d'auteur*

In their superimposition of the personal (the distinctive style, recurrent themes and the presence of autobiographical elements) and the historical (in the sense of the wider cultural, political and socio-economical framework in which the films are elaborated) Denis' films may usefully be described as *auteur* cinema. But the concept of authorship, especially when applied to film,[11] remains fraught with ambiguities, and in the present instance, it needs to be understood in its complex, contemporary meaning. The *auteur* cinema concerned here cannot be defined merely as the individual expression of a singular vision and personal concerns. It designates a body of works that are, on the one hand, readily recognisable as the output of the same person and/or team, but on the other hand avowedly inscribed in a wider historical context, including a background of cultural and artistic references and a framework of cinematic traditions. As such, the practice of always referring to 'Denis' films' needs to be qualified. From the initial writing stage to the actual shooting and editing, the films directed by Denis are clearly a collective creation and the impact of regular collaborators in particular cannot be overvalued. The work of contributors such as scenarist Jean-Pol Fargeau, camerawoman Agnès Godard, editor Nelly Quettier, soundman Jean-Louis Ughetto, the scores of musicians like Abdulla Ibrahim and the group the Tindersticks, together with the performance of actors such as Isaak de Bankolé, Grégoire Colin , Béatrice Dalle, Alex Descas or Denis Lavant, has proved crucial to the development of the style of filmmaking as a whole. Denis co-wrote most of the scripts of her feature fiction films with Fargeau. Their collaboration is driven by the recognition that the script should be used essentially as a detailed but loose framework, in preparation for the actual filming. Based on the dismissal of elaborated series of dialogue and conventional narrative causality (where a system of cause-and-effect motivations determine the ordering of the scenes and the characters' actions), the written stage thus lays the foundations for the construction of a highly visual cinematic world. In

11 The term *auteur*, inherited from the critics of the French magazine *Cahiers du cinéma*, is useful to designate a body of work that constitutes a unique, original vision. It is, however, a problematic concept to apply to such a collective creation as filmmaking. In addition, *auteur* cinema in itself has been criticised as over-individualistic in two ways. On the one hand, films narrowly focused on one artist's concerns have been described as self-centred (or even self-indulgent) and easily de-politicised. On the other hand, the very idea of authorship was undermined by the post-structural de-centering of the self: both 'I' and my discourse are predetermined by the environment in which I was born and live (see Louis Althusser). As such, to believe that an author speaks his or her own voice is an illusion. Moreover, films arguably exist only when screened, and each spectator, in his or her process of viewing is arguably the actual 'author' of the films being screened (see Roland Barthes).

turn, and relayed by Agnès Godard's camerawork, much of the actors' performances are built around movement and silences. Godard's camera seizes fleeting details and gestures that participate in the construction of the fluid narrative thread, but it also explores the meaning of the actor/character-as-body. While the bodies are always inscribed in a particular space (the location, its geography, its light, but also its history, all determine the way the characters are shot), they are also often captured in close-up, and in their presence as flesh (as living elements of the filming process and not merely as signifiers of a pre-existing story) is inscribed their mystery (the body 'obscures' the screen) and their mortality.

Similarities in training and professional experience no doubt played an important role in establishing the successful collaboration between the director and the *chef opérateur*.[12] Godard started as a photographer but later trained at the IDHEC (the Institut des Hautes Etudes Cinématographiques), where Denis was also a student. Both women were thus exposed to the work and teaching of personalities like Henri Alékan (former *chef opérateur* to Jean Cocteau), Peter Brook or Philippe Garrel, and developed an early interest in independent filmmaking that led them to work with leading figures of art cinema. Godard worked with Sacha Vierny on the sets of Peter Greenaway, whose films are renowned for their photography – the painterly composition, framing and baroque beauty of their images. She also collaborated with Agnès Varda, in the making of *Jacquot de Nantes* (1993). Varda's ability to convey the poetic or symbolic qualities of banal objects, her experimentation with photography, composition and framing, and her work on close-up and the filming of the human body, proved highly inspirational.

When Godard came to work for Wim Wenders in the 1980s, assisting the German director's own *chef opérateur*, Henri Alékan, Denis was working on the same films. Denis was in fact employed as assistant director for fifteen years. During these fifteen formative years she was able to observe some of the seminal *auteurs* of Western cinema at work, and to participate in the making of some of the

12 Together with the director, the *chef opérateur*, is responsible not only for the camerawork during the shooting, but for the framing, the composition and the way they combine with the light; in other words, she supervises the elaboration of the actual 'look' of the image. The nearest translation is director of photography.

classics of contemporary independent cinema (*Paris Texas*, 1983, *Wings of Desire*, 1987, *Down by Law*, 1986, etc.). She was a regular collaborator of Wim Wenders but also of filmmakers such as the politically committed Costa Gavras, veteran *nouvelle vague* director Jacques Rivette, and the *enfant terrible* of independent American cinema, Jim Jarmush. Rivette was a crucial source of reference for Denis, who shot a documentary portrait of him. *Jacques Rivette, Le Veilleur* (1990) was produced for the Television channel *La Sept* as part of the *Cinéma de notre temps* collection, a series of documentaries on influential directors. Rivette himself suggested Denis whom he had worked with, to direct the film. Shot in two parts, 1. *Le Jour* (Day), 2. *La Nuit* (Night), the portrait takes the form of a free conversation with the *Cahiers du cinéma* critic Serge Daney, interspersed with interviews of actors. Rivette evokes his beginnings and the other *Nouvelle Vague* directors (Jean-Luc Godard, Eric Rohmer, François Truffaut),[13] talks of his conceptions of cinema and of the making of his films. The filming starts in a gallery, to underline the filmmaker's habit of crossing over to other forms of expression, from performance to visual arts and literature. This hybrid quality of Rivette's work certainly finds echoes in Denis' own filmmaking, as does his unconventional approach to cinematic narration. For instance, he compares the notion of a plot with the French word *pelote* (a ball of thread or wool) that needs to be unravelled only as the film gets made. Rivette and Daney are occasionally filmed in long travelling shots, accompanied by the camera while walking, but a great deal of the documentary is filmed in steady medium shot, often privileging chiaroscuro effects during the day time, while during the night time, obscurity threatens to swallow the two men's bodies. At some point, Rivette evokes *Paris nous appartient* (*Paris Belongs To Us*) a collection of short films directed by *nouvelle vague* directors and put together to constitute a portrait of Paris. Quoting poet Charles Péguy, he then remarks that Paris 'belongs to no-one', or, perhaps, to those who wake-up early or live at night. The comment could also apply to Denis' two-part documentary. In effect, *Jacques Rivette, Le Veilleur* is also a portrait of Paris that betrays Denis' fascination for urban spaces (she shoots in the subway, in the streets and in cafés) and cityscapes. The

13 The French *Nouvelle Vague* (new wave) of the 1960s revolutionised cinema. The movement's ideas and films still exercise a widespread influence.

camera follows with curiosity as the two men explore a post-industrial site of wasteland, and the film includes sequences dedicated to the changing spectacle of the Paris-scape shot during the day and at night. Poetic variations on the theme of the city are developed in many of Denis' fiction works, and the opening sequence of her latest release, *Vendredi soir*, is evocative of some of the images included in *Le Veilleur*.

Denis embraced Rivette's rigorous dismissal of the meaningless, pre-packaged images that fill commercial cinema. In this, her work is also indebted to the cinema of Jean-Luc Godard, elements of which resurface in her films (Chapter 3). In her interviews, she also mentions a number of other influential directors such as Jean Renoir, but her set of references was never restricted to French cinema. There appear to be strong echoes, for instance, between the central concerns of the 'New German cinema', and the kind of problematic Denis was to address in her own work. Together with Rainer Werner Fassbinder and Werner Herzog, Wenders was one of the filmmakers of this movement whose work captured Denis' imagination early on (Denorme and Douin 2001: 23). Emerging in the 1960s, from a group of young filmmakers addicted to American B movies, the *New German Cinema* reflected the deep feelings of unrest of a generation that had grown up without a proper sense of its past. In the aftermath of World War II, the guilt and shame that befell the German nation was more or less buried under a process of collective amnesia. The defeat, the holocaust, the question of individual responsibility became part of a largely unspoken area of the national past. The period of the reconstruction, and the take-over, by the US, of Germany's cultural life (and, in particular, its cinema) and economy, helped to consign the recent past to oblivion (as one of Wenders's characters famously exclaimed: 'The Yankees have colonised our unconscious'). Repressed memory, and the sense of loss and doubt inherited from a muted past, were motifs that Denis thus encountered in a cinematic form early in her career, and aspects of the approach she was to adopt in her own exploration of such issues are akin to the metaphorical and stylistic solutions developed by the directors concerned. One could find in her films echoes of Herzog's work in Africa, of his grinding sense of absurdity and of the surreal quality of his images both in his documentary and in his fiction work. Wender's mix of minimalism and poetic lyricism, the recurrent figure of the passing stranger, the deliberate play on time and space, and the use of the road-movie format as an allegory for the search for memories also find resonance in Denis' filmmaking. Also echoed in Denis' work are Fassbinder's play on established genres to attack the conventions of bourgeois culture, his denunciation of the new cult for money and economic power that filled the gaps left by the erasure of history and the failure of the traditional systems of values.

As we will see, Denis is highly critical of certain aspects of Hollywood cinema. Conversely, her filmmaking is often compared to that of independent directors who work in the margins of the large studios system such as David Lynch, David Cronenberg (see discussion of *Trouble Every Day*) and Jim Jarmush. In common with the German directors, and in particular with Wenders, Jarmush has been held as a master in the art of de-familiarisation. Like Wenders's, his films excel at the representation of displacement and exile, at combining the realistic and the lyrical to generate the uncanny even from the most ordinary aspects of existence. One needs only recall the classic wide shots of a desert that threaten to engulf the dwarfed silhouettes of the characters of Wender's *Paris Texas*, or the unfamiliar sight and outlandish beauty of a deserted Florida beach in the winter cold in Jarmush's *Stranger than Paradise* (1984), to perceive how inspirational Denis might have found working with these directors.

Whereas Denis' body of work stands apart from the trends and genres that have dominated the French production since the 1980s, she does entertain close links with some of her contemporaries. Denis' thematic choices are sometimes compared to those of Catherine Breillat's and the two directors have been interviewed together on several occasions. Denis' occasional cameo appearances and small roles in other directors' features (in Laetitia Masson's *En avoir (ou pas)* (1994) for instance, or in Tonie Marshall's *Vénus Beauté* (1999)) also testify to her interest in the work of other French filmmakers of her generation.[14]

14 Denis' work is not discussed as the work of a *woman* director in this book. An exhaustive analysis of women's filmmaking in France has been published by Carrie Tarr and Brigitte Rollet: *Cinema and the Second Sex*, New York and London: Continuum, 2001.

The aesthetics of the unsaid

To a certain extent, Denis' film work could be compared to a kind of palimpsest. Just as the memory of a certain cinema seems to inhabit some of her documentary work and short films, the tales told in her feature fiction films appear haunted by the ghost of another, buried story. Her films rest on elliptical, fragmentary narrative constructs, where the erased traces of a repressed past seem to constantly threaten to resurface, and cyclically, mysteriously, as in a traumatic expression of forgotten memories, violently erupt. Only *Chocolat* and *Beau travail* directly visualize France's colonial past, but all of her films in some way explore how History (*Histoire*) permeates stories (*histoires*), the way the individual is affected by the historical and the social, and how the individual body is marked and controlled by the body of society. Indeed, not only do the films partly generate their troubling impact by portraying a past that inhabits the present, with its scars unhealed and its conflicts unresolved, but the themes of exile and alienation, and the question of the definition of contemporary identities, serve as a starting point to a renewed investigation of cinematic language.

In the tradition of nineteenth-century Western fiction, remarks Marguerite Alexander, authors shared with their readers certain assumptions 'about the ultimate value of society, whatever specific criticisms of it might be made; about the place of the individual within that society; about the existence, if not of God, then of a body of universal truths which included an agreed concept of human nature. But that concord can no longer be said to exist, at least as far as postmodernist novelists are concerned' (Alexander 1990: 5). If these comments were applied to cinema, Denis' fiction work would readily be described as postmodern. The director stresses that for her,

> Cinema is not made to give a psychological explanation. For me, cinema is montage, editing. To make blocks of impressions or emotions meet another block of impressions or emotions, and put in between pieces of explanation, to me it's boring ... Our brains are full of literature – my brain is. But I think we also have a dream world, the brain is also full of images and songs, and I think that making films for me is to get rid of explanation. (Romney 2000)

Denis' filmmaking resists conventional narrative approaches bent on explanation and psychological definitions. Her films do not depict situations and tensions in order to resolve them. The protagonists are not endowed with personalities that justify their actions. In effect, in the way characters and narration become emancipated from pre-established codes and causalities, Denis' filmmaking seems to combine aspects of modernist fiction and of philosopher and film theorist Giles Deleuze's concept of a 'cinéma-temps' (in 'time-cinema', time and vision do not merely function as a codification allowing for the smooth unfolding of movements and actions towards a logical resolution, they become the actual texture of the film) (Deleuze 1994). As such, Denis' films generally fail to meet many of the expectations associated with more traditional work. As one journalist put it to her: 'the way you tell stories, you don't make it easy for the audience' (Romney 2000). Her stylised approach has occasionally baffled critics and viewers and has even recently earned her work the qualification of 'pervertissement formaliste' ('perverted formalism') (Prédal 2002: 102). Yet, when they are considered in context, her films appear far from being empty exercises in stylistic composition. The denial or abandonment of certain conventions that opens onto less explored territories of cinematic expression contributes, I would argue, to the elaboration of a provocative, analytical representation of our contemporary world. From *Chocolat* to *Vendredi soir*, the formal and aesthetic experimentation appears intrinsic to the expression of a poetic insight coupled with a profoundly ethical vision.

Indeed, with reference to the historical backdrop sketched out at the beginning of this chapter, the director's specific approach already takes on a particular resonance. Her films indisputably capture the spirit of a time; a body of work like Denis' echoes and contributes to some of the debates that have recently become central to the work of modern thinkers and to the Western socio-political arenas. It is the more troubling and provocative elements of these debates, however, that she seems drawn to: the renunciation of the certitudes upon which identities have been constructed and orders established, of the belief in an immutable, inherently rational human nature and of the justification of History as a logical, progressive enfolding of causal events. This is reflected not only in her thematic choices, and in her references, but also in her filmmaking. The rules of the causal chain that continue to govern the fictional constructs of the conventional novel and mainstream cinema tend to be ignored in Denis' cinema. Her films shun well-defined, stable characterisation and situations and favour transitory, mutating spaces. They never offer an ending that could be described as a 'closure'. They do not form finished entities. Rather, they provide a wealth of connections and potential interpretations, and a multitude of lines of flight. Hence, from *Chocolat's* taut silences to the labyrinthine structure of *J'ai pas sommeil* and the rhythmical flow of *Beau travail*, a specific stylistic approach emerges, which privileges a cinematic language proper (where meaning is conveyed through images and sound) over plot line and narration.

Time and narration

Two images from *J'ai pas sommeil* could encapsulate the elaboration of narrative space[15] in Denis' films. The opening sequence is shot from within a police helicopter flying above Paris, providing an aerial view of the city sprawling beneath it. Later on, a brief scene shows a forensic expert looking at samples – hairs or maybe a few threads from a piece of clothing – through the magnifying lens of a microscope. As the camera takes the place of the microscope, we are shown enlarged threads overlapping web-like, resembling wires or roads on a map. The criminal whom these samples could identify is lost amidst the interlacing of streets of the old Parisian district of Montmartre, and, as he roams amidst the city's nocturnal crowd, his path will cross that of a multitude of other characters. Much of the narrative structure of Denis' film evokes a fluid, changing perception of time and space. It eschews logical, progressive story lines of the 'organic' mode.[16] Instead, it posits a maze of links and interconnected trajectories that run within the diegesis[17] or in excess of it, and plays

15 The expression 'narrative space' designates actual locations but also the spatial organisation of the film, in terms of narrative progression and editing (which scenes, and what kind of scenes, take place in which kind of space). It also designates the way the characters occupy the space and are filmed within it, how the space determines their existence both as individuals in a story, and as characters in a movie.

16 Here, 'organic' designates the way the logical unfolding of a story hides its constructed quality, makes the series of events that compose it appear 'natural'. Deleuze uses the term to describe a narrative approach where 'the real that is assumed is recognisable by its continuity – even if it is interrupted – by the continuity shots which establish it, and by the laws which determine successions, simultaneities and permanences' (Deleuze, 1994: 127).

17 The world created by the film itself: a music, for example, is *diegetic* if its source can be located within the universe described by the film – when it corresponds

on different times and scales, from the smallest detail or moment to a global environment where past and present coexist.

Flashbacks (*Chocolat, Beau travail*), parallel editing[18] (*US Go Home, Nénette et Boni, Trouble Every* Day, *J'ai pas sommeil*), dissolves and superimpositions[19] (*Beau travail, Vendredi soir*) contribute to create a narrative space where a multitude of lives, of realities, and several time zones seem to collide or to overlap. Through editing, a multiplicity of connections are created without strict chronology and the necessities of explaining or justifying a scene: there are always potential exchanges of gazes, closeness between characters suggested through graphic cuts[20] and apparent eye line match[21] rather than dialogues or actions. *J'ai pas sommeil* represents an elaborate example of such narratives in terms of parallel individual trajectories, and has spurred comparisons with the style of narrative launched by Robert Altman in *Short Cuts*. *J'ai pas sommeil*'s characters appear in turn, and live related but separate lives. They often seem to wander aimlessly and, linked by cuts that suggest a spatial and emotional proximity, always seem to be on the verge of meeting. Yet the expected encounters rarely take place. When the recently arrived Daïga takes her first stroll in the glittering street lights of the boulevards near her hotel, the sequence is interspersed with images of another, yet unknown character, Mona, sitting alone in a café. The editing, the lighting, the isolation of the two women alone in the crowd, all stress their closeness, yet, in the actual diegesis, they will never physically meet. Even the main male protagonists, the brothers Théo and Camille, only briefly meet and exchange but a few words in the course of the

---

to the score played by a musician on screen, or by a radio that one of the characters has switched on for instance.

18 Here, parallel editing (*montage alterné*) describes a montage or editing technique where the film cross-cuts between two or several coexistent situations or actions so as to compare or generate contrast or to create an effect of simultaneity.

19 In the transition between two shots for instance, the last image of the second shot only fades gradually, while the first image of the following shot emerges, creating an effect of superimposition.

20 Two successive shots which contain similar compositional (colour, shape, movement within the frame, etc.) elements.

21 A combination of shots that create a spatial/directional link between two things or two individuals. If a shot shows a person looking left for instance, and the next shot shows the person they are supposed to be looking at, the second individual may be looking right, as if returning the gaze.

film. Through chance, Camille and Daïga happen to stay in the same hotel, but they only share the same frame for a fleeting instant, a few seconds at the counter of a bar, time enough to drink a cup of coffee and exchange a glance, and for their hands to brush against each other. In *Trouble Every Day*, Shane travels from the States to Paris in search of the doctor who could perhaps cure him, but that he will never actually encounter. In *Nénette et Boni*, a crowd of secondary characters, otherwise completely unrelated, unknowingly share a phone line via a collection of forged phone cards. A haphazard web of communication thus surrounds the mutism and loneliness of the central characters. *Vendredi soir* is the first of Denis' films that actually focuses on two characters together, yet the first part of the film is but a series of fleeting apparitions, tentative exchanges and aborted meetings: an exploration of potential stories where chance will ultimately prevail.

Whilst various characters' trajectories cross or parallel each other within separate diegetic worlds, passages are open between the films themselves, so that even in the works that focus on a handful of figures, a more complex array of implicit connections seems to establish itself. There are fleeting, often playful signs of such overlaps. These are created through music, as with the ballads of the Tindersticks, whose melancholy, atmospheric tones connect several of the films. They also operate through the brief appearances of known faces and recurrent figures suggesting that two separate diegeses temporarily come into contact. Hence, for instance, the discrete presence of Jacques Nolot in *J'ai pas sommeil*. The main actor/narrator of Denis' short, *La Robe cerceau*, and the father of the two youths in *Nénette et Boni* can be glimpsed sitting in amongst the spectators of the porn cinema Daïga enters to escape a flirtatious stranger.[22] Alex Descas and Richard Courcet, central figures of *J'ai pas sommeil*, hold cameo roles in *Nénette et Boni*. Grégoire Colin (Alain in *US Go Home*, Boni in *Nénette et Boni*, and the young soldier Sentain in *Beau travail*) appears briefly in *Vendredi soir* as an anonymous passer-by who, in spite of the bitterly cold night, declines Laure's offer of a sanctuary in the warmth of her car. Like another memory from another tale, there is also the figure of the legionnaire who sits alone in the background in the bar where Laure and Jean meet again. But the quotes are not

22 Interestingly, Nolot's latest release as a director, *La Chatte à deux têtes* (2002), takes place almost entirely in an old porn cinema.

limited to self-references: Denis' narrative maze seems to expand into a kind of macro-mapping, where the universes of her films appear to meet those of other filmmakers. As if the camera had zoomed out in between films, before focusing in again at the beginning of another story, one could imagine that Wim Wenders's angels also patrol the skies of Denis' films. While the helicopter pilots at the beginning of *J'ai pas sommeil* evoke Altman's *Short Cuts*, they also resemble degraded incarnations of Wender's angels in *Wings of Desire*. The music that accompanies *Vendredi soir*'s opening sequence also recalls the German director's 'angel movies', as does the gaze of the camera as, in city-symphony style,[23] it surveys the cityscape before focusing on one lit window, one set of characters amongst the crowd. At the beginning of *Trouble Every Day*, the shots of the varied Parisian cityscape are compared to views of Denver at night taken from the plane and looking like a 'computer chip'. The contrast establishes a resonant link between the old continent and the States, but also between two dominant types of mapping, of seeing the world, of making cinema.

In effect, Denis' work as a whole could be compared to a continuing wandering. In the complex narrative structure of her films, time is rarely bound to plot. Not only does the editing favour elision, but it allows for the narrative to stray, creating a 'porous' kind of time, where the present is constantly inhabited by the past. Denis once remarked that 'even if I work on a script and I try to make a plot ... because I am told to make a plot ... something comes up and it's time' (Denis 1996). In this way, and increasingly so with each of her successive features, her approach calls to mind Deleuze's description of the emergence of a 'time-cinema' as a cinema where time becomes tangible, elastic and changing, and where situations exist in themselves and not simply as the premise to an action.[24] In *S'en fout la*

---

23 The city-symphonies designate a group of ambitious documentaries from the 1920s and 1930s, a series of films that sought to capture the kaleidoscopic movement of urban life.

24 Deleuze talks of a cinema where a situation 'is not extended directly into action: it is no longer sensori-motor as in realism, but primarily optical and of sound, invested by the senses, before action takes shape in it, and uses or confronts its elements ... Between the reality of the setting and that of the action, it is no longer a motor extension which is established, but rather a dreamlike connection through the intermediary of the liberated sense organs. It is as if the action floats in the situation rather than bringing it to a conclusion or strengthening it.' (Deleuze 1994: 4).

mort, for instance, much more screen time is granted to the scenes of the training of the roosters than to the actual fights on which so much of the film's symbolic and actual violence rests.

> You are speaking of time when you speak about the training scene of the rooster ... On paper I would have thought it was a matter of seconds or very short scenes, but when I watch the real training of a rooster I find it is a question of time. I thought it was important to show the difference with an actual fight which sometimes will last a minute ... I think it is very interesting for me as a filmmaker – this aspect of time. (Denis 1996)

While certain scenes expand, converting a gesture or a series of gestures into a ritual, or transforming an apparently banal episode into a poetic digression, other sequences of events are reduced to the briefest of allusions, appear out of context or with no regard to strict chronology, or are completely eluded. Very little is known of a character's past, and, often, even less is revealed of their future. In *Nénette et Boni*, the story of the bakers, which calls forth its own tradition of classic French cinema and a mythic Marseille (see discussion of *Nénette et Boni*), also unsettles the time structure within the film itself. The love story between the baker and his wife is suggested through an elliptical series of interspersed sequences that appear throughout the film without preliminaries, like free-floating sheets of memory. Jean-Luc Godard's *Le Petit soldat* (1960), a film that connotes a particular period of French history marked by war and censorship, infused the project that resulted in the making of *Beau travail* (Dobson 2002). Probably the most 'Deleuzian' of Denis' films, *Beau travail*'s intricate time structure and rhythm is informed by the unreliable tale of its central protagonist. The discrepancies between the images and the voice of the narrator, legionnaire Galoup, are relayed by contradictory camera movements and the time-lags created by the editing. The penultimate sequence portrays him seemingly preparing for suicide, yet the film finishes with a scene that shows him dancing in a night-club. As in a time loop, the setting, presumably in Marseille, nevertheless uncannily resembles the set of the club frequented by the soldiers in Djibouti at the beginning of the film. In addition, the soldier's training sessions punctuate the film like strange moments of suspended time. In these ritual performances, between dance and martial arts, the group of men moves in sync, participating, like an ancient chorus, in the symbolic representation of unspoken bonds and hidden tensions.

Freed from their functions as mere links in a chain of causes and effects, images are thus offered up to contemplation and observation. Screen time is granted equally to small details that often weave the story together and to the wider context in which the characters exist. Even when, as in *S'en fout la mort* or *Vendredi soir*, restricted, claustro-phobic spaces and close-ups dominate, the films are punctuated with long travelling shots, panoramic movements or single fixed-frame shots and series of stills, depicting the landscapes and the characters within them, looking and walking. The individuals portrayed in her films are wanderers. In the urban space where the camera follows them, walking or driving, often through streets and roads at night, they occasionally take on the role of the contemporary flâneur or flâneuse,[25] who passes through as a detached observer. Those who, like Galoup in *Beau travail*, have forgotten to look and pay attention to the world around them, find themselves at odds with a space and time where they have become redundant.

Image and sound: crossing the borders of perception, sensations and art forms

The status of silences and music, and the prevalence of the optical and sound over the verbal, are striking aspects of Denis' fiction films. 'Les personnages principaux parlent peu. Ils ne se disent que les paroles de politesse en usage entre gens de classes différentes. Aucune voix hors champ ne vient combler ce silence'.[26] (Beaupré 1989: 30). This particularity of her approach, which Denis initially related to her African background – 'In Africa, nothing is ever said, but the weight of things is always there' (Denis 2000) – was developed through her

25 The concept of the *flâneur* was originally proposed by Charles Baudelaire, writing at the height of the urban mutation of Paris. In the late nineteenth century, the city, so far understood and experienced primarily as a space to live and work in, was transformed into a spectacle, organised and presented so as to captivate the gaze. The *flâneur*, or wanderer, emerged as a new kind of urban dweller, who walked the streets not out of practical necessity, but in order to observe the development of a space where architecture, goods, images and people were offered for actual or virtual (visual) consumption.

26 'The main characters say little. They only exchange the polite words that are customary between people of different classes. There is no voiceover.'

work with scriptwriter Jean-Pol Fargeau in particular. As discussed earlier, her collaboration with Fargeau has resulted in the elaboration of cinematic universes where the implicit and the implied prevail over exposition and dialogues. There is, for instance, no voiceover in *Chocolat*, a film close to the heritage genre and a childhood tale, and, as such, one where such a device could have been expected. Indeed, what we glimpse of the travel diary of *Chocolat's* heroine herself at the beginning of the film is not a written account, but a drawing. In *S'en fout la mort* and in *Beau travail*, the voiceover commentaries are more streams of consciousness than informative frameworks. Indeed, Dah's reflections appear to be part of a grieving process, and Galoup's subjective tale, which accompanies *Beau travail's* images, seems anything but consistent and reliable. In *Vendredi soir*, Denis manages to adapt a literary text that describes the inner feelings of a character without resorting to the voiceover at all. The information comes indirectly, through the connections that the editing creates, and through visual and sound compositions that never seek to demonstrate:

> Quand j'ai commencé à faire du cinéma, je penchais vraiment pour la famille des cinéastes qui font confiance à l'image ... Le dialogue devient un son, au même titre qu'une musique ... Il faut utiliser les dialogues presque pour détourner l'image. Des choses non-dites peuvent se passer pendant ce temps-là.[27] (Lifshitz 1995)

Agnès Godard's role as *chef opérateur* has been crucial in developing a complex visual grammar that does not rest on the plot and dialogue structure, but in establishing what Deleuze calls the '*inventaire du milieu*' (the 'inventory of the context', Deleuze 1994: 5). For instance, her use of lighting, framing and photography has been particularly noted to bring out the aesthetic and evocative value of ordinary locations and apparently meaningless, banal objects. Yannick Lemarié talks of the

> parti pris d'Agnès Godard, cette réponse à de 'muettes instances', qui la poussent parfois à animer son plan en partant d'un simple objet. Tout en se méfiant d'un excès qui consisterait à réifier le monde, elle

---

27 'When I started to direct, I really opted for the family of directors who trust the image ... The dialogues become a sound, just like music ... Dialogues have to be used to subvert the image. Unspoken things can happen during that time.'

puise dans l'étoffe des choses une vitalité nouvelle.[28] (Lemarié 2000: 128)

Although it overlooks its potentially morbid connotations (see below the effect of the *décadrage*), the term vitality underlines the sensual effect of the technique. The camera gleans objects – often picking out the more humble ones – that may provide a scene with a metaphorical dimension, or simply inhabit a space to which they grant significance by virtue of the evocative effect they may exercise on the viewer. Though Denis claims that she has no talent for lightness and comedy, such 'inventories' occasionally provide a humorous or ironical touch even in the most melancholy of her films, and daringly court the kitsch and the grotesque. Crucially, they operate as a relay between the sensual (texture, shape, colour, smell, sounds ...) and the emotional (desire, memory, loss ...). Textures combined and caught in close-up, sounds captured to their utmost detail and complexity, thus contribute to create a confusion of the senses, a kind of set of 'correspondences' in a Baudelairian[29] sense (Chapter 3). In *Nénette et Boni*, fluffy, creamy cakes and the malleable pastry of Boni's pizzas come to incarnate the fantasies that inhabit the young pizza maker's obsessive mind. The pizzas reappear in *Vendredi soir*, smiling their anchovy smile to the lovers. Laure's woolly glove, abandoned, crumpled onto the humid asphalt, is a playful signal of her own abandon to the rule of desire. Drops of blood dripping from grass blades are enough to evoke the unspeakable that lies at the heart of *Trouble Every Day*, and to simultaneously call forth a whole tradition of dark cinema. Marking out the male world of *Beau travail*, the soldiers' barracks stand out in the desert, but are surrounded with lines of drying clothes, floating against the sky like notes on a music scale.

Godard's camera scrutinises bodies as well as inanimate objects, but eschews the voyeuristic[30] mode: the use of the macro lens in love

28 'Agnès Godard's deliberate choice, her response to "silent entreaties" that sometimes lead her to begin a camera movement with a simple object. Suspicious of a systematisation that would result in objectifying the world, she draws from the texture of things a renewed vitality.'

29 French Poet Charles Baudelaire (1821–67) is famous for the analogies that his poetry created between symbolism and the senses, and between the senses themselves. The term 'correspondences' is also the title of a poem where he associates colours and textures with particular smells.

30 By voyeur, one designates an observer who secretly watches a scene (intimate, erotic, and so on) that he or she should not be seeing. In some aspects, as a

scenes or scenes of intimacy in particular denies the necessary distance for this kind of objectification. In an opposite process, bodies and objects are thus de-familiarised: while the objects singled out by the lens become endowed with an anima, a kind of personality, when filmed in close-up, as flesh, the bodies become texture, matter. As the image hovers at the frontier between the figurative and the abstract, the gaze is less one of observation calling for identification or objectification[31] than one of sensual closeness inviting empathy. At the same time, the attention granted to the face, and the recurrent presence of a small group of actors in successive films, act as counterpoints to the potential effect of de-personification that the framing and the *mise en scène* may create:

> Il y a un respect de l'homme, à l'évidence, et plus précisément du visage dont elle ne cherche jamais à violer l'intégrité, qu'elle tourne en 35 mm ou en super-16. Le visage reste, selon la belle expression de David le Breton 'puissance d'appel'.[32] (Lemarié, 2000: 129)

Godard and Denis' filming techniques are a fundamental aspect of the representation of the tension between the affirmation of the self (or person) and the threat of its return to the animal or of its dissolution into death, a theme which will emerge in the more

---

regime of the gaze, film viewing appears close to a form of voyeurism (and as such, the concept is central to psychoanalytical approaches to cinema). Films are generally watched in darkness. The cinematic mimetic power make actors on screen seem 'real', make them look like a 'live' spectacle, and can show what is usually hidden of people's lives since at the same time, the presence of the spectators is rarely 'acknowledged' as such.

31 In classic theories of identification, the analogy between the gaze of the camera and that of a character (occasionally combined with techniques such as the voiceover), encourages the spectator to identify with this character in particular, to adopt his or her point of view and 'step in his or her shoes' as it were, for the duration of the film. Conversely, the figure who, devoid of a point of view, is presented to the gaze of the camera as a spectacle, to be looked at, can appear 'objectified': his or her function is to be 'consumed' visually. Traditionally, in classic and mainstream cinema, agency and point of view tend to be associated with male characters, while the female figure remaining the passive object of the gaze, the object of desire and the 'reward' of the hero at the end.

32 'There is an obvious respect for the human being, and, more precisely, a respect for the face, the integrity of which she never seeks to violate, whether she shoots in 35 mm or in 16 mm. The face retains, as in David le Breton's beautiful expression, "its power to captivate".' Quote from *Des Visages*, Paris: Metailié, 1992, p. 266.

detailed analysis of the films as central to Denis' cinema. Indeed, in films like *Trouble Every day*, an abundance of what film theorist Pascal Bonitzer calls *décadrage* ('de-framing') – 'les champs vides, les angles insolites, les corps parcellisés en amorce ou en gros plan' ('empty frames, unusual angles, fragmented bodies at the borders of the frame or in close-up') (Bonitzer 2001: 126) – contributes to a pervasive feeling of displacement and anxiety. The human figure is broken up or driven to the periphery of the images while empty spaces and inanimate objects (or objects that are mechanically animated like the rotating flasks in the neurological labs) take over the screen. 'L'œil habitué (éduqué?) à centrer tout de suite, à aller au centre, ne trouve rien et reflue à la périphérie, où quelque chose palpite encore, sur le point de disparaître' ('The eye, used to (or educated to?) immediately centre things, or to direct its gaze to the centre, does not find anything and withdraws back to the periphery, where something on the brink of vanishing still quivers') (Bonitzer 2001: 127). In such instances, the void suggested by the image seems like an extension of the sense of anguish that the film's scarce dialogues, isolated heightened sounds and silences generate.

In effect, sound is never a mere 'accompaniment' to the image in Denis' filmmaking. Music, silences and dialogues are more likely to act as counterpoint to the image. In *Trouble Every Day* for instance, the violence of certain sequences is offset by the mournful tunes of the Tindersticks. Sound also functions as a further structuring principle that combines with the editing and the montage to create the narrative rhythm. In *Trouble Every Day* and in *Vendredi soir*, the richness of the soundtrack grants a particular density to sounds, and imbues them with an almost tactile quality. In *Trouble Every Day*'s cannibalistic scenes, as the images become obscured and their effect turns from the graphic to the impressionistic, the sound is essential in suggesting the pain and conveying the horror. Conversely, in the almost wordless *Vendredi soir*, the most ordinary sounds are enhanced and seem to foretell pleasure. Throughout, the narration seems to slow down and to pick up in accordance with the musical tempo. The emotional fluctuations experienced by *Vendredi soir*'s characters – fear and withdrawal, temptation and elation – are suggested almost solely through visual details, fleeting gestures and the changes in the musical score. Because of this ability to combine image and sound, to digress rather than follow a tight plot structure, and to create variations on a theme, Denis' cinema has sometimes been compared to free Jazz (Romney 2000). Often, the music associated with a film is already present at the writing stage. It can function as an initial inspiration and as element of the scenario. In *US Go Home* and in *Nénette et Boni*, for instance, much of the information pertaining to the relations between the various characters is suggested through the musical choices and the lyrics of the songs. '*Nénette et Boni* was completely nourished at the very beginning when we were writing the script, by a song by the Tindersticks called *My Sister*'[33] (Romney 2000).

Denis nurtures a deep love of music expressed in her work through the presence of a wide range of sounds: from opera (*Beau travail*) to Beat music (*US Go Home*) and to traditional and contemporary African music. Like Jarmush (with Screamin' Jay Hawkins, John Lurie, the Lounge Lizards and Tom Waits) and Wenders (with Nick Cave and the Bad Seeds, Ry Cooder and the Cuban musicians of *Buena Vista Social Club*), Denis has always worked in close collaboration with musicians. As described earlier, the music of the Tindersticks, specifically composed for each of the films in which it features, is an essential element in the elaboration of the atmosphere of her story worlds. She has also made films on music, recently completing, for instance, the shooting of a musical clip with singer Alain Bashung on the occasion of the release of *L'imprudence* (a record whose haunted tunes and lyrics create an atmosphere not unlike that of Denis' fiction works). *Man No Run*, her first documentary, shot shortly after *Chocolat*, focused on a group from Cameroon on tour in France (Chapter 2).

If music always features prominently, visual arts and performances arts are equally inspirational to Denis. As will emerge in the detailed analysis of some of her films, techniques associated first and foremost with painting and photography feature prominently in Denis' filmmaking. In addition, the short film format has allowed her to confront or combine certain cinematic principles with that of other visual arts: *Duo* (1995), a film on a painting by Jacques de Loustal shot for the BBC, and *A propos d'une déclaration* (*Declaration of love*) (1995), a commission from the contemporary art centre Fondation Cartier, are discussed in Chapter 3.

In her latest work, Denis explores themes that are directly connected to the world of theatre and dance. She is currently shooting images of

33 *Tindersticks II*, Polygram, 1995.

contemporary dance in Montpellier, the city that houses the national company directed by Mathilde Monnier as well as the largest dance festival in France. Prior to this, however, for *Beau travail*, she had collaborated with choreographer Bernardo Montet, subjecting the actors to an intense training prior to the actual shooting of the film. Through dance, Denis composes a complex and stylised vision of her subject – the elite corps of the legion. The military world, with its rituals, its mythical aura, is revealed through the prism of collective movement and physicality. This overlap between cinema and dance highlights a crucial aspect of Denis' filmmaking: the *mise en scène* of the tension between physicality and transcendence, between the dimension of the body (present and changing) and that of the ideal (immanent and inaccessible).

Denis' interest in forms of expression that challenge the dominant conventions of filmmaking extends to literary material insofar as her approach to the written source is not connected to the establishment of plot lines and dialogue. A means to address a specific thematic issue, the literary source adds another layer of depth to the *mise en scène* and contributes to the creation of the films' particular atmospheres. As evoked earlier, a whole tradition of underground literature feeds into the intertextuality[34] of her films. But Denis has also adapted existing texts to the screen: *Beau travail*, based on a novella by Herman Melville, and *Vendredi soir*, a faithful adaptation of an Emmanuèle Bernheim novel. In addition, if her films often adopt the form and pace of largely silent ballads (in the visual and musical sense: in French, *ballade*, for a poem or a song sounds like *balade* – a stroll), she has nevertheless shot films based on monologues and conversations: her documentary on Jacques Rivette, for instance, as well as her adaptation of a text written by Jacques Nolot *La Robe à cerceau*. In this 1992 short, an anonymous customer, sitting in a deserted bar at closing time, reads a text based on his memory of a woman. Providing a poetic but subdued framework to the text written and performed by Nolot, the film is an exercise in simplicity, eschewing the explanatory mode to explore the status of the written and spoken word as triggers to the imaginary.

34 The concept of intertextuality stems from the realisation that no text can be created or can exist in isolation. The term, first coined by Julia Kristeva, designates the mosaic of references and quotations that are woven into a work of any kind.

Figures in space: characterisation, *mise en scène* and ideology

Even as her approach eschews the expository form, the prevalence of
the implied and the unsaid in Denis' work is qualified by an acute
consciousness of the power of the image to carry latent messages or,
to paraphrase Roland Barthes, to reinforce contemporary mythologies.[35] As one white character in *J'ai pas sommeil* pointedly reminds
the black man whom she employed illegally and is now reluctant to
pay, this was, after all, nothing more than: 'du travail au *noir*'
('moonlighting', literally 'black work'). Just as preconceptions and
discriminatory attitudes continue to permeate contemporary society
through its most ordinary customs and its language, they still inform
its modes of representation, including cinema. Often, it is by simultaneously using and underlining them that Denis' filmmaking subverts
or undermines certain strategies of representation. Already in
Chocolat, while the camera attaches itself to the characters and gives
them a powerful presence, at the same time, through *mise en scène* and
framing, the unspoken boundaries that trap them are marked out.
Protée may be the most engaging amongst the protagonists, one
whose point of view the camera is likely to adopt (thus arguably
facilitating spectatorial identification). Yet, when he serves Aimée's
white guests at the table, Protée is mercilessly beheaded by the frame,
reduced to the anonymous, faceless presence of the black servant.

Denis' filmmaking never ceases to investigate the functioning of
the cinematic gaze, to question the conventions of *mise en scène* and
characterisation and the discourse of differentiation and categorisa-
tion – by race, by gender, by class – that they contribute to create.
From a reflection on the normalising powers of language and
representation unfolds a questioning of preconceptions, and in
particular, a questioning of the very notion of race. In his study of the
status of whiteness in representation, Richard Dyer remarks:

35 In the well-known essays published as part of the *Mythologies* collection, French
philosopher Roland Barthes pointed out the ability of images to present certain
facts as unquestionable, 'natural', and in that way to reinforce or create myths.
Myths are symbolic tales accepted as truthful by force of tradition. They evolve
with time, and continue to shape our contemporary understanding and systems
of belief. A whole 'mythologising' discourse accompanied the colonising
process for instance: images, texts, and stories presented the western hegemony
as a natural and beneficial process. (*Mythologies*, Paris: Seuil, 1957, reprinted in
London: Vintage, 1993.)

> As long as race is something only applied to non-white peoples, as long
> as white people are not racially seen and named, they/we function as a
> human norm. Other people are raced, we are just people. (Dyer 1997:1)

As we will see, the problematic of a racial discrimination that rests on
the principle of a white race posing as the non-racial norm, in
particular, finds strong resonance in a study of Denis' films. The
refusal to define and categorise extends to all her characters, defying
the rule of appearances so central to a visual media like cinema: in the
world of Denis' films, people, places and situations are never
reducible to one dimension, never equated to what they may look like.

> Elle a constamment eu ce désir de mélanger les situations concrètes
> avec d'autres, fantastiques; les êtres pleins, entiers, terriens (le
> personnage interprété par Line Renaud dans *J'ai pas sommeil*) avec
> d'autres plus éthérés, plus légers et absents; ou encore l'indicible des
> individus avec les réalités de la chair.[36] (Chauvin 2002: 80)

Claire Denis has often been praised for her ability to combine the
mundane and the bizarre, the down-to-earth and the aloof, both in
terms of narration and *mise en scène* and in terms of characters. The
subverting of genre conventions and the singular atmosphere created
by her films may destabilise usual patterns of identification[37] both
with the characters and with the structure of the fiction itself (see, in
particular, discussion of *Trouble Every Day*). Focalisation[38] (the structuring of the story according to a point of view, a narrative instance
with which the viewer can identify) in Denis' films is never unilateral
or simple. Even in the films that include a voiceover narration, the
process is experienced as unstable and fragmentary. In effect, the

---

36 'She shows a renewed desire to mix concrete situations with fantasy; fully-
fledged, earthly beings (the character interpreted by Line Renaud in *J'ai pas
sommeil*) with other figures, ethereal, light, absent; or the indescribable part of
the individual with the realities of the flesh.'

37 Some theorists designate the process of identification with both the characters
and the fiction as 'secondary identification' (as opposed to the primary
identification that is the merge of the viewer's gaze with that of the camera).
(Alain Bergala, *Le Cinéma en jeu*, Aix en Provence: Institut de l'Image, 1992. Joël
Magny, *Le Point de vue*, Paris: Cahiers du cinéma, 2001.)

38 Gérard Genette talks of 'focalisation zéro', 'focalisation interne' and
'focalisation externe' to designate, respectively, story worlds described by
omniscient narrators, experienced through the vision of one or several
characters, or from the outside, with no access to the characters' inner thoughts.
(Gérard Genette, *Figures III*, Paris: Seuil, 1972.)

principal characteristic of the main protagonists in her films is probably
this elusiveness described by Chauvin – an aloofness occasionally
rendered more manifest through the presence of (seemingly) familiar,
solid, figures amongst secondary characters, and that the critics and
viewers may experience as highly frustrating or as mysterious and
seductive. Part of the attraction exercised by the characters of Protée
in *Chocolat*, Jocelyn in *S'en fout la mort*, Daïga, Camille and Théo in
J'ai pas sommeil, and Jean in *Vendredi soir*, rests with their silences,
their impenetrability, and their unpredictability. The characterisation
and the actors' performance often elude psychological definitions and
create fluctuating figures that always retain a degree of inscrutability.
Understatement prevails over expressive demonstration: the impact
of emotions and reactions tends to remain hidden, or it is merely
suggested, anger and violence explode unannounced, the expression
of feelings remains equivocal. The last ritual that binds France and
Protée ambiguously mingles love and hate, as does officer Galoup's
obsession with the soldier Sentain. Camille the serial killer is a soft-
spoken young man, an affectionate son and a pitiless killer. 'I am
happy', repeats the newly married Shane, holding his wife in his arms
while simultaneously beset by bloody fantasies and horrific images of
the young woman being eaten alive. Tough guy Boni elaborates
pornographic fantasies about the local baker woman, yet when face to
face with the object of his lust, he remains shyly quiet. In spite of all
expectations, his sister Nénette is resilient till the end to the maternal
instinct that society and the narrative logic would require her to
acknowledge. Though they are complete strangers, Laure and Jean's
night together is imbued with tenderness and affection as much as
with sexual passion.

Central characters could be described as incarnations of postcolonial uncertainties, of the fluctuation of contemporary identities.
Inherited from the nineteenth-century novel, and still dominant in
mainstream cinema, the conventional protagonist remains a stable,
consistent creature, whose destiny and actions are determined and
explained by what is assumed to be his or her (good or bad) 'nature'.

> Un personnage, tout le monde sait ce que le mot signifie. Ce n'est pas
> un *il* quelconque, anonyme et translucide, simple sujet de l'action
> exprimée par le verbe. Un personnage doit avoir un nom propre,
> double si possible: nom de famille et prénom. Il doit avoir des parents,
> une hérédité. Il doit avoir une profession. S'il a des biens cela n'en

vaudra que mieux. Enfin il doit posséder un 'caractère', un visage qui le reflète, un passé qui a modelé celui-ci et celui-là. Son caractère dicte ses actions, le fait réagir de façon déterminée à chaque évènement. Son caractère permet au lecteur de le juger, de l'aimer, de le haïr.[39] (Robbe-Grillet: 2002, p. 27)

Like Robbe-Grillet and the proponents of the *nouveau roman* before her, Denis clearly refutes such a tradition, but inscribes her approach within the context of a discourse of discrimination. Characterisation in Denis' films thus ignores the conventions of the traditional occidental hero and, by extension, preconceived categories of 'others':

[Il y a] une espèce d'injustice à considérer que dans le monde qui nous entoure, chacun a une place qui lui est attribuée d'office, que ce soit le Maltais ou l'Asiatique fourbe, le Noir niais et rigolard, la femme noire chaude, etc., etc. On peut décliner longtemps comme ça les fonctions du corps des autres.[40] (Lifshitz 1995)

By establishing parallel trajectories, her stories often depict a multitude of characters entrapped by different sets of preconceptions showed as equally arbitrary. Protée, the central character of *Chocolat*, is reduced to his role as the black 'boy', while in spite of her dominant status, Aimée is also limited by the definition of her function as the white woman in Africa, the wife of the colonial administrator. In *J'ai pas sommeil*, Daïga, the young woman from Lithuania, faces a range of preconditioned attitudes, different, but comparable to the more or less overt prejudices experienced by Théo, the young man from the West Indies. In *Beau travail*, the individual is literally subsumed by the precise role and rituals that the army dictates. Conversely, the precious chance that befalls the two characters caught in the immense

39 'A character – everybody knows what it means. It is not just a *he*, anonymous and transparent, merely the subject of the action expressed by the verb. A character should have a name and a double one if possible: family name and first name. He should have parents, hereditary links. A character should have a profession. If he has some property it is an advantage. Finally, he should possess a "character", a face in accordance with this temperament and a past that shaped them. His character determines his actions, makes him react in a certain way to each event. His character allows the reader to judge him, love him, hate him.'

40 'There is something unfair in considering that in the world around us everyone has been attributed a place, whether it is the deceitful Maltese or treacherous Asian, the simple-minded, grinning black, the 'hot' black woman, etc., etc. You could go on listing the functions of the others' bodies'.

traffic jam that immobilises the Paris of *Vendredi soir* is to be granted a moment of suspended time, where they can be no more and no less than two lovers.

A similar refusal of certitudes marks the visual treatments of the characters as bodies. Rather than disclosing information or signalling traits of personalities, the actual bodies of the individuals portrayed in Denis' fiction often function as screens. External looks are difficult to read, and, in some of the films, the bodies, obscured rather than exposed, tend to stand 'too close' to the camera, sometimes literally blocking out the view. On the one hand, this suggests that, as part of a process of internalisation, the impact of the environment (social as much as geographical) remains largely hidden. At the same time, the technique directly questions the authority of the cinematic representation as a visual mode that fetishises difference, and in particular racial difference.[41] Very early on, Denis was made aware of the defining power of the look:

> En Afrique, je me sentais étrangère, parce qu'on comprend assez bien, quand on est un petit enfant blanc, qu'on est pas de cette terre-là et que les gens de là-bas, ils sont différents dans le sens où ... la couleur de la peau, déjà, *ça saute aux yeux*.[42] (Denorme and Drouin 2002: 21)

As a visual medium, cinema is particularly apt to capture outward signs of difference such as the colour of one's skin. Yet the significance and the value allocated to these signs is relative and variable, depending on the point of view: when Godard's camera comes close to Camille's body as the young man undresses to take a shower, his skin loses any definition; the camera scrutinises the texture of the skin of a man that could be white or black. In the effect created by these images is condensed the initial idea of the whole film:

41 A character can be evoked in writing with a degree of uncertainty with regard to his or her race, and, in some languages, with regard to his or her gender, but the image that shows bodies also foregrounds the outward marks of identity. As discussed in the case of colonial cinema in the previous chapter, however, the necessity of insisting on these visible differences, and of qualifying them through the *mise en scène*, shows that they remain in fact relative, dependant on the way they are shown to and read by the spectator: ultimately, it is not the outward difference in itself that counts, but the characteristics assigned to it.

42 'In Africa, I felt foreign because you understand pretty well, when you are a white child, that you are not from this land, and that people there are different, that is ... the colour of skin, *makes it obvious*.' (literally: 'it leaps to your eyes' – my emphasis)

the impossibility of finding the answer on the surface of things, in the investigation of the isolated, a-historical[43] body. No matter how close, how intimately with the physical presence of the criminal (the body that Denis described in one interview as the 'corps du délit' ('corpus delicti' or 'body of evidence') the camera takes us, it reveals nothing to the viewer if not a similarity, an irreducible sameness. With reference to the subject of *J'ai pas sommeil*, Denis reflected that 'Y'a une part de reconnaissance de soi et de l'autre, même dans ce qu'il y a de plus monstrueux' ('Even in the most monstrous entity, one finds part of oneself and of the other') (Lifshitz 1995).

The uncertainty that surrounds the characters denies the rule of the principle of essence – the belief in immanent, unchanging elements that would predetermine each individual's 'nature' and destiny. In turn, it refocuses the attention on the impact, visible or internalised, of the changing historical context onto individuals. As the monstrous acts of Camille, the serial killer of *J'ai pas sommeil*, are not accounted for through a psychological depiction, through the revelation of a unique 'flaw' in his character, they are reinscribed in the wider background provided by the film. It is not an isolated, human accident, but the social setting as a whole that is at stake:

> C'est bien dans les films, de donner une chance à ceux qui n'en ont pas, de leur prêter un regard. Parce que finalement, même quand ils sont l'objet de faits divers, ils sont décrits comme des accidents, ou des raisons de se dire 'Ah ben oui, encore un immigré'.[44] (Lifshitz 1995)

The recontextualisation of characters and stories within a wider framework cannot be dissociated from the choice of setting or from the *mise en scène* and framing: the way the body is filmed and located in space and time is never anodyne in Denis' films. The extensive use of still frames, of long travelling and sequence shots, contributes to

43 What is meant by historical here is not merely something that belongs to a recorded past. Historical refers to the relative nature of reality, past or present, to values, beliefs, structures and systems that are changing and belong to a particular era. An individual's identity for instance, depends on the 'historical' context he or she inhabits, that is, the particular social, economic and cultural factors that are at play at the time and in the place where he or she lives.

44 'It is a good thing, in films, to give a chance to those who are denied it, to lend them a gaze, because in the end, even when they appear in the tabloid press, they are described as *accidents*, or as reasons to tell oneself "of course, it is an immigrant again".'

the depiction of the environment, inviting a contemplative gaze but also calling for the viewer to exercise his or her attention to detail. The sequence shot also allows for the elaboration of a visual expression of the relationship between characters and environment: 'Le plan séquence pour moi, c'est le temps nécessaire pour qu'un rapport s'établisse avec un personnage ... c'est le corps lui-même de l'acteur qui développe la chorégraphie' ('The sequence shot is the necessary time to establish a relation with a character ... it is the body of the actor that develops the choreography') (Lifshitz 1995). Denis' characters may express little as far as the dialogues are concerned, but their bodies, their place in space, and, even when sparse or highly stylised, their gestures and movements convey a lot of information. At the same time, their existence is always beset by a more or less marked sense of displacement. The off-centred framing, the dwarfing of the characters in landscapes, the contradictory directions of the travelling shots that follow their wanderings, but also the melancholy sound-track and the mixing of languages, all participate in a process of defamiliarisation and estrangement. Depending on the norms set by their social environment, it is their age, their social status, their race, their nationality, or their sexuality which mark the characters in her films as outsiders. They tend to live at the fringes of society, and the narrative space they inhabit is often a space of exile, borderline, changing and unfamiliar. Denis favours those moments when perception becomes uncertain, fraught with misreading. Her films privilege nocturnal settings, when bodies are likely to become obscured, to be swallowed by darkness; or those ambiguous times where night and day merge, with dawns almost indistinguishable from sunsets. Her characters are always, in one sense or another, out of place, marginalised, and sometimes alienated. Like the black American she meets during her trip in Cameroon, the young white woman who, in *Chocolat*, has come to Africa in search of her roots, finds that she is no more than a stranger and a visitor in the country of her childhood. For the musicians of the African band touring Europe in the humorous documentary *Man No Run*, the journey, punctuated by monotonous drives and stays in dull hotel rooms, is in part an experience of estrangement and homesickness. *S'en fout la mort* focuses on two friends, one from Benin the other from the West Indies, who arrive in a nondescript suburb of Paris alongside a motorway, to live in the bowels of the club where the illegal cockfighting they organise is to take place. *J'ai pas sommeil*'s main characters are immigrants and marginals, living in a Paris that belongs to the indefinable time zone between night and dawn. The suburbs are again the set chosen for *US Go Home*, but this time in the form of the housing estates emerging outside Paris in the 1960s. A non-picturesque Marseille serves as a backdrop for the portrayal of *Nénette et Boni*'s two unanchored youths. The legionnaires of *Beau travail* form an alien, obsolete presence in a landscape that threatens to swallow them. As in *US Go Home* and *S'en fout la mort*, it is partly on the other side of the *périph'* (*périphérique* or ring road) that *Trouble Every Day* is set, a no-man's-land that separates the centre of Paris from its suburbs and where the film's bloodthirsty heroin hunts for her prey. *Vendredi soir*'s tale of love between two strangers also unfolds under the sign of the transient: cars, nameless streets, hotel rooms. The film's poster shows a bright neon hotel sign glittering in the night. If hotels feature so prominently in Denis' films, it is because of the nature of such places: transitory spaces where anonymity meets intimacy.

Location and space thus emphasise a sense of displacement and function as metaphors for the process of potential exclusion of the individual (body) from (the collective body of) society. But the metaphor also evokes an inner sense of exile and longing, a feeling of foreignness that is played out at the level of the individual and of the individual's body through relations of desire, fear and rejection.

As the simultaneous affirmation of the self and of its dependence on an 'Other', desire, in Denis' films, is always disruptive, always associated with transgression. In *Chocolat*, a doubly unlawful attraction develops between Aimée, the wife of the white colonial administrator, and Protée, the black servant. The teenager of *US Go Home* sets her heart on a figure of love and hate: an American soldier from the nearby military base. The teenage girl of *Nénette et Boni* resents and ultimately disowns the new life that is growing in her womb. The arrival of a new recruit, the perfect Sentain, in his battalion, threatens to disrupt the impeccable order of legionnaire Galoup's world in *Beau travail*. In *Trouble Every Day*, a man and a woman whose bodies and minds are colonised by a mysterious illness are driven to commit horrific murders. Invaded, inhabited, beset by desire and aversion, threatened in its entity, the body thus appears as the actual and metaphorical vector of covert struggles.

Trouble Every Day is the most explicit in its evocation of a trespassing that opens onto the realm of the unspeakable and the forbidden. Conversely, *Vendredi soir* stands out because it concentrates less on the potentially disruptive force unleashed by desire than on the poetics of its actualisation. The two lovers steal some time to engage in a brief but intense sexual and emotional experience under the cover of anonymity. Until *Vendredi soir*, however, the films had focused more on the anarchistic nature of nascent or unavowed passions than on their fulfilment. Sex is only alluded to, it remains off-screen, unless it is, as in *Trouble Every Day*, indistinguishable from a death.

Like desire, the violence at play in Denis' films is of a complex, hybrid nature, of which, as we will see, films like *Beau travail* and *J'ai pas sommeil* explore several facets. It is the violence exerted on the individual who not only has to don a predefined identity, but does so in order to fit into a system of value rendered absurd by the disappearance of ideals (*Beau travail*). Conversely, it is the violence perpetrated by those individuals who turn blindly against the system, or push the logic of the hidden social violence to extremes of meaninglessness and destruction (*J'ai pas sommeil*). And, in a circular process, the violence ultimately becomes part of the process of retribution and punishment set in motion by a body or a social system that must protect itself and its community.

Whether they refuse to integrate it, or try to conform to an established system of values, as individuals who do not fit within the wider social framework, some of the central protagonists in her films come to incarnate such extreme feelings of inner as well as physical exile that the result is a loss of identity, a dissolution of the self. Coextensive with the disintegration of the self is the disappearance of the frontier between rational and irrational, between evil and good. The quote from American underground writer Chester Himes, which appears at the beginning of *S'en fout la mort*, could serve as a heading to many of Denis' stories: 'Every human being, whatever his race, whatever his country, creed or ideology, is capable of everything or just anything' (Himes 1976). The aberration incarnated by one or several characters, in most of the films, is present as a potential in everyone; the monstrosity is but an expression of a wider social unrest, of a latent side of human existence that emerges given the right environment. In many of Denis' fiction films, the critical observation of the contemporary world thus finds its expression through the *mise en scène* of a-typical 'heroes', disenfranchised and sometimes repellent figures, and in the investigation of some of humanity's more taboo areas: lawlessness and crime, abjection, incest, psychosis. In this, as we shall see, Denis' cinema draws close to a rich and complex tradition of counter-culture that focuses on the darker, irrational sides of humanity and explores the philosophical but also the aesthetic potential of transgression. Denis sternly dismisses cinemas which purport to represent an unquestionable, transparent concept of right and wrong (Morice 2001, Lifshitz 1995). On the contrary, she prophesies a sustained interest in artists and forms of discourses that deal with the relative and changing nature of points of views, truths and value systems.

Conclusion

The ending of Denis' films can never be said to provide a 'closure' as such. The destiny of her characters remains open to the speculations of the viewer's imagination. France is never seen to meet Protée again. There is no place in the life of the teenagers of *US Go Home* for the American soldier, other than as a memory linked to the rituals of coming-of-age. The implications of the dramatic ending of *Nénette et Boni* remain unknown, as does the fate of those linked to the tortured creatures of *Trouble Every Day*. The ending of *Beau travail* hovers ambiguously between death and rebirth, and in *Vendredi soir* time and the narrative logic catch up, but without bringing a resolution. Denis' films belong to the postmodern in so far as their denial of the comfort of the progressive unfolding and of the 'logical' ending seems to echo the contemporary fading of the belief in safe, 'grand narratives'. Her work belongs to a cinema that does not aim to present a vision of a set, immanent truth, but seeks to reflect the changing nature of human reality and time. The attention is thus refocused from the predominantly narrative to the specifically cinematic: Denis' films simultaneously present an analytical vision of the world, and stand as explorations of a cinema of the senses.

References

Alexander, Marguerite (1990), *Flights from Realism: Themes and Strategies in Postmodern British and American Fiction*, New York, Routledge.

Austin, Guy (1996), *Contemporary French Cinema*, Manchester, Manchester University Press.

Beaupré, Sylvie (1989), 'Chocolat', *Séquence* 139, p. 30.

Beugnet, Martine (2003), 'French Cinema of the Margins', in E. Ezra (ed.), *European Cinema*, Oxford, Oxford University Press.

Bonitzer, Pascal (2001), 'Décadrages', first published in *Cahiers du cinéma* 284, 1978, reprinted in *Théories du cinéma*, Paris, Cahiers du cinéma, pp. 123–33.

Chauvin, Jean-Sébastien (2002), 'Panne des sens', *Cahiers du cinéma* 571, 80–1.

Deleuze, Gilles (1994), *Cinéma 2: L'Image-temps*, Paris, Editions de minuit, 1985, reprinted as *Cinema 2: The Time-Image*, trans. H. Tomlinson and R. Galeta, London: The Athlone Press.

Denis, Claire (1996), www.worshipguitars.org (accessed July 2002).

Denis, Claire (2000), 'Lifetime series', www.ammi.org/calendar/SeriesArchives (accessed September 2002).

Denorme, Vincent and Douin, Emmanuel (2001), 'Travelling Light', *Modam* 1, 20–7.

Dobson, Julia (2002), 'From *Le Petit soldat* to *Beau travail*: Sequels of Engagement', conference *Contours of Commitment in French Cinema*, Nottingham Trent University, 22 September.

Dyer, Richard (1997), *White*, London and New York, Routledge.

Ezra, Elisabeth (2000), *The Colonial Unconscious*, Ithaca and London, Cornell University Press.

Himes, Chester (1976), *My Life Of Absurdity*, New York, Thundermouth Press.

Lemarié, Yannick (2000), 'A Propos d'Agnès Godard', *Positif* 471, 128–30.

Lifshitz, Sébastien (1995), *Claire Denis, la Vagabonde*, 48 minute documentary, colour, Prod. La Fémis.

Morice, Jacques (2001), Entretien avec Claire Denis, *Télérama*, 11 July, 27–9.

Prédal, René (2002), *Le Jeune cinéma français*, Paris, Nathan.

Robbe-Grillet, Alain (2002), first published 1963, *Pour un Nouveau Roman; 'Sur quelques notions périmées'*, Paris, Editions de Minuit.

Romney, Jonathan (2000), *The Guardian*/NFT interview, www.filmunlimited.co.uk, (accessed January 2003).

Sherzer, Dina (1996) (ed.), *Cinema, Colonialism, Postcolonialism – Perspectives from the French and Francophone Worlds*, Austin, University of Texas Press.

Silverman, Max (1999), *Facing Postmodernity: Contemporary French Thought on Culture and Society*, London and New York, Routledge.

Young, Lola (1996), *Fear of the Dark: Race, Gender and Sexuality in British Cinema*, London and New York, Routledge.

2

Screening exile

The films that launched Claire Denis' career as a filmmaker deal with aspects of France's recent history that had previously remained all but invisible. Chapter 1 briefly outlined how both at the level of the discourse, by the state laws limiting the rights of expression, and on the unconscious level, as a form of collective amnesia, the decolonisation and the lasting impact of imperialism had long been relegated to the shadowy areas of a little spoken past. But these are precisely the themes that inform Denis' filmmaking. Issues relating to colonialism and postcolonialism, to exile and alienation, always at play in her work, are central to the films discussed in this chapter.

Chocolat's lush natural and historical setting and *Beau travail*'s stunning open landscapes on the one hand, and *S'en fout la mort*'s claustrophobic atmosphere and spare *mise en scène*, and *J'ai pas sommeil*'s unusual portrayal of a *noir* Paris on the other, seem like aesthetic antinomies. It is because, although the films are part of a thematic continuity, they deal with different aspects of the same topic. The first features bear witness to a colonial reality recreated from memory, the latter are projections of the internal alienation generated by that reality. From Africa to France, from the external evidence to the hidden stigma, the films evoke a colonial past that has left visible and invisible marks on ex-colonisers and ex-colonised alike. *Chocolat* and *Beau travail* are filmed in Africa, and their entry point is the colonial and military settlement. *S'en fout la mort* on the other hand, eschews historical reconstruction to explore the insidious effects of the colonial past in the present time, and approaches the issue from the point of view of the black man, the ex-colonial subject in France. In *J'ai pas sommeil*, the *mise en scène* of alienation extends into a challenging exploration of transgression and evil. Together with the documentary *Man No Run*, Denis' first feature films thus signal, through the movement they initiate, a wish to explore the colonial inheritance and the phenomenon of exile and otherness in its complexity, without privileging a single point of view. Each time, the primacy of the suggested over the stated allows for the characters not to be trapped into categories and stereotypes, even if this means abandoning certitudes and conclusions. The techniques at work in the films appear radically different, yet in all instances, through narrative structure and camerawork, through music and visual symbolism, Denis pursues an investigation of cinema's unique capacity for dealing with the past, and in particular with its repressed memory:

> Le cinéma français n'est pas très bon en géographie. Ses parcours manquent généralement d'inventivité sur son propre territoire et frôlent l'errance touristique désœuvrée dès qu'on s'éloigne de l'Hexagone. Ce n'est pas simplement le signe d'un manque de curiosité de l'œil. Si le cinéma français n'est pas bon en géographie, c'est qu'il est également assez cancre en histoire, et précisément sur la question de l'histoire de sa géographie. Passer la frontière, c'est prendre le risque de rencontrer les fantômes d'un ailleurs refoulé: l'impérialisme et son image taboue, la colonie. Ce risque, Claire Denis l'a pris il y a deux ans avec Chocolat.'[1] (Strauss 1990a: 29)

Chocolat

Although it was a first film, *Chocolat* was widely talked about. Elected to represent France in the Cannes Festival's official selection, it was noticed for its unusual approach to a sensitive subject. With *Chocolat*, Claire Denis had chosen to depict one of the taboo areas of recent French history, the final years of the colonial empire, without giving in to the temptation of the nostalgic 'retrospective' trend.

---

[1] 'French cinema is not very good on geography. Generally speaking, explorations of its own territory lack inventiveness, and as soon as it leaves France, it starts to resemble tourism's idle wanderings. It does not merely signal the absence of a curious eye. If French cinema is not good on geography, it is because it is rather hopeless on history, and, more precisely, on the history of its geography. To go across the frontier is to take a risk to meet the ghosts of an elsewhere that has been repressed: imperialism and its taboo, the colony. This risk, Claire Denis took it two years ago with Chocolat.'

The film is composed of a long flashback, framed by two sequences in present time. A young woman, aptly called France (Mireille Périer), has come back to Cameroon on a pilgrimage to the place of her childhood. On the road, she encounters a young boy and his black American father, Mungo Park (Emmet Judson Williamson), who offers her a lift to a nearby town. During the drive, France reminisces about her years as a young girl growing up in a remote region in the north of the country where her father, Marc Dalens (François Cluzet), a *commissaire* (a colonial administrator with military powers) in the colonial administration, has been posted. During his frequent absences, seven-year-old France (Cécile Ducasse) remains in the settlement's whitewashed house with her mother Aimée (Giulia Boschi) and her 'boy' Protée (Isaac de Bankolé) with whom she has developed a close, secretive relationship. The daily routines of the small community are first disrupted by the visit of an Englishman, Boothsby (Kenneth Cranham), whom Aimée proceeds to entertain in a manner fitting to their station. Later on, after a plane crashes nearby, a motley group of colonial figures descends upon the house. The stranded passengers include a stereotypical intrepid pilot, a racist white planter and his black mistress, and a young couple of new settlers who will later refuse to be treated by the local black doctor. Luc (Jean-Claude Adelin), an ex-seminarist who is pretending to go native, joins them and stays on, imposing his ironical stance and self-indulgent pose on servants and masters alike. Without any explicit signs, the attraction between Aimée and Protée grows, provoking a jealous, cynical outburst from Luc. But when eventually, in a brief but intense scene, the young woman silently expresses her desire, she faces Protée's dignified refusal. As a result, Protée is dismissed from his function as house servant. France seeks him out in the garage where he is now working maintaining the generator. The two characters share one last ritualistic gesture that leaves them both physically marked: Protée lays a hand on the burning hot mechanism, and the little girl trustingly imitates him. The end sequence returns to an adult France, and to a contemporary Africa. After thanking Mungo for the lift, she returns to her hotel room overlooking an airport where Protée, perhaps, works as a baggage assistant.

Although the film benefited from the *Avance sur recette* (a state loan offered on the strength of the scenario, to be reimbursed after the release of the film, depending on box office results), and in spite of the help provided by Wim Wenders and Jean-Paul Belmondo, putting together the necessary financial backing for the shoot was a struggle, reflected in the long list of producers included in the credits. One reason would have been the relatively high budget proposed: filming on location in Africa, with a historical setting, was, for a first feature, a rather ambitious remit. Denis settled for Cameroon, where she had lived as a child, filming the contemporary part of the film in the capital Yaoundé, and the childhood episode near the small town of Mindif, in the north of the country. 'La dent de Mindif' ('Mindif's tooth'), the strange peak that so dramatically dominates the landscape, immediately captured the director's imagination, and she had a colonial style house rebuilt close to the nearby village. Shooting on location allowed Denis to surround herself with Cameroonian technicians. Though she admits that Chocolat was 'un film de Blanche' (Tranchant 1988) ('a white woman's film'), Denis nevertheless underlined the importance of the collaboration, of the presence of a 'regard de Noirs sur mon regard de Blanche' (Frodon 1988) ('black people's gaze on my white woman's gaze'), a theme that also underpins the mise en scène of the recent Beau travail.

Colonial memory

While aspects of the film recall Ferdinand Oyono's book Une vie de boy,[2] considering the approximate period of the flashback (the mid-1950s), the location, and the choice of a young girl as one of the central protagonists, the project's autobiographical basis is apparent. Yet, while she recognised that much of the material was linked to situations and places she had experienced as a child, Denis constantly played down the connection, insisting on the film's more universal basis. The initial idea for Chocolat, she stresses,

> n'était pas tellement liée à mon expérience personnelle, elle était plutôt liée à une accumulation d'idées reçues sur la colonie, de sensations et de souvenirs. Je pourrais dire que c'était davantage la grande mémoire collective des coloniaux qu'une histoire particulière entre un boy et une petite fille.[3] (Gili 1988: 15)

2 Paris: Julliard, 1956.
3 'was not particularly linked to my personal experience; it was linked to an accumulation of preconceived ideas about colonial settlements, as well as of

This insistence on the wider context and on critical analysis signals a deep suspicion towards three aspects of the cinematic discourse that, in her subsequent films, Denis will continue to sidestep: the resort to psychological exposition, the elaboration of moral tales and the retreat into the nostalgic.

To begin with, however, *Chocolat* appears rather traditional in form, a far cry from the more experimental approach adopted by the director in her second fiction feature for example. The premise of the film and its visual treatment seem hardly different from that of the conventional heritage cinema evoked in Chapter 1. The remembrance of the past, which forms the main part of the film, is based on the detailed reconstruction of a historical setting, and from costumes to set and props the production obviously strove for a feeling of authenticity. As mentioned earlier, and rather ironically for a film set to underline the absurdity of the colonial presence, the house of the *commissaire* even had to be built by local people, based on the memory of the village's eldest inhabitants. In its *mise en scène* and lighting, the film seems to oscillate between vivid, sensual evocations and a nostalgic feel. The feverish atmosphere is almost palpable, captured in chiaroscuro shots that contrast the darkness of the interiors and the unforgiving brightness and heat of the sun-drenched exterior. At the same time, the limited range of colours, beige and brown and rusty tones, endow many of the domestic scenes with an appearance akin to that of the old sepia photographs that would have been taken at the time. Denis and Godard also make a striking use of an impressive natural setting, depicting the stupendous landscape through those sweeping panoramic shots that have become a staple technique of the heritage genre.[4] In heritage cinema, such lyrical and spectacular images are usually seen to 'create a veil between us and the events which happened prior to the end of the colonization, and lyrically lead

---

sensations and memories. I could say that it was more the common collective memory of the settlers than the specific story between a boy and a little girl.'

4 The film thus arguably rests on three main characters, France, Protée, and the African landscape of North Cameroon – a landscape of mythical dimensions. Man and child have been given symbolic names. Like many of the children of French colons at the time, the little girl is called after a *métropole* that she has possibly never seen but that, through her mere presence, she stands for. As for Protée, like the God from Greek mythology whose name he bears, he has many talents, many jobs, and a multiplicity of roles in and around the house.

the spectator astray from the problematic appropriations taking place within these narratives' (Blum 1996: 65). The poetic, idealised aspect of the colonial memory, and, more specifically, of the colonial childhood, is undeniably present in *Chocolat*; however, this nostalgic dimension is both framed and qualified. Denis repeatedly underlined her refusal of both the concept of a 'love of the land', and of a romanticised vision that would justify, in retrospect, the colonial presence. *Chocolat*, she insists, does not attempt to give an untainted, 'truthful' vision of the past. It approaches it through the *memory* of childhood – a memory that is subjective, ambiguous, haunted by implicit, unspoken conflicts, and questioned by the reality of the present time.

> La mémoire enregistre beaucoup d'éléments plus ou moins mystérieux, qui méritent d'être réexaminés plus tard. Toutes ces impressions sont la matière du film, et j'ai voulu me servir de la mémoire comme d'une loupe, pour montrer les petits aspects de la vie. Mais à partir de ces choses minuscules, j'ai essayé de me poser des questions plus vastes. C'est la mémoire enchassée dans le présent.[5]
> (Tranchant 1988)

Denis' filmmaking plays on the scale of things, both literally and symbolically. Like the tiny bodies of the ants that, as described in one of Protée's riddles, draw black lines along the road, the human body and the travellers' caravans are but small black specks in the vastness of the African space. Aimée's project of planting a vegetable garden around the house appears as doomed as Marc's well-meaning attempts to regulate the life of the communities scattered in the bush. The African hinterland remains hostile to the sensibilities of such colonial ambitions. The land continues to erase traces of successive colonial powers (the vanished German settlers whose graveyard has been reclaimed by the wilderness) and to defeat technology (once stranded, it will take weeks for the passengers of the damaged plane to take off again).

From the banality of the family chronicle to the stupendousness of the imperialist project, the critical vision at play in *Chocolat* is exercised through the recording of details that can only take on their

---

5 'Memory records many more or less mysterious elements to be re-examined at a later stage. All these impressions form the material of the film, and I wanted to use memory like an enlarging glass, to show the small aspects of life. But from these tiny elements, I started to ask myself broader questions. It is memory inscribed in the present.'

full meaning when related to the wider context. Just as the framing and camera work never attempt to compensate for the presence of the off-field, the observations open on to a web of inferences that constantly refer back to a larger context of historical determinants. The description of a particular moment and place – one small settlement, a few years before the wars of independence – only takes its full signification when it is replaced within a larger time frame. In this way, Denis demonstrates that memory must be inserted within, and framed by, the present. Her narrative approach thus departs radically from the heritage genre's conventional reconstruction of the past, with or without the help of flashbacks. Whilst traditionally heritage films have set extraordinary individual trajectories against a backdrop of major historical events, Denis focuses instead on the daily reality of domestic life in a colony. Arguably, it is in particular the sensitive portrayal of those slow moments of inertia, brought on by an unbearable heat and boredom, that grants the film its quality.

In 1990, critic Frederic Strauss identified, from among the films dealing with France's colonial past, and in contrast with the dominant heritage trend of the late 1980s, a cinema of 'films historiques en marge des fresques édifiantes' ('historical films that remain separate from moralistic sagas'). Bringing together Denis' work and that of several other female filmmakers, he defined this cinema as the *Féminin colonial* (Strauss 1990a: 29). Along with the films of Marie-France Pisier (*Le Bal du Gouverneur* 1990) and Brigitte Rouän (*Outremer* 1990), a film like *Chocolat* functions, he argues, as a foil to an epic cinema of war exploits and historical sagas, by evoking instead 'la conscience anti-coloniale' ('the anti-colonial consciousness'), 'l'infiltration pernicieuse de rapports de force dans un paradis perdu' ('the pernicious infiltration of relations of force in a lost paradise') (Strauss 1990a: 30). Crucially, in Denis' case, the focus on the ordinary and the autobiographical element contributes to the reconstruction of a past that is never severed from the present:

Je ne voulais pas que ce soit seulement l'Afrique du passé parce que quand la colonisation s'est arrêtée, on a dit 'c'est la fin d'un empire, ce monde est fini'. Même si l'économie va mal, en Afrique, le pays continue à exister et il faut le montrer.[6] (Strauss 1990a: 30)

6 'I did not want the film to only show the past because when colonisation stopped, people said "it is the end of an empire, that world has ended". Even if the economy is in a bad state in Africa, the country continues to exist. It must be shown.'

Whereas heritage cinema's appeal rests partly on its ability to recreate dramatic historical chapters presented as 'closed', *Chocolat*'s narrative structure denies such closure. The past that is evoked in *Chocolat* is still present, its impact felt through the contemporary depiction of the same country. As such, *Chocolat* initiates a thematic – the exploration of the lasting impact of colonial rule, an impact that Denis' subsequent films will develop in the present tense.

More generally, *Chocolat* demonstrates a desire to question cinema's particular relation with the representation of time and history,[7] a theme that reappears throughout her cinema of exile. Film can play with time, and with its representation: the flashback, for instance, is arguably one of cinema's most efficient devices for evoking the emergence of memories, voluntary or traumatic (Turim 1989), that are played out with the immediacy of the present tense. Like the trauma (the emergence of repressed memories from an intolerable past), the flashback is a fragment of past time that is recalled in relation to a present: it is a situation in the film's diegetic present that explicitly or indirectly triggers the flashback. *Chocolat* first operates a smooth passage from present to past, through the sight of the unfolding landscape, changed yet familiar, and the lulling movement of a car journey. But it also eventually reveals the scars left by the past. In effect, *Chocolat*'s symbolism plays on the etymology of the term trauma, for, as Marreem Turim reminds us, 'the metaphor of psychic trauma relies on a comparison to the more visible damage done to a physical body' (Turim 2001: 205). From her childhood and from the story she shared with Protée, France has kept such a scar, the burnt palm of her hand, the smooth skin of one who has, as the befriended driver eventually remarks, 'no past, no future'.

Through its narrative rhythm, *Chocolat* also initiates an approach to the depiction of time that shuns the conventional cinematic treatment imposed in much of the mainstream practice. The epic framework of the grand narratives and the clear segmentation that serves the logical unfolding of a plot towards an expected conclusion are dismissed in favour of a non-linear, indefinite filmic and diegetic time. Freed from the necessities of the plot-driven time structure, the

7 Cinema has the ability to capture or to recreate events and to present them as if first-hand. Furthermore, and even more so since the popularisation of the video format, a filmed representation can be endlessly 'replayed', like vivid memories that the mind screens again and again.

film creates a specific cinematic tempo, where long takes are used to capture a particular atmosphere, a specific moment, rather than to demonstrate or to depict series of actions. The introductory sequence sets the tone, with its slow panoramics and long takes, placing the human figures within the space, establishing a sense of scale, without revealing anything of its enigmatic characters: 'Elle excelle à saisir un temps et un rythme très particulier, ceux de l'Afrique coloniale. Temps non strié, sans repère précis ...'[8] (Jousse 1988: 132). In effect, this particular sense of time and rhythm, already Deleuzian (Chapter 1) in its evocation of free-floating sheets of duration, will become a characteristic of Denis' filmmaking as a whole.

Much of *Chocolat*'s narrative avoids conclusions, and its unresolved ending may have left some of its viewers frustrated. Yet the resistance to the construction of a filmic time regulated by strict conventions of chronology and of cause and effect not only emphasises the fluctuations and incertitude inherent in memory itself, but also allows for Denis' fictional universe to question and overlap with non-diegetic realities. This predilection for the suggested and the unexplained have become the trademark of her cinema, an approach that also contributes to the enigmatic appeal of its characterisation. Already in *Chocolat*, characters are not treated in isolation, and there is no attempt to define them according to set psychological features. Causality is not to be found in their individual qualities and stories, but in their conditions of existence and in their relationship to their environment and to each other, entwined in the historical and geographical context. *Chocolat* may be recalled through the eyes and memories of France as an adult woman and as a child, but the young woman will never actually speak about her past, and the childhood memories are not elucidated through the expected voiceover account. Similarly, Protée's 'personality' does not elucidate his actions. He is not to be defined in terms of 'good' or 'bad', and his being cannot be dissociated from the description of a particular system that condemns him to subservience. Isaak de Bankolé, praised for his performance, remains largely silent, his character understated, yet powerfully present. Interestingly, the casting also defeats expectations, thus indirectly contributing to the fluctuating nature of a characterisation that resists definitions. With Bankolé (as in the case of Valérie

8 'She excels in capturing the very specific time and rhythm of colonial Africa. A time that is not patterned, that is devoid of precise points of reference.'

Lemercier, for *Vendredi soir*), Denis chose an actor whom she asks to play the opposite of the roles he had been known for. Bankolé's previous work on-screen had seen him cast as the stereotype of the resourceful, fast spoken black man with the large smile in the comedy *Black mic-mac* (Thomas Gilou 1986). In *Chocolat*, he assumes an introverted presence and a guarded performance, where each gesture becomes significant.

The thematic and aesthetic principles that have been outlined so far are present from the very beginning of the film. The images that compose *Chocolat*'s opening sequences hint at the autobiographical basis but suggest a universal dimension. They combine the realistic and the symbolic, privilege the unsaid over dialogue and exposition, and play on our perceptions of time and space .

The film starts with images of two people playing in the sea. There is a joyous carelessness in the scene, but also a symbolic overtone. The scene is filmed in long shot so as to take in a large section of the landscape, and the silhouettes are at first too distant to be identified, too far for us to tell, for instance, what the colour of their skin might be. There is a certain timelessness and a kind of mythical flavour to these images – man and child playing in the sea, that is, surrounded by the founding, maternal element. The soundtrack is dominated by the sound of the waves – comforting and powerful. One of the traditional images that is associated with the waves, in Western culture, is that of Aphrodite, the goddess of beauty, coming out of the water in all her dazzling whiteness. Such a white mythical construct has no bearing here: a black man and his son emerge from a dark sea to run on dark sand. Later on, they will be shown lying in the sand, side by side, the man, arms extended high above his head, adopting the position of Leonardo da Vinci's drawing of the perfect male figure. In the first instance, however, the two silhouettes exit the frame on the left, while the camera starts a panoramic movement in the opposite direction. Typical of Denis' and Godard's style, in this unexpected, contradictory use of movement, the human figure leaving the frame, draws attention to the existence of an off-field. The ensuing panoramic shot, almost 180 degrees to the right, slowly leaves the sea to turn inland. Again, the long shot stresses the immensity of the landscape, as does a depth of field that allows us to glimpse the faraway mountains. In the middle ground appears a tiny white silhouette sitting in the sand. A medium shot gives a closer picture of a young woman in T-shirt and shorts looking towards the right of the frame, before the film cuts directly to a close-up of the child's head resting in shallow water. This link is slightly confusing because, while it creates a connection between the two characters, the shot of the child cannot be interpreted as from the woman's point of view. She is far too far away and will not, in fact, approach the two bathers. A gap is thus created, a first sign of the discontinuity that exists between reality and representation; between childhood memories, the reality of the past and that of the present; between the observer, the white woman, representative of the old (colonial) order and the new Africa. A close-up on the child's hand elaborates on the theme, and forms a counterpoint to the film's closing sequence. The palm of the child's open hand shows deep lines, where France's own hand, which Mungo examines at the end, is devoid of any of the marks that would allow the deciphering of her past and future. In addition, the images, like the close-up on France's foot later on, further challenge our usual perception of things: the sand that clings to the young woman's skin, like the sand on which the child rests, and like the water around his head and over his hand, appears black.

Almost imperceptibly, the rest of the sequence continues to undermine our sense of a spatial and temporal whole. A series of shots alternate from the young woman to the sea, before the panoramic shot resumes. Again, the movement stops inland, but reveals a different perspective, a dirt track lined by large trees, in between which the young woman, now dressed, is seen walking away. The circular movement, conventionally associated with continuum and disclosure, with spatial and temporal continuity, thus becomes, in this case, unexpectedly elliptical.

In the following sequence, France is walking along a road until a passing car, driven by the man from the beach, stops to pick her up. When the car first overtakes the young traveller, it is as if the past and the present were simultaneously catching up with her. Not only the driving sequence triggers a flashback, a scene where she travels in a truck as a little girl, but the more recent past and the future also mingle with the present, in the shape of the black American father, a new kind of expatriate, and of his little boy, born in Cameroon. There is a certain aggressiveness in the man's comments: he takes the young woman for yet another tourist, a white occidental in search of a bit of adventure, the embodiment of a new, hidden form of colonialism.

When they reach the town, a brief series of long shots show the young woman thanking her driver then setting off to find her next means of transport across the busy, ramshackle street. Around her, from the corrugated iron roofs to the church tower, from the Texaco petrol station to the old-fashioned Peugeot cars and the ads for the Panach' beer, signs of past and present forms of colonial presence abound. Similarly, in the film's concluding scene at the airport, the baggage assistants are shot loading African artefacts into the plane – an image that also works as an unspoken reminder of a continuing system of economic and cultural exploitation.[9]

France does not find a bus and ends up pursuing her trip with Mungo and his son. Under the little boy's inquisitive stare, the young woman, now the one observed, clings to her father's old sketch book. The gesture hints at the nature of the film, revealing *Chocolat* as a sort of visual diary. Through this journey, both in space and time, a character is attempting to elucidate part of her past, and to recapture a sense of her identity. The close-up on France's book is followed by a scene that shows the little boy name parts of his father's face in the local language. Witnessed by the adult France, and repeated, with an inversion of roles, by France and Protée in the flashback, the scene has an explicit symbolic significance: to name is to define, and to assert one's own language (in this case, as opposed to the language of the colonial power) is to assert one's own identity and culture. As it turns out, the father is no less an outsider, in search of an identity, than the young woman in the back of the car. As a black American, he sought to find his roots in his ancestors' country of origin. Through him, another part of the colonial history is evoked: hers is linked to the end of the colonial era, his to its very beginnings, to forced emigration and slavery. To local people, however, Mungo's presence is synonymous with postcolonial realities, with the existence of an economic regime determined by the American international domination. Times have changed and neither the colour of the skin nor childhood affinities are sufficient to allow France or Mungo to feel 'at home'. The young man has not found his place, and France can be little more than a passing visitor in the country were she grew up.

9 In 1961, Chris Marker and Alain Resnais shot *Les Statues meurent aussi*, a powerful documentary about the transformation of African art from a way of life into an industry under the pressure of the colonial economy and fashion. The film was banned by the state censorship board.

At first, the landscape, filmed from inside the car, unravels from left to right – the direction of Western writing, the conventional sign of progression in time. A shot of France's thoughtful face is inserted, and the music starts, indicating a new beginning in the narration. The ramshackle houses with their corrugated roofs are replaced by traditional clay huts, as the landscape now passes in front of our eyes from right to left, a movement towards the past, given rhythm by the hearty, lyrical accents of Abdullah Ibrahim's timeless music.

Space, gaze and taboos: the *mise en scène* of discrimination

Chocolat debunks the nostalgic stereotype not only through its narrative structure, by looking at the past in the light of the present, but also through its choice of protagonists. Although it is France's father, the explorer and 'enlightened' administrator of the region, the author of the travelling diary, who is the typical colonial hero, the film does not focus on him. A few sequences document his missions to the remotest part of the hinterland, giving shape to his romantic dream as an adventurer; the film concentrates principally on the life of the colonial settlement, on the relations that link Protée the servant, the little girl France and Marc's wife Aimée. The main setting is thus the house, and not merely the masters' quarters, but also, at the back of the principal building, the servants quarters and the dependencies. As such, the film draws a series of parallels between an exploited majority primarily represented by the character of Protée, and the status of women and children, even if they are Western occidental. Like Protée and France, Aimée, though she stands as a representative of the colonial order, is excluded from the more glamorous aspects of the colonial venture. Restricted to the domestic sphere where her role is mainly decorative, she faces the void and absurdity of a largely obsolete existence, and experiences the latent tensions generated by the law that rules colonial life.

Women, children and servants alike thus occupy the lower positions in the hierarchy of a colonial myth of adventure and conquest. They all belong, in some ways, to the realm of the Other that the traditional male colonial discourse has tended to make invisible, or to use as a foil. As discussed in the first chapter, the colony occupied a crucial function in the construction of the *métropole*'s self-image as a unified nation. Cinema, as we saw, was one of the media that played on strategies of difference where the racial Other stood as the antithesis against which white Western identity was asserted as the norm. In some ways, the strategies of representation at play were comparable to those applied to gender (Young 1986). The very basis of feminist film theory was to question the process whereby the female figure was objectified and used as the foil for the affirmation of the male figure as subject and as norm. In her psychoanalytical critique of such processes, Mary-Ann Doane has drawn attention to Freud's use of the trope of the 'dark continent' in his description of female sexuality, and on the collapsing of femininity and race as the Other (Doane 1991). The woman, in film, often stands as the mysterious entity, the *terra incognita* to be explored and conquered. In the margins of representation and subjectivity, the realm of child-hood, because it still eludes the defining, normalising process of adulthood, also remains in the margins. It is therefore not surprising that the colony, as the land of mystery and danger, should so often be described in feminine terms, or as an unpolished, childlike entity, and filmed from the point of view of the white male subject.

That in *Chocolat* the primacy of the point of view should be related almost entirely to characters that are peripheral to the colonial project is thus crucial in establishing the film's economy of gaze:

> Dans ce rapport très dynamique avec la mémoire, le projet autobiographique échappe à la banalité minimaliste du simple désir de raconter des choses très personnelles pour affirmer le lien avec le cinéma qui marque toute la logique du regard ... L'autobiographie impose un point de vue ... [qui] n'est pas celui des hommes, donc pas celui de l'autorité. C'est un certain regard sur la colonie qui se révèle ici, une mise à distance de la Loi dont la violence revient en échos intimes, quotidiens, dramatisés et secrètement douloureux.[10] (Strauss 1990a: 30)

In *Chocolat* the camera does not seek to unveil, but to observe and record, paying a particular attention to those details that appear, on

10 'In this very dynamic relation to memory, the autobiographical project escapes the minimalist banality of the mere desire to recount very personal things, in order to stress the link with cinema, upon which rests the whole logic of the gaze ... The autobiography imposes a point of view ... [which] is not the point of view of men, that is, of authority. It is a particular look at the colonial settlement that is at play here, distanced from the Law whose violence returns daily in intimate echoes, dramatised and secretly painful.'

the surface, anodyne. The point of view is most often associated with that of the child, who adopts the same distanced, observing attitude as that of her 'boy' towards the white adults. Hers is a fairly mute presence, relayed by fixed frames and medium to long shots which evoke a child's neutral stance – the partly disengaged position of one that senses rather than comprehends and judges. Even when the point of view is an objective one (dissociated from any of the characters), long takes abound, capturing the movements of human figures that enter and leave the fixed frame while the gaze of the camera lingers on the landscape or on the deserted set. At the same time, the spare use of camera movements, together with the framing and the distance, grant importance to the overall context, to the environment and the unspoken rules that regulate each character's movements. The shot/counter-shot on the other hand, as the most familiar figure of explanation in cinematic language (showing the cause, and then in the next shot its effect, showing the face of a speaker, then that of the listener ...), is rare, as is conventional dialogue. The lack of explanatory statements, of narrative demonstration, thus challenges the spectator to engage in an analytical viewing experience, where each detail calls for critical attention. At the same time, the *mise en scène* plays on the relation between bodies and space, favouring gestures and gazes over speech:

> L'une des forces du film est justement de ne rien expliquer ... Claire Denis est incontestablement très à l'aise pour filmer l'inaccompli, le silence, l'insistant, tout ce qui rôde mais demeure invisible.[11] (Jousse 1988: 132)

The approach corresponds to the desire not only to sidestep the conventional, dominant point of view, but also to evoke the colonial order through its most insidious aspects.[12] It is around the evocation

---

11 'Indeed, one of the strength of the film is that it does not explain anything ... Undeniably, Claire Denis has a singular ability to capture the unaccomplished, the silence, the pervasive, that which lurks but remains invisible.'

12 The rise of opposition that would eventually overthrow the colonial power is only indirectly evoked, in the scene where Marc goes in search of the local doctor. As the car stops in front of the school, where some of the local people organise secret nightly gatherings, its front lights throw a bright halo on the building's door. The men inside come slowly out, blinded, covering their eyes with their hands: though the context is not one of confrontation, the *mise en scène* strongly evokes the scenes of group arrests that would punctuate the period leading to the uprising.

of the 'douceur rampante et abominable du "chacun à sa place"' ('the abominable, creeping softness of the "everybody in its place"') (Strauss 1990a: 32), that the film is organised, progressively hinting at a whole scheme of established rules and unspoken assumptions that regulate each and every individual, assigning every woman and man a precise place and a prescriptive status.

One of the first shots of the flashback shows France and Protée sitting together at the back of a truck, where they each get an equal share of the frame space. Man and child face the camera, silently contemplating the unfolding landscape, unaware of the dialogue exchanged by Marc and Aimée in the front. Later, as they stop for lunch, France chooses to remain in Protée's company. One critic, sensitive to the fairy-tale quality of the story, mentions the *Alice in Wonderland* feel that the relation between 'l'enfant lilliputienne et le géant Protée' ('the tiny girl and Protée the giant') calls forth (Lefort 1988: 44). To the child, Protée is both servant and mentor, protective and awe-inspiring. The man and the child share an arcane complicity sealed by mysterious rituals that skirt the prescriptions and rules imposed in the adult world. Protée tells riddles and garnishes France's buttered bread with live ants, and, when he waits at the table while she eats, France forces him to kneel down to taste her soup, and spoon-feeds him. In one episode, the pair even go on a nightly hunt, Protée brandishing a useless rifle, and carrying France perched on his shoulders. As he walks into the darkness that surrounds the house, repelling the hyenas' laughter with his loud incantations, the two bodies merge, becoming one tall silhouette. However, if, on the surface, the relationship between Protée and France appears to eschew the Law that governs the realm of adulthood, it nonetheless depends on it. The closeness that unites the two characters also reveals the 'boy''s inferior status. Protée is an adult, yet, as a black servant, his is a position that is, at best, comparable to that of the (white) child. Protée waits and takes orders, dependent on the will of the white settlers, and, even though he appears to exercise a strong influence over the child, he is also at the whim of a little girl, jealous of 'her boy''s rare moments of private life.

In her interviews, Denis recalls how the colonists' children, separated from the local children and marginalised from the adult world of their own parents, functioned as intermediaries, between the world of the white settlers and that of the adult natives. In *Chocolat*,

France's status as go-between is emphasised through the techniques associated with the representation of her movements and point of view. The ex-seminarist, Luc, is the only other white character that is seen mingling with the servants. But whereas Luc's behaviour is recorded as a deliberate gesturing, an attitude destined to provoke his white counterparts, the fluid camera movements or the long fixed takes that document France's movements around the settlement suggest a largely innocent presence. Drawn to the community of black workers through solitude, curiosity and unspoken affinities, the child repeatedly escapes the attention of her mother and leaves the masters' house to stand at the edge of the servants' lodgings, at the border between two worlds. When the arrival of an English friend of the family disrupts the normal routine, she is excluded from the preparations and from the celebrations that take place, but observes them from afar, hiding in the dark and exchanging comments with a female servant.

Mirroring the colonial system as a whole, the spatial arrangements of the domestic setting thus reflect the existence of a strict hierarchical system. France's mother Aimée never crosses the unmarked boundary that separates the main house from the servants' quarters. Even when Luc defiantly leaves the house to sit and eat with the employees and coarsely addresses her, Aimée does not leave the raised veranda that surrounds the house. If her gesture of desire towards Protée, at the end of the film, is so potent, it is because it breaches an extremely powerful taboo. Whereas children like France can still enjoy a physical closeness to all adults whatever their status and colour, white adults do not mingle with, and do not touch the servants unless it is absolutely necessary.

Equally significant is the ambiguous status of the father figure, a sympathetic presence that embodies the dangerous pull of romanticism. A benevolent representative of the colonial power, Marc nevertheless seems to look upon the land of others as if it was his own gigantic playground. The insidious nature of his role as a sympathetic occupier is made clear from the start, in the first sequence of the flashback, through a brief, almost unnoticeable situation and throwaway comment. Marc is driving his family and Protée back home on a dirt track. The group stops for lunch, and before the journey starts again, the two men are framed together in long shot, standing with their back to the camera, urinating while facing the immensity of the bare landscape. The triviality of the gesture in contrast with its setting, the two men's silhouettes, one in shorts, the other in the white colonial uniform but equally sharing the frame, all seem to indicate a kind of nonchalant fraternity. Yet, before turning back to the truck, Marc flippantly comments, 'L'année prochaine, j'élargis la route!' ('Next year, I will widen the road!') Seemingly anodyne, like the context in which it is uttered, the sentence is nevertheless significant. As a representative of the colonial power, Marc is able to take lightly a decision that could have important implications for the indigenous population (one could imagine that for the local people this might mean additional heavy work performed far from their homes). Most importantly, these few words show his implicit mastery, his power to modify the landscape, demonstrating ownership over a land that does not belong to him. As he later explains, unwittingly voicing the legitimising discourse of an imperialistic conquest disguised as adventure, discovery is his motivation, following the continuing trail towards an endlessly receding horizon.

The Dalens may be a liberal couple, enjoying the friendship of the local chief, they nevertheless fall prey to the almost unconscious mode of behaviour of the colonial oppressor. Before the dinner with Boothby, for instance, Aimée commands Protée to take a shower, but only just before he dresses up to wait at the table. In a few seconds, one sentence and an exchange of glances, a whole system of humiliation and repressed anger is revealed. Similarly, very little is said in the brief sequences that involve Delpich, the uncouth coffee planter, and his servant and mistress Thérèse. After a meal taken with the rest of the white guests, Delpich, observed by Protée and France, furtively collects some left-overs from the kitchen, and brings them back to his room, where Thérèse awaits. Even more than Delpich's painfully coarse statement ('Voilà ton picotin, ma cocotte') ('Here's your ration, pet'), it is the *mise en scène*, and Thérèse's silence, that suggest the brutal nature of the situation. The young woman, a mere silhouette in the darkened room, sits motionless on the floor, at the foot of the bed. The image is sufficient to imply the limbo that Thérèse is doomed to inhabit as the incarnation of the taboo of cross-racial sexual relations. The same taboo, this time involving a white woman and a black man, is brought forth in the scene where the local doctor is called in to give medical care to the young wife of a recently arrived colonial administrator. Not only is the idea of a black man as qualified doctor inconceivable to this couple of new settlers, but they cannot envisage the possibility that he might touch the body of a white woman.

It is, however, through Protée and Aimée's largely unspoken relationship that the tensions generated by a whole system of prejudices and taboos emerge most poignantly. The film often refers to the stereotypical representations of gender and race that would have forbidden or poisoned any relation involving a white woman and a black man. From the white woman's nymphomania to the sexualisation of the black man, the myths attached to these two figures of the colonial discourse, and elaborated in order to diffuse the threat they represent to a dominant male white order, are necessarily present here. But in *Chocolat*, the *clichés* are simultaneously played out, questioned, and debunked. In one ambiguous shot for example, Protée is presented to the gaze in a stereotypically objectifying manner: he is filmed washing himself outside the house, covering his muscular body with soap. In effect, the outdoors servants' shower does not allow for proper privacy, and in a later scene the process of objectification and voyeurism is framed by the experience of shame. This time, as Luc, Aimée and France arrive back at the house while Protée takes his shower, the young man cringes in anger and humiliation at the possibility of having been seen.

One scene in particular, halfway through the film, manages to crystallise the complex web of issues at stake in the portrayal of the connection that unwittingly comes to bind Aimée and Protée. Aimée, preparing for her formal dinner with Boothby, calls Protée for last-minute assistance. While the young man hesitantly stands in the dark doorway of her bedroom, she orders him to come in and help her tie the back of her dress. Aimée steps in front of her full-length mirror and Protée comes to stand behind her. In the following, heightened moment, Protée and Aimée, the servant and his master, the black man and the white woman, framed together, look at each other silently and their exchange of gazes suffices to outline the subversive meaning of that brief instant. Although, in an earlier scene, craving for privacy, Aimée had ordered Protée not to enter her bedroom, her request regarding the tying of the dress is not in itself equivocal. As illustrated in a subsequent scene, where Boothby's manservant caters for his completely drunk master, the presence of servants is considered inconsequential. Aimée and Marc can kiss in front of Protée; their guests can hold racist conversations while he waits at the table, unnoticed and rendered faceless by the framing. The scene featuring the mirror is thus particularly powerful because Protée, by returning the gaze, asserts himself as a full subject, able to reciprocate both the gaze and the desire felt by Aimée. Recognition, shame and desire ambiguously mix as the young woman briefly lowers her eyes. At the same time, the symbolic dimension of the *mise en scène* captures the two characters together, but, as reflections, foregrounds the almost inescapable web of appearances and rules in which they are caught. Yet, for this intense moment, it is the two conventional 'others', the feminine and the racial other, that take over the screen and gaze at themselves and at the camera.

Throughout, Denis resisted the pressure to elucidate the complex relationship that develops between Aimée and Protée, and between Protée and France, and to bring the film to a dramatic climax that would also provide an acceptable, conventional closure. The last confrontation between Aimée and Protée is again silent, and its depth and intensity come from the compelling presence of the unsaid, of the taboo that weights on both protagonists. The scene is shot in one take, in fixed frame and low light, avoiding visual dramatisation. Aimée sits prostrate on the floor next to a French window, barely visible, as Protée steps in to close the curtains. As the young man stands close to her, she touches his leg. Protée closes the blinds before he bends down to reach for the young woman who he roughly raises back on her feet. The repressed violence of the gesture may be a sign of contained anger or of contained desire. But by forcing her to stand before he leaves, Protée also extends to Aimée the irreducible sense of dignity that prevents him engaging in a relationship steeped in inequality.

The title of Denis' film is representative of its deceivingly soft tone: chocolate is the warm, sweet drink that one associates with the comforting safety and innocence of childhood. But it is also a highly valuable substance, imported from ex-colonies where, like so many of the goods produced for the *métropole*, it was synonymous with exploitation and harsh work in the fields. In the context of the colonial past, chocolate also brings back memories of the racist imagery that came to symbolise the imperial rule: *Banania* boxes of instant chocolate appeared on the breakfast table of most French families, adorned with a slogan in pidgin French and stereotypical images of smiling black soldiers in colonial uniform.

Ultimately, *Chocolat*'s title thus signals the deception inherent in the imperialist project. 'Être chocolat', in French, also means to be unsuccessful and disappointed, and the phrase accurately describes France and Mungo's experience of contemporary Cameroon. France in particular, as a girl and as an adult, stands as an incarnation of the dilemma of colonialism. Having grown up in a country where they were representatives of an occupying power, ex-colonial settlers can never claim that particular country and its history and culture as their own. Torn between the 'motherland' and the adopted country they remain forever in exile, lacking a full identity.

Man No Run

Denis met the *Têtes Brûlées* (literally, the *burning heads*, also meaning the daredevils) in Cameroon's capital Yahoundé, when she was filming *Chocolat*. She was attracted to the group's bizarre blend of ethnic tradition and postmodern cool: a mix of old and new instruments to play variations on the traditional *Bikutsi* music, and a combination of body painting and shaven heads in the punk style. Denis planned to feature the group and their music in *Chocolat*, but was unable to do so due to copyright problems. After the completion of *Chocolat*, however, she managed to put together the necessary resources for a documentary shot with minimal technical means, and, rather than filming in Cameroon, she ended up following the group through a French tour of concerts.

Man No Run stands as a striking demonstration of the fundamental role played by music in Denis' work, but also of the direct impact of the environment and of chance over her directorial choices. In the absence of a precise scheme, the director shows her ability to probe the real and bring out those seemingly less significant details that ultimately form the film's thematic framework and a mood. The film initiates the move back from Africa, and the reframing of the theme of exile within the context of the old *métropole*, which also applies to *S'en fout la mort*. One critic aptly renamed the film a '*détour*' (Mazabrard 1989: 53): Denis' atypical road movie is shot from the point of view of the group, and this time the foreign land is France itself. In addition, while the film starts with extracts from a concert, it is primarily the other side of the performance, the margins of the stage that the director chooses to portray. The film thus becomes a chronicle of daily life on tour, with its anonymous hotel rooms, its late night discussions in the local bars, and its monotonous, ever recommencing journeys. This is a voyage of initiation, and not only for the musicians, but also for the French spectator, who is invited to consider hidden facets of familiar environments, from the dull, nondescript anywhere places to the *cliché* tourist location, commented upon by musicians speaking a mix of Ewondo, Saoussa, and French. The sense of displacement culminates with the sequence at Mont Blanc, the discovery of the mythical white snow, which the men contemplate through the windows of a suspended cable car. 'The cabin slides through the landscape, isolating them as in a bubble. The feeling of exile then reaches its paroxysm: blacks amongst the ice.' (Mazabrard 1989: 54). Occasionally, anecdotal cultural differences are discussed, as when one of the musicians recalls how his grandfather broke a radio in order to see whose voice it was that was addressing him thus, and reflects that a white man would have opened the machine merely to see how it functioned. At the same time, the film does not seek to create unbreachable gaps between the visitors and the country they pass through. Through fluid movements and long-sequence shots, the camera goes back and forth, gathering some details in passing, and linking the human figure to the environment, the public to the performers. The music inhabits the whole film without ever becoming a mere accompaniment to the images. Silences, words and music are given the same status, the same signifying function. The pace is never forced, neither constructed in order to fit a message or a particular narrative nor to turn a situation into a drama. The information thus seems to come in its own time, to appear in accordance with the film's rhythm, and with its title, *Man No Run* (also the title of one of the group's songs), which advocates patience and obstinacy.

S'en fout la mort

After *Chocolat*, the shooting of the documentary *Man No Run* brought Denis back to France, but away from its more picturesque countryside, to the anonymous land that borders its roads and motorways. The move is confirmed in *S'en fout la mort*, where the wide, sun-drenched expanses of African landscape characteristic of *Chocolat* have been replaced by a claustrophobic, subterranean world in a shady suburb of Paris. In the image of its setting, the feeling of exile evoked in *S'en fout la mort* is an internalised one, an inner sense of lack and alienation that the character of Jocelyn incarnates and which imbues the film as a whole. The film thus charts a double movement: the 'return' to the French *métropole*, and a fall back into the inner recess of human existence:

> L'histoire des deux personnages de *S'en fout la mort* est inscrite en eux, comme est inscrite dans ces premières images du film, la propre histoire de Claire Denis cinéaste: de retour d'ailleurs (*Chocolat*), après un voyage sur les routes (*Man No Run*), elle débarque sur les routes de Rungis.[13] (Strauss 1990b: 64)

Dah (Isaak de Bankolé) is from Bénin, Jocelyn (Alex Descas) from the West Indies (Martinique or Guadeloupe). The two friends get by as small-time traffickers, in pursuit of the big job that will allow them to pay their debts and fill their pockets. To this end, Jocelyn agrees to put his knowledge of cockfighting in the service of Ardennes (Jean-Claude Brialy), a white man who spent part of his life in the West Indies, where he became addicted to the game. Ardennes is a ruthless petty crook who handles a multiplicity of more or less legal businesses in association with his son from a first wife, Michel (Christopher Bucholz), and with his new spouse, Toni (Solveig Dommartin). He also nourishes an ambiguous nostalgia for the past. Once the lover of Jocelyn's mother, he greets the young man as if he was his long-lost son, and indulges in paternalistic reminiscences. Dah and Jocelyn enter into a contract with him, agreeing to open a cockfighting pit in Ardennes's sordid kingdom in Rungis, south of Paris. Thus, the two newcomers start a clandestine life, alternating between the training of the cocks and the nocturnal fights, where the hysteria of the crowd is fuelled by frantic betting. Toni, who has become the object of desire of all the men, keeps Michel at bay, but appears attracted to Jocelyn. When Jocelyn's favourite cock, *S'en fout la mort*, is blinded, the claustrophobic existence and sordid violence start to defeat the young

13 'The story of *S'en fout la mort*'s two characters is inscribed in them as is inscribed in the first images of the film the story of Claire Denis the filmmaker: returning from elsewhere (*Chocolat*), after a trip on the roads (*Man No Run*), she arrives on the streets of Rungis.'

man. He admits to his growing longing for Toni, and to his need to get away from the pit. Bound by debts and contract terms, however, Dah agrees to one last fight. This time, the animals will be armed with deathly steel spurs. As his contender, a white cock called Toni, is being butchered, Jocelyn's anger explodes. Amidst the confusion of the crowded room, Michel stabs him. In their subterranean chambers, Dah lays out the corpse and washes his friend's body before being taken to the police station. The film ends with Dah's departure the following morning.

If the material for the film appears far from *Chocolat*'s largely autobiographical inspiration, the subject nevertheless partly originated in the director's own experience, which accounts for the urgency that marks the project. The director explained, without divulging any detail, that it was the disappearance of one of her close relations that spurred the need to make a film about loss and grieving. Fargeau and Denis wrote the script in a few weeks, and the project of focusing on a friendship was confirmed by the choice of the two main actors (Strauss 1990b: 85). Not only did Isaak de Bankolé, the Protée of *Chocolat*, agree to play one of the leads, but he also introduced Denis to actor Alex Descas. In reality as in the film, the two men, one from Africa, the other from the West Indies, were long-time friends.

An unclassifiable film

S'en fout la mort, like *Chocolat*, was selected to represent France, this time at the Venice Festival. It did not, however, attract the same amount of interest. This was due no doubt to the harsher, more visceral vision it orchestrates, but also, probably, to the film's unclassifiable nature. Whilst, particularly with reference to the tradition of colonial cinema, *Chocolat* could be related to and distinguished from the conventional heritage trend that dominated the French production at the time, *S'en fout la mort*, on the contrary, resists genre comparisons. The film does indeed rest on a thorough research into the tradition of breeding cocks and of cockfighting, and the actors trained with an experienced breeder in preparation for it. Yet neither the effect of the hand-held camera, nor the long sequences devoted to the care of the animals, suffice to transform the film into a docudrama. Like Dah's voiceover commentary, a deep murmur that flows with the images, the descriptive sequences are more poetic than explanatory. Resting on his knees, in front of a deep-red carpet, framed by the uprights of a door, Jocelyn balances the cock on its legs from right to left, then throws the animal in the air. A whirl of beating wings and feathers fills the frame. It is the movement of the bodies, the seductive choreography binding man and animal that the camera records. Ultimately, this kind of preparatory 'dance' performed by the birds acts as a metaphor for the unspoken, violent destiny that besets the protagonists.

S'en fout la mort's first image is one of Dah sitting in his car. He is framed in medium close-up, from the back, the outline of his profile almost swallowed up by the surrounding darkness. His deep voice, heard as a voiceover commentary, quotes Chester Himes' dark words about man's equality in sin.[14] Soon, the lights of a passing truck briefly illuminate the car and its passenger. The truck parks in front, and three men, two truckers followed by Jocelyn, disembark in the wan halo projected by the light of Dah's car. Dah and Jocelyn exchange a smile, boxes are extracted from the back of the truck where they had been hidden, money changes hands. The two friends go back to the car, having barely exchanged two words. As the car starts, the basic elements of plot are spelt out by Dah's voiceover tale: where the two men come from, where they are going and why. The music that Dah chooses to play, and that becomes his theme music throughout the film, Bob Marley's *Buffalo Soldier*, introduces the film's implicit problematic: at stake is the history and identity of two protagonists who are two outsiders.[15] The rest of the sequence, on which the credits unfold, is composed of a long series of shots/counter-shots of the two men. Again, the features of the faces, sketchily drawn by the scarce light, seemed forced out of a dark background barely animated by the smoke of Jocelyn's cigarette. As previously, no words are exchanged, yet the alternation of close-ups stresses the men's deep complicity,

14 'Every human being, whatever his race, whatever his country, creed or ideology, is capable of everything or just anything'.
15 The title and lyrics of the song refers to black soldiers enrolled in the American army to fight the war against native Indians: 'If you know your history/Then you would know where you're coming from/Then you wouldn't have to ask me/ Who the heck do I think I am/I'm just a Buffalo Soldier/In the heart of America/Stolen from Africa, brought to America/Said he was fighting on arrival/Fighting for survival/Said he was a Buffalo Soldier/Win the war for America.' (Bob Marley, *Buffalo Soldier*, 1983).

just as Dah's internal monologue did, by addressing Jocelyn directly.
Dah's friend nods and smiles in agreement, as if his companion had
spoken aloud. With its nocturnal setting, its voiceover introduction,
its mysterious exchange of money and smuggled goods, the opening
sequence of *S'en fout la mort* deceptively sets the film as a thriller or as
a film noir:

> Claire Denis introduit *S'en fout la mort* comme un film policier, ou qui
> pourrrait le devenir. Mais de la police, on ne verra qu'un ou deux
> uniformes silhouettés dans un des derniers plans. Et c'est logique. La
> réalisatrice va filmer une implosion. Pas du tout le choc ou l'explosion
> naissant du contact entre l'interdit et l'ordre.[16] (Sartirano 1990)

The set-up and the muffled rhythm of the single bass chord that
runs on this first sequence create a sense of expectation and suspense.
Yet it is not on dramatic shifts and twists that the intensity of the film
is built. In effect, the basic elements of the plot, evacuated at the very
beginning of the film, leave space for an observation of the mechanisms and circumstances that will draw some of the protagonists
towards their fate. But *S'en fout la mort* cannot be described as a social
film or as a psychological drama either. As ever, Denis' approach
eschews the expository mode and direct social comment. At the same
time, for all the restriction which marks the spatial organisation of
S'en fout la mort, Denis' filmmaking also shuns psychological or
essentialist causality. As the quote from Himes forcefully recalls, the
individuals that the characters represent are not biologically determined – they remain inseparable from a specific historical and spatial
environment. A specific set of circumstances imbues Jocelyn's
trajectory in particular with a false sense of fatality. The force of the
weight that slowly drags him down is exacerbated by the fact that the
lingering influence of the colonial logic, operating in a diffused way,
beyond the realm of official laws and hierarchies, cannot be easily
identified and named.

16 'Claire Denis introduces *S'en fout la mort* like a thriller, or like a film that could
   become a thriller. Yet we only get a glimpse of the police: two silhouettes in
   uniforms in one of the last scenes. It makes sense. The director is about to film
   an implosion. Not at all the shock or the explosion born out of the contact
   between order and the unlawful.'

The unspoken rule

While the defining features of established genres fail to provide a relevant framework for Denis' second fiction film, the continuity with her previous work is undeniable. Signalled by Isaak de Bankolé's presence and Abdullah Ibrahim's involvement, by the title (a saying, as for *Chocolat* and the documentary *Man No Run*), this continuity is also explicit in both the treatment of the subject matter and in the restricted function of the spoken word. Like Protée at the end of *Chocolat*, Dah and Jocelyn settle close to the boiler room, the secret heart of a structure that denies them an official existence. In *S'en fout la mort*, as in *Chocolat*, blacks only enter the realm of the white man as stowaways. They are kept at the margins, on the lower floors, amongst the menial workforce. They belong to the shade and to nocturnal time. In *S'en fout la mort*, the past weighs on the characters' fates, but, if it finally determines a tragic conclusion, it is because the circumstances allow for this unresolved past to be alternatively repressed and replayed. Implicitly, the same traditional hierarchies persist, the same structures of subjection and humiliation, rendered more anonymous by the implicit rule of money. As such, the film echoes the writings of Frantz Fanon, whose work Denis evoked as one of her inspirations. Indeed, Jocelyn's origins are not an element of chance. Fanon, who was born in Fort-de-France, used the West Indies,[17] which remains a French *département*, as a case study in his exploration of the psychological impact of colonisation: 'Je suis noir, et mon ami est de la même couleur' ('I am black, and my friend is black'). This declaration, one of Dah's first sentences, is superfluous since Dah appears on the screen as it is uttered. Yet it directly calls forth the ambiguity at play in the establishment of the racial Other's identity. Dah and Jocelyn are from different countries, they like different types of music, and have diverging interests. Arguably, the colour of their skin is but a subjective factor in their friendship, an element of identity defined as such by historical, external circumstances: Dah and Jocelyn are two black men travelling through white France. By default, the force of the dominant model is thus posited: as underlined in Richard Dyer's study (Dyer 1997), the white race poses as the non-race. There will be no need to define Ardennes, Toni, or Michel in terms of the colour of

17 The West Indies or *Antilles* is an archipelago of islands first colonised in the seventeenth century. It includes Guadeloupe, Martinique and Dominique.

their skin. Theoretically an equal, the black man (and Fanon studies not solely but principally the case of the male) from the West Indies still has to define his identity with reference to a norm, that of the old *métropole*, and of the white man. At the same time, this ubiquitous, mythical model, impregnates all aspects of his existence, from his history, to his education, to his future:

> However painful it may be for me to accept this conclusion, I am obliged to state it: For the black man there is only one destiny. And it is white. (Fanon 1986: 12)

In many ways, the character of Jocelyn could be read as an incarnation of the schizophrenic experience of the contemporary black man in France as Fanon so provocatively described it. His pride and his self-worth constantly undermined by a reality that denies him any existence outside with that of being a small-time hired hand, Jocelyn finds himself in the service of a white man who pretends to know his past and his future and ultimately poses as his father. By selling his skills to a sordid end, Jocelyn signs a form of pact with the devil, but daylight, desire, success, and the wide horizon remain the preserved realms of the white. Fanon thus sketches out the backdrop against which *S'en fout la mort*'s drama unfolds:

> The effective disalienation of the black man entails an immediate recognition of social and economic realities. If there is an inferiority complex, it is the outcome of a double process: primarily, economic; subsequently, the internalisation – or, better, the epidermalisation – of this complex of inferiority. (Fanon 1986: 13)

Like the character himself, Jocelyn's predicament remains, on the surface, highly enigmatic. Yet his destiny is signposted and framed by several potent entities whose presence is as tangible as that of the characters. Money, for instance, literally permeates the universe of *S'en fout la mort*. From the payment of the truck drivers to Dah's sharing of his last reserves with Jocelyn; from the thick wads of banknotes frantically waved by the betters during the fights, to the final laying out of the corpse, money inhabits the frame and colonises the vision. Crushed between fingers and in pockets, punctuating Ardennes's recriminations and verbal digressions, it also dominates the dialogue. Ardennes bitterly argues about the terms of the contract that will rule the fights, and his pettiness extends to all details: the two men that he houses on his premises are required to pay for all the drinks and meals ordered. Profit and money rule over his relations, professional as well as emotional: he introduces his wife as a prized part of his property ('Elle est belle ma Toni hein?') ('Isn't my Toni beautiful?'), and, when the young woman bets large sums of money unwisely, he complains that she is trying to 'hurt' him. Significantly, Jocelyn, who, according to Dah, 'never has a penny on him', has delegated the task of discussing money to his friend. Dah's ability to deal with Ardennes partly emanates from his knowledge of the discourse of money.

The Hotel *Formule 1*, where Dah first asks Ardennes to meet them, prefaces the arrival at the Rungis stronghold. Run like a gigantic automaton (it cannot be entered unless payment has been provided to the credit card machine that replaces the customary receptionist), the hotel's outlandish construction sits alone on a parking lot just off the motorway. The dark red walls of the entry hall provide a suitable backdrop to Dah and Ardennes's settlement of their contract, and, with its narrow bedroom and bunk beds, it announces the claustrophobic atmosphere of the men's future lodgings. Once the contract is agreed, however, Dah and Jocelyn drive down to Rungis. There stands the embodiment of Ardennes's shady power and ubiquitous trafficking skills: the Pondorly. Ardennes's property includes a partly derelict structure, once boarded up by the police and declared unsafe. A covered footbridge over the expressway towards Orly airport, the Pondorly houses a shabby night club and is flanked by a bar-restaurant. The boundaries are set almost immediately: the two men arrive during the day and park in front of the main building, but Ardennes quickly orders them to go around to the back. In daylight, they will not be allowed within the restaurant, the legal front of Ardennes's business, run by his wife Toni. As Ardennes, unshaven and clad in his customary worn-out leather coat, leads them through his domain like a seedy Faustian figure, the two men, closely accompanied by the camera, appear to be descending into a kind of cold, metallic inferno. Ardennes first invites them to admire the night-club, and the three men sit down as Ardennes's son Michel operates the light system. Daylight is shut out as the roof slowly closes up above their heads, and a swirl of coloured neon lights illuminates the vault. In the absence of music, it is the noise of machines that fill the air, exposing the shabby theatricality of the display. Michel's role as the orchestrator of this show signals the character's symbolic function: it is Ardennes's son who, like a deathly *Deus ex machina*, will strike the blow and bring the tension to its conclusion. Throughout the nights that follow, however, the throbbing pulse of the club's music expresses the growing tension that first finds its outlet in the orchestrated violence of the cockfights.

The way to Dah and Jocelyn's own quarters is an endless row of corridors and closed doors that leads them beyond and below the restaurant's kitchen and storerooms. On the way, Ardennes introduces them to his employees, all of them immigrants, mostly from African countries and from the West Indies. Ardennes's realm is a primarily nocturnal world. Every night, a motley crowd of people gather in and around the place – men with the weary, pallid faces of somnambulists.

The little known suburb of Rungis is home to Paris's largest wholesale markets. Denis and Godard managed to capture its atmosphere without giving in to the temptation of exploiting the place's expressionistic, post-industrial character to overtly symbolic or primarily aesthetic ends. Though imbued with sordid overtones and a vague sense of threat, the vast parking lots with their rows of trucks, and the long facades of the warehouses standing in the dim light of the street lamps are filmed without emphasis. A fixed shot records Dah searching for left-over material along the warehouses in the cold waning light at the end of the day, and fluid camera movements accompany the two friends as they run along the parking lots at night, passing by groups of silhouettes intent on their mysterious deals. Often, the backdrop blurs into a mass of artificial glare: street lamps, and passing truck lights. The deceptive warmth of the bar-restaurant's illuminated window attracts a crowd of noctambulist workers, who come to have a drink at the end of their shifts: truck drivers mingle with the butchers of the local abattoirs still clad in their bloodied aprons. A motley mob also presses around the cockfighting pit to watch and bet. Brought out by the hand-held camera style, and structured by a taut editing, the fight sequences combine Godard's circling long takes with close-up on hands shaking bundles of notes, and shots of the roosters throwing themselves at each other to the deafening clamour of the audience. Asian, African, Arabic, and Western faces are pressed together, and communing in the same sordid, hysterical frenzy. The strong contrasts, generated by the artificial glow of the lamps, further add to the intensity of the scene and give those episodes a painterly, Goyaesque quality. The natural light is scarce in *S'en fout la mort*, and limited to hybrid moments that hesitate between night and day: a few cold, blue mornings, and a dull eventide. Bodies are always hovering at the frontier between darkness and light: their existence is restricted to the borders drawn by the glow of electric lights and neon lamps that often transforms them into mere silhouettes.

The only sequence shot in Paris is equally dominated by the artificial glow of urban night-light. While *S'en fout la mort*'s hand-held camera style spurred comparison with John Cassavetes's filmmaking, Denis' ability to capture the atmosphere of a city at night, and to approach the city space as if it was an entity in itself, evokes a more mainstream tradition in American cinema. (The urban *flânerie*, though a feature of some the French *nouvelle vague* films, is less common in French cinema.) Denis' subsequent films, and, in particular, *J'ai pas Sommeil* and *Vendredi soir*, testify to a renewed interest in experimenting with the cinematic depiction of the city. In *S'en fout la mort*, the portrayal of Paris is ambiguous: a relief from the no-man's-land of Rungis, and from the stifling environment of the Pondorly, the spectacle of the city streets is both familiar and removed. It is as if the characters, after their immersion in the violence-ridden space where they have locked themselves up, could only contemplate the city centre from a distance, from behind the windows of a car. Significantly, the place where Dah finds a drunk Jocelyn is also a maze of underground corridors and rooms, like a small replica of their space in Rungis.

Within *S'en fout la mort*'s fluctuating nocturnal environment, the camera work imbues the presence of the main characters with a particular density, as if the images were generated through a clinch between the camera and the bodies of the protagonists. Originally, and before, thanks to the propagation of the small DV, this style became popular, Denis had planned to film in 16 mm to benefit from the freedom of the hand-held shooting. Godard, however, suggested 35 mm, and realised the remarkable feat of shooting the whole film while carrying the heavy equipment on her shoulder. The result is a combination of the richness of the 35 mm picture with a rare fluidity of movement. Unusual lenses, used to underline the feeling of entrapment, alternatively stress the endlessness of the corridors, and, in the scenes shot in the cafés at night, on the road and in parking lots, transform the wider backdrops into a blurred mass of crude colours. In the restricted field of vision, bodies appear and disappear, closely followed by a camera that shoots at shoulder level and accompanies the characters without pre-empting their trajectories. The mobility of the camera and the fragile balance of the frame do not merely create a feeling of urgency. They express the tension created by the constant tyranny of racial appearances: the impossibility of escaping the rule of skin as signifier. It reflects the blinding lack of distance of the protagonists trapped in a swirl of ritualistic aggressiveness and vio-lence. In effect, to borrow from Fanon's wording, it is this *epidermic* quality of the filming that gives *S'en fout la mort* its intensity.

As in her first feature, but with an added physicality in the shooting style, the gestures, the movement of the bodies in space, their relation to the environment, to the frame, and to each other, say more than the dialogues. The strength of Dah and Jocelyn's bond for instance is expressed with hardly any recourse to spoken exchanges. Established through the internal dialogue and in the series of shot/counter-shot of the opening sequence, it also shows in the way the two characters share the frame and the screen time equally, in the gestures and attitudes that bind them together. It lifts the atmosphere of certain scenes, as when they push each other or exchange complicit, knowing glances behind Ardennes's back. Medium long shots of the two men walking together, their gait in perfect sync, suffice to suggest the existence of a strong friendship. At the same time, as they stroll by the side of the motorway in the barren landscape of Rungis, huddled in their black coats, the sight of their two silhouettes calls forth this powerful sense of displacement that already imbued the documentary world of *Man No Run*. This unspoken feeling, the obscure longing for a faraway land, for a different landscape and a different climate, is carried through by the character of Jocelyn with one simple gesture: the tightening of his coat or jacket around his body.

Throughout the film, Ardennes, the surrogate father and symbolic figure of authority, is the master of the spoken word. But his kingdom, with its night-club and deafening music, the shouts that surrounds the pit, and the constant movement of bodies, is not a place of communication: if Ardennes tends to take over the rare moments of potential silence, his speech is first and foremost a monologue. Like the character himself, the banter is a strange mixture of boasting and cynicism, of genuine longing and of manipulation. Trafficking has granted him far-reaching connections, and, when he threatens the two friends, only Dah's warning that he will expose Ardennes's dodgy dealings in army goods can placate him. Punctuated by money-related comments and nostalgic tales of his time in the West Indies, Ardennes's diatribes are only interrupted when he gives an order to one of his employees. Progressively, the reminiscing takes up a larger part of his addresses to Jocelyn, and he starts rewriting the young man's history, evoking Jocelyn's mother as his long-lost love. But in the image of the shady world that he inhabits, Ardennes's perverse nostalgia for an exotic, adventurous past has sordid overtones. In the West Indies as in France, Ardennes ran a series of businesses, and, like most of his contemporaries from the *métropole*, had set out to fill his pockets as quickly as possible. From the faraway islands, he thus brought back tales of dubious authenticity, memories of a lost love and an addiction to gambling. Ardennes's projection of his longing and 'love' onto Jocelyn culminates in his verbal appropriation of the young's man past and future. Arguing that, had Jocelyn not been so 'black', he could well have thought him his son, Ardennes finally vents his anger at the young man's ungratefulness: 'Ils ont pas tous eu quelqu'un comme moi derrière eux! Et toi tu t'en rends même pas compte!' ('They haven't all had someone like me to back them up! And you don't even realise it!')

Confronted with Ardennes's logorrhoea, Jocelyn leaves the talking and the negotiating to Dah, and progressively withdraws into silence. As the young man finally breaks down at the end of the film, it is in his native créole (the language of the West Indies) that he cries out his anger and his disgust. The scene finds its contradictory echo at the end of *J'ai pas sommeil*. Even when he is face to face with his own mother, Camille, the central character of *J'ai pas sommeil*, refuses to speak in his own mother tongue: Jocelyn and Camille thus embody two contrasted forms of alienation. Compared to Camille's voluntary amnesia, Jocelyn's silence, and his eventual return to his first language, is the clearest sign of his initial denial of Ardennes as the embodiment of the White Man, as an interlocutor or as a figure of identification. In pointing out the implicit hierarchy at work in the persisting dominance of the colonising country's language, Fanon outlined the problematic that underlies *S'en fout la mort*'s *mise en scène* of power through a particular form of language and its silent refusal:

The Negro of the Antilles will be proportionately whiter – that is, he will come closer to being a real human being – in direct ratio to his mastery of the French language ... Every colonised people – in other words, every people in whose soul an inferiority complex has been created by the death and burial of its local cultural originality – finds itself faced to face with the language of the civilising nation. (Fanon 1986: 18)

Dah's own use of the spoken language mediates between Jocelyn's progressive disavowal and the hijacking of the diegetic word by the character of Ardennes. In front of this Faustian figure, Dah does not merely take on the symbolic role of a black Orpheus, failing to bring Jocelyn back to the land of the living. Neither is the character reduced to the function of the antique chorus whose comments punctuate the ineluctable unfolding of a drama. Directed to the audience and, every so often, to Jocelyn, the seductive flow of his voiceover commentary overrules Ardennes's control of the first degree enunciation. If Dah is powerless in avoiding his friend's death, throughout the uncertain time during which their story unfolds (How long do the two men stay in the Pondorly? Is the film a long flashback or a tale told in the present tense?), the command over the narration remains his. Dah, unlike Jocelyn, is not French. His history and his present are not as closely embroiled with that of the white man, their employer. This difference, stated in his introduction, may explain the character's ability to withstand the seedy reality that surrounds him. Ultimately, Dah is the only one amongst *S'en fout la mort*'s protagonists who walks out free. Before he leaves, he collects a few clothes, pockets some money, and fills his bag with the books that Jocelyn and himself had piled into their den. In a distant echoing of *Chocolat*'s ending, he is then seen driving in the direction of the airport.

If communication is largely absent from the universe of *S'en fout la mort*, around the pit, the men nevertheless come together to scream. Around the circular enclave, mouths open and faces contort, as an unknown violence is exposed and vented out in the crude abandon generated by the fight's suspense. The cockfighting functions as a metaphor for the hidden violence imposed by the established order on men who, in turn, repress and internalise it.[18] The cere-

18 It is also a sign of the persisting presence of the colonial. The fact that Jocelyn and Dah have come via Spain, in itself an anodyne element of the scenario, takes on extra significance in the light of Denis' preparatory research in the subject

monial that might have given this ritualised form of violence its
nobility is crushed by the sordid expediency that governs life in this
small community at the margins of society. While the training of the
roosters is shot in long takes, with an emphasis on the poetics of
arcane rites binding the animals to their guardian, the chaotic reality
that surrounds the pit unavoidably bears the mark of the sordid.
Between each fight, the two men withdraw to the nearby toilets to
clean the winning animal and dispose of the loser's corpse. Next to
the bustle and reddish semi-darkness of the room that houses the pit,
the toilets provide a brutally sobering environment, a cold white
space where the bodies of the dead birds are unceremoniously
shoved into rubbish bags. In contrast with the banal abjection
suggested by those scenes, the laying out of Jocelyn's body at the end
of the film is an attempt at recapturing a sense of respect of the other
and of oneself. But around the pit Ardennes rules, and his interest in
the fights is superficial and motivated primarily by profit: soon, the
dead cocks end up served as Sunday lunch. Ultimately, the rituals
have to be disposed of to make place for utmost efficiency and profit,
and new animals are brought in to be trained as quickly as possible.
In order to attract the crowds and raise the bets, the fights have to
become shorter and more deathly. Dah and Jocelyn are forced to
replace the traditional corn spurs with steel ones: the fights are
transformed into fast-paced bloody butcheries. Significantly, it is
another set of outsiders that Ardennes and Michel have attracted to
their pit for this new type of show: a group of gypsy men. In a distant
echo of the Marley's lyrics at the beginning of the film, two 'Others'
thus face each other. But the camera's closeness precludes a lyrical
treatment of the scene: the confrontation has little of the mythical
about it, it merely sets representatives of the underclass against each
other. For all the poignancy of Jocelyn's fury and solitude, the white
man's greed remains the principle that underpins a pitiful escalation
of violence.

Within this almost exclusively male environment, and in spite of
the fact that she represents the only individual that withstands the

---

(Bouzet, 1990). Known in most countries outside of the African continent,
cockfighting was first popularised there by the Spanish settlers. Hence, the two
men, under Ardennes's orders, are not so much introducing an exotic custom
as 'bringing back' a tradition.

hysteria of the fights, Toni's character has little space to develop beyond its symbolic function. Yet there is a curious, almost comical resonance in the choice of Solveig Dommartin to play the role. In Wim Wenders' *Wings of Desire*, for which Denis worked as the director's first assistant, Dommartin played a trapeze artist. Like Jocelyn, her character had to make sense of a self-split between performance and the dull reality of everyday life.[19] However, whereas in *Wings of Desire* the character conducts long internal monologues, Denis offers Dommartin a character locked into its function as appearance, as a body-as-sign. In addition, in *S'en fout la mort*, aside from a brief sequence in the night-club, she is the only feminine presence. As such, she crystallises the desires and the tensions, becoming the objectified centre of a relay of gazes and repressed violence. If an unspoken hierarchy rules the relations between white French men and men from other ethnic backgrounds and countries, Toni is the ultimate Other, a female amongst males, or, to quote Jocelyn speaking through Dah's voiceover, the carrier of bad vibes. *S'en fout la mort* thus illustrates how 'the fascination with oppressed ethnic minority men can lead to the marginalisation or stereotyping of women' (Tarr and Rollet 2001: 225), a tendency, Carrie Tarr and Brigitte Rollet add, which Denis avoids in later films.

The sexualised dimension that the fights bring out is obvious: as Denis remarks in one interview, in several languages, the word cock is associated with the male sex, and in creole (in the language of the West Indies), *coquer* means making love (Bouzet, 1990). In *S'en fout la mort* as in *Chocolat*, desire cannot be dissociated from a highly determined context. Like Aimée and Protée in *Chocolat*, Jocelyn and Toni are caught in a web of stereotypes that corrupts desire. Toni's isolation and her empathy and attraction towards the young man are thus not sufficient to breach a gap that is both racial, economical, and historical. Just as Jocelyn and Dah carry with them the myths associated with the black man as sexualised body, Toni incarnates the myth of the white woman as transgression. In Jocelyn's case, the myth also bears on a personal history: Toni is white and she is Ardennes's wife.

19 For the circus shows, the character dresses as an angel, and, during rehearsals, she bemoans the inability of her 'chicken wings' to protect her against a deathly fall, but also to lift her above the banality of existence.

Transferts déments, identifications perverses: à travers la surchauffe des combats de coqs, le film traduit une mythologie mâle et femelle irrationnelle qui aboutit aux duels virils et meurtriers.[20] (Audé 1990: 72)

In *S'en fout la mort* as in *Chocolat*, desire is another form through which the past inhabits the present, re-emerging in the folds of elliptical narratives that bear the mark of the repressed.[21]

Le meurtre de Jocelyn (qui recherchait la mort), résulte d'une longue histoire de captation mentale des dominés et des colonisés par les dominants colonisateurs ... Jocelyn et Ardennes sont fils et père putatifs d'une même histoire rancie qui a le mauvais goût de resurgir au présent.[22] (Audé 1990: 72)

Permeated by a morbid violence, the universe depicted in *S'en fout la mort* often seems closer to the world of the dead than to the land of the living. Jocelyn finds himself doubly trapped: caught in the resurgence of the past and in the tyranny of profit that rules over a seedy world of illegality and misery. Such characters, locked in a muted, obscure inner torment, reappear throughout Denis' filmography. There is arguably an element of romanticism in the sense of displacement and exile that marks them and in their silent refusal. But this romantic dimension is always framed within a determining historical context, and the depth of the process of alienation in which the characters are caught is signalled by the gap that opens between unspoken aspirations and the excluding and sordid nature of reality.

Contre l'oubli (*Against Oblivion*)

A year later, Denis was one amongst thirty directors and personalities of French cinema to agree to contribute to the project *Contre l'oubli*,

20 'Mad transference, perverse identifications: through the over-heated atmosphere of the coq fights, the film expresses an irrational male and female mythology that ends in virile and deathly duels.'
21 The myth of a racialised sexuality reappears as the theme of two of Denis' short art films discussed in Chapter 3.
22 'The murder of Jocelyn (who was seeking death) is the result of a long history of mental capture of the dominated and colonised by the colonising dominants ... Jocelyn and Ardennes are the presumed son and father of a same rotten history that, in bad taste, dares to reappear in the present.'

launched on the occasion of the thirtieth anniversary of *Amnesty International*. Each of the participants volunteered to film a three-minute declaration, to denounce or to protest against the treatment of a victim of political oppression. Denis shot a film in defence of the Sudanese activist Ushari Ahmed Mahmoud. Together with Costa Gavras, she was amongst the few participants who chose the musical clip format: produced in collaboration with French singer Alain Souchon, her film follows, through long travelling shots, the wanderings of a black man in the popular multi-ethnic district of Belleville. The images are set to songs about freedom in Sudan sung by Souchon, and alternate with close-ups of the singer's face. The films were separately broadcast on French television before being released as a 90 min feature in the cinemas. Judged too indirect, Denis' contribution got mixed reviews (Frodon 1991). However, the project, indeed fraught with risks, raised questions of ethics that are present in many of Denis' fictional works: the issue of transforming suffering into a form of spectacle, the difficulty of exposing and denouncing without becoming sanctimonious.

Keep It For Yourself

The theme of exile also lies at the heart of a short film that Denis shot soon after the release of *S'en fout la mort*. *Keep It For Yourself* explores the theme of displacement but this time through the story of an encounter between two disenfranchised individuals in the US. Sophie (Sophie Simon), a young French woman, travels to New York to join a man she has recently met. However, on arrival she finds herself alone in a strange flat and in a strange city, until a young Puerto Rican man on the run attempts to break into the apartment. The film is shot in striking black and white, and set to the music of John Lurie, like a distant homage to Jim Jarmush's *Stranger than Paradise*. In its wistful tone and its poetic approach to camerawork and light, it pre-empts Denis and Godard's work for later feature films. It was also the beginning of Denis' collaboration with actor Vincent Gallo.

These short films illustrate the director's renewed interest in addressing the issue of exile not merely from an exotic, foreigner's point of view or, conversely, as the expression of a 'white' individual's rite of passage. Through her films it emerges as a multi-faceted experience, one that leaves its marks on the new immigrants, the inhabitants of ex-colonies but also on those who belong to the old imperialistic cultures. The feeling of displacement and alienation that inhabits her work is part of the spirit of the time; it affects people in their native land as well as abroad, shapes the life of the disenfranchised individual as well as of the ordinary citizen that has always conformed. Denis' films thus seem to be traversed by a movement, thematic, geographic, and formal that corresponds to the drive to capture the changing nature of contemporary differences. From the native soil to the foreign country and back, abroad or in his or her own territory, the spectator, like the characters, always finds him or herself in a strange land.

J'ai pas sommeil[23]

While Protée and Jocelyn prefigured many of the characters that feature in Denis' later works, *S'en fout la mort* signalled the director's predilection for a particular type of environment. At the borders of social recognisance, the underworld of the outsiders and dropouts will repeatedly attract her, while at the same time, between death and desire, her thematic explorations pull her towards the frontiers of transgression.

From the beginning, the exploration and strategies of representation of the Other that underlie Denis' cinema, have eschewed traditional categorisations and the temptation of binary oppositions. The issues of identity and alterity initially emerge as complex and fluctuating, a nexus of external, social and historical determinants, of circumstances and of internalised feelings of belonging and alienation. Cynthia Marker's remarks that

> The ultimate implication of the thematic and stylistic masquerade in *J'ai pas sommeil* is that there is no possible separation of the mask and the identity the disguise conceals. There is, therefore, as the *mise en scène* attests, no distinguishable boundaries between inside and outside with regard to identities the film imagines. (Marker 1999: 147)

---

23 Part of the material included in this chapter was originally published in Beugnet 2000 and 2001.

With *J'ai pas sommeil*, the tension created by the presence of enigmatic figures and the denial of explanation (psychological in particular) is exacerbated by the film's focus on an extreme form of transgression:

> Les gens sont captifs de quelque chose d'insupportablement mal, ce qui est compréhensible, et point final. Comme si on ne pouvait pas expliquer que ces monstres aux yeux de la justice ne sont pas les premiers, que ça a toujours existé. Ils concrétisent des fantasmes que les gens trimballent depuis des temps immémoriaux.[24] (Kaganski and Bonnaud 2001: 34)

Stylistically, the refusal to equate filmmaking with a process of elucidation also leads to the extension or the subversion of the conventions of the genre that Denis draws from, film noir (as with Gore in the case of *Trouble Every Day*). While she initially appears to venture into territories primarily associated with American cinema, Denis not only continuously blurs the frontiers of genres, but she also retains a crucial feature of the French tradition: the primacy and ambiguity of the criminal or monstrous figure. In the introduction to *French Film Noir*, Robin Buss remarks that in the French tradition of noir literature and film, the focus has been on the criminal rather than on the enforcer of law and order. In addition, in the margins of binary definitions of good and evil, the representation of 'evil' has remained essentially complex and elusive.

> Departing from a long-standing tradition drawing on concepts of evil as a form of human transcendence and provocation, French cinema is rich in representations of evil as banal – the mere expression of the spirit of a particular era – on the one hand, and as manifestations of apparently repressed but ineluctable, deadly traits of the human psyche on the other. (Beugnet 2000: 196)

With *J'ai pas sommeil* and, later, with *Trouble Every day* and *Beau travail*, Denis creates controversial works that explore the limits of the acceptable, the moment where the borders of identity and sanity are crossed. In the worlds represented in these films, it is not only the

---

24 'People are trapped by something unbearably wrong, which is understandable, and that's it. But it is as if it was impossible to recall that these people, monsters in the eyes of the justice system, are not the first cases, that this has always existed. Through them, fantasies that people have carried with them from time immemorial are made concrete.'

established order of things but the very notion of a coherence of the self, social and individual, that is beset and threatened.

Loosely inspired by a criminal affair of the 1980s,[25] *J'ai pas sommeil*'s premise almost seems like a calculated challenge to the rules of political correctness: at the heart of the film is the character of a serial killer, a murderer of old women, who is black, homosexual, and HIV positive.

> L'expression 'politiquement correct' ou 'politiquement incorrect' était constamment présente dans l'idée de ce film. Je sentais qu'il était impossible qu'on aille vers cette notion, dont la question se posait évidemment avec ce personnage qui tue plus de vingt vieilles dames, les êtres les plus fragiles de la société après les enfants, qui est noir, homosexuel et vaguement drogué, l'inverse absolu de ce que devraient être les personnages noirs au cinéma selon les schémas du 'politiquement correct'.[26] (Jousse 1994: 27)

In the shadow of this provocative criminal figure, looms the memory of many accursed anti-heroes of literature and cinema. *M* (1931), Fritz Lang's portrayal of a child murderer, comes to mind and was indeed mentioned in relation to Denis' film. The work of director Rainer Werner Fassbinder, renowned for his talent at subverting genre conventions in order to stigmatise the social establishment, is another reference that Denis acknowledges (Jousse 1994: 28). In the case of Fassbinder, the resonance is even greater when considered in the light of Richard Dyer's analysis of the work of French writer and *poète maudit*, Jean Genet,[27] and of the German director's screen

---

25 Thierry Paulin, a young man from the West Indies, was arrested in 1987 and charged with the murder or attempted murder of twenty-one elderly women, all residents of the eighteenth district where the young man also lived. Some of the crimes were perpetrated with an accomplice who was also arrested and charged. Paulin was HIV positive and died in prison before he was put on trial.

26 'The expression "politically correct" or "politically incorrect" was constantly present in the idea of the film. I felt it was impossible to move towards this concept. Yet it was obviously an issue, with a character who not only kills more than twenty old women, who are amongst the most fragile members of our society after children, but is also black, homosexual, and addicted to certain drugs. The complete opposite to what black characters in film should be according to the rules of the politically correct.'

27 The expression *Poètes maudits* designates French literary figures that were reproved by the society and times in which they lived. A writer, dramatist and filmmaker, Jean Genet (1910–86) is one of the prominent figures of French

adaptation of Genet's *Querelle de Brest* (1953). In his novel, Genet depicts the systematic descent of the young sailor Querelle – a homosexual, a traitor, and a murderer. In effect, if the racial element is added, Denis' remarks on her film's controversial premise precisely echo Dyer's, when he writes about Jean Genet's work as often seen as 'a gift to homophobia, easily appropriated as the living proof of how sick, neurotic and degraded homosexuals are' (Dyer 1990: 75). Significantly, however, the analogies are suggestive but limited: in *J'ai pas Sommeil*, the criminal's actions bear none of the tragic compulsion that determines Lang's character in *M*, nor of the provocative overtones which characterise Genet's work. On the contrary, as we will see, *J'ai pas sommeil* appears as a complex exploration of a perverted drive to conformity.

In spite of the presence of the *serial killer*, who represents a prominent contemporary figure of fascination and generated a mass of pseudo-scientific inquests and fictional 'types', *J'ai pas sommeil* is neither constructed like a case study, nor like an investigation. From the narrative mode to the stylistic choices and the actors' performances, Denis avoids turning the film into what she repeatedly evoked in her interviews as a customary and futile search: an inquiry seeking to reveal the nature of an evil suddenly incarnated by an extraordinary individual. As such, her approach is in stark contrast with the Hollywood sub-genre of serial killer films popular in the 1990s, but comparable to that adopted by a handful of contemporary French directors working on similar themes at the time.[28] In Denis' film, the

---

avant-garde literature. In his youth, Genet was charged with theft, vagrancy, and homosexuality and spent time in various European prisons as well as in the foreign legion. However, supported by Jean-Paul Sartre and Jean Cocteau, he later came to fame in particular through his work for the theatre.

28 See my article 'Negotiating Conformity: Tales of Ordinary Evil', which includes a brief analysis of *Docteur Petiot*, Christian de Challonges, 1990; *L'Appât*, Bertrand Tavernier, 1994; *Le Boucher*, 1970, and *La Cérémonie*, 1995, Claude Chabrol. Other instances of films with similar thematic and formal explorations and released in the following years include Philippe Grandieux's *Sombre*, 1998 and Gaspard Noé's *Seul contre tous*, 1998. Shot by an independent American filmmaker, also indebted to Fritz Lang's *M* and bearing interesting similarities to the premise of *J'ai pas sommeil* in its thematic and parallel or simultaneous narrative threads, Spike Lee's *Summer of Sam*, 1999, with its more stereotypical incarnation of the deranged killer figure, provides a thought-provoking contrast to Denis' film.

enigma embodied in the criminal only makes sense as one element in the complex depiction of the environment the figure of the killer inhabits.

J'ai pas sommeil is set almost solely in the eighteenth district of Paris, one of the oldest parts of the city and a hybrid space, with Montmartre and the church of the Sacré-Cœur at its heart, and Pigalle, known as the traditional Parisian hive of sex, at its border. Once the centre of artistic bohemia, Montmartre has been turned into a favoured tourist hangout. But beyond its picturesque facades and rows of restaurants, it houses a mixed population of old and new poor. Within the district's concentric web of streets, Godard's camera accompanies an array of characters whose trajectories cross till they form a kind of pattern, a circular movement that leads to the central figure of the criminal.

The film starts and ends with Daïga (Katherina Golubeva), a young Lithuanian woman, who initially arrives in Paris with the address of an old aunt (Irina Grejbina), and the fake promise of a job by a Parisian theatre director (Patrick Grandperret) she met in Vilnius. She briefly encounters the unfriendly local police and visits a small community of illegal Eastern immigrants, before she ends up working as a cleaner in the hotel owned by the energetic Ninon (Line Renaud) and her elderly mother. The same hotel houses Camille (Richard Courcet) and his lover Raphaël (Vincent Dupont). The couple live a nocturnal life, mingling with the crowd that inhabits the Parisian night, and supplementing Camille's job as club performer with the spoils from their crimes: the two men assassinate old women to rob them. Camille also keeps irregular contacts with his family: his mother and his brother Théo (Alex Descas). A dedicated musician forced to moonlight to earn his life, Théo dreams of taking his young son back to his native West Indies, but faces the downright refusal of his French wife Mona (Béatrice Dalle). The characters cross each other's paths throughout the film till Camille's arrest. While the young man is being interrogated, Daïga searches his room and takes off with the remains of the criminals' booty.

A contemporary film noir

The title of the film hints at its film noir filiation.[29] In effect, after
S'en fout la mort, the noir genre, with its hybrid, Franco-American
origins, its essentially urban nature, and its tradition of anti-heroes,
seemed a particularly apt direction for Denis' work. Named after the
French *Série noire* thriller collection, the roots of the genre go back to
the German cinema of the 1930s. In the States, the movement grew
at a time of social and moral uncertainty, its stories of despair and
entrapment replacing the customary 'triumphant good' Hollywood
ending. Denis adapts the genre to her vision of a postcolonial urban
world, extending the noir ambivalence to race and gender identities:
in the word of one of the critics, the enigmatic Camille, with his
androgynous name, is a 'very feminine man' (Jousse 1994: 20). *J'ai
pas sommeil* successfully creates an equivocal cinematic world in
which Denis continues an exploration of alienation and marginality
started in *S'en fout la mort*. Throughout, the light fluctuates between
sunset, dawn and the artificial glow of the city at night, generating a
feeling of incertitude that the film's elusive characters come to
embody. Indeed, *J'ai pas sommeil* is a journey into an urban world
where, just as day and night mingle and become confused, conventional morality and transgression lose their contrasts and clear
boundaries. On the one hand, the film attempts to sidestep simplistic moral judgements in order to investigate certain forms of
collective anxieties, to evoke a contemporary social malaise. At the
same time, it seeks to 'mark out society's darker spheres, this
doomed area inhabited by the outcasts, those who haunt the nooks
and crannies of the city'[30] (Jousse 1994: 22). Like Thierry Jousse,
Michel Pascal draws comparisons between *J'ai pas sommeil* and Fritz
Lang's film:

> C'est effectivement *M le Maudit* qu'évoque *J'ai pas sommeil*. C'est un
> récit en cercles concentriques, qui part du boulevard périphérique

29 There is a wealth of studies on this genre. For example, Foster Hirsch, *The Dark
   Side of the Screen*, San Diego, A. S. Barnes, 1981; and Dana Poland, *Power and
   Paranoia – History, Narrative and the American Cinema 1940–1950*, New York,
   University of California Press, 1986, both give good insights into the genre's
   history and characteristics.
30 'cerner les zones d'ombres du social, cette part maudite habitée par les
   réprouvés, ceux qui hantent les coins et les recoins de la cité.'

pour arriver au cœur des secrets d'un assassin au calme et au détachement effrayants.[31] (Pascal 1994: 32)

But whereas in *M* a gigantic hunting game is organised by Berlin's underworld in order to catch the killer that disrupts the city's life and business, in *J'ai pas sommeil*, the narrative's slowly narrowing circles are the work of chance. In one interview, Denis even compares the film's structure to a game of snakes and ladders (Jousse 1994: 25). The crimes are omnipresent in the diegesis. The decomposing body of a victim is discovered at the beginning. The murders are discussed by people. They make the front page of the newspapers that litter Camille's hotel room, fill the radio broadcasts with warnings and debates. The film includes two scenes of Camille and Raphaël committing murders. At the same time, the police are depicted as bystanders, who appear more preoccupied with harassing a young Lithuanian woman about the parking of her car than with the search for the murderer.

The film is thus imbued with a contemporary sense of horror's banality. Within the maze of the streets of Paris where he operates, the criminal is but a small element of a larger game. At the same time, old women are of little social and economical value in the modern city, where their murderer's eventual arrest may ultimately be left to chance. The tone is given from the very beginning. The film opens with aerial images of Paris, taken from a police helicopter. Though this flight over a sprawling city may seem like one amongst a number of quotes, in Denis' films, of the influential *Wings of Desire*, the two uniformed pilots have little in common with the angels that survey the sky of Wender's Berlin. Filmed in close-up, from the back or in a low angle shot, the two men fill the exiguous space of the cabin with their bodies and with their bawdy laughter. In an indifferent sky, the omniscient point of view, *God's eye shot*, belongs to two policemen sharing crude jokes. Their hysterical laughter rings like a sinister omen as the gaze of the camera leaves the helicopter and plunges through the clouds and fumes towards the ring road's flow of cars. From then on, from the motorway that encircles the capital to the narrow circular streets of Montmartre, the parallel editing intertwines

31 'In effect, it is *M* that *J'ai pas sommeil* brings to mind. It is a circular story, which starts from the city ring road to get to the heart of a criminal's secret life – an assassin of terrifying calm and detachment.'

snatches of the existence of a series of characters all connected, in one way or another, to the murderer.

In the typically complex narrative structure of the classical film noir, more importance is generally granted to the exploration of the ambiguous relationships that link the characters than to the advancement of the actual thriller plot. In *J'ai pas sommeil*, this strategy of the noir scenario rules to utmost effect. The initial element of criminal plot is but a premise to the *mise en scène* of the trajectories of the three main protagonists, Camille, Daïga, and Théo, coming across a series of microcosms inhabited by a multitude of secondary characters. Because of its opening sequence and narrative organisation, *J'ai pas sommeil* was often compared to Robert Altman's *Short Cuts* (1993), which rediscovered the potential of multi-plot narratives and parallel editing. But in *J'ai pas sommeil*, the tactic is explored as an end in itself, disengaged from the rule of strict cause and effect structure, from the necessity of bringing all the elements and loose ends to a logical conclusion. The film follows the aimless, solitary wanderings of characters brought close to one another through parallel montage or by virtue of the depth of field (several characters share the frame but on different planes). They cross each other's path in places of transit: in hotels, cafés, night-clubs, neon lit streets, or in the dark theatre of a cinema. They exchange gazes, sometimes appear obscurely conscious of a particular presence, but often they simply miss each other. Through editing, Daïga and Camille's trajectories appear to run parallel, and they end up living in the same hotel. Thus, the encounter between them becomes a moment that is both expected and awaited. Yet it lasts but an instant, time enough to drink a coffee standing at the counter of a bistro. Captured in close-up, a fleeting moment of contact, two hands brushing against each other with an almost imperceptible slow-motion effect, suffices to create an ambiguous feeling, where threat, unspoken desire, and closeness mingle.

Together with her editor, Nelly Quettier, Denis played on two effects in the montage of the scenes. On the one hand, the editing generates jarring antagonisms between atmospheres and settings. On the other, it creates a network of links that bind together certain characters whether they have met or not. One of the rare moments of harmony is depicted in a sequence shot on the roof of the tall building that houses Théo and Monas's flat. In contrast with the constricted space of their apartment, and away from the disturbing sound of the neighbours' violence, the roof opens the perspective onto the endless spectacle of the nocturnal Paris cityscape. The couple decides to spend the night there with their small son Harry, and the sequence closes on an image of Théo stroking Mona's hair against a soundtrack of distant traffic. This scene imbued with tenderness is directly followed by images shot in the claustrophobic space of the night-club where Camille performs, and where one of his shady friends, the doctor (Laurent Grévill), is seen stroking the hair of a very young man, possibly a male prostitute. Similarly, from the scene at the hospital, where policemen interrogate one of Camille's victim, an old woman left for dead by her attackers, the film shifts to Camille and Théo's mother's birthday party with its atmosphere of familial celebration. The editing thus stresses the contradictions and the compartment-alisation of urban existence. In effect, one sequence is actually dedicated to the theme: this time, the sense of fragmentation, visualised within the frame, is simply suggested by the architectural setting. Whilst the soundtrack reproduces a radio programme about today's insecurity and what it means to feel safe, one long shot slowly pans across a facade, going from one window to the next, as if moving through a series of microcosms shut off from one another. The impossibility of communication lies at the very heart of the film. The characters speak little, and often don't understand each other's language. Dialogue proper (questions and answers, characters exchanging information) and shots/counter-shots are non-existent, and the incessant ringing of the telephone is never answered.

A tenuous but complex web of affinities nevertheless links the characters. Images, graphic cuts[32] and soundtrack create correspon-dences where the characters' gestures, or their *mise en scène*, echo each other. From one window to another, from one face or one gaze to another, equivocal connections are created that don't necessarily materialise. When Daïga and Mona's path cross for instance, the editing and the composition of the images create a contiguity that functions like the preamble to an encounter. The sequence mingles images of Daïga, walking down along the brightly lit facades of the cafés of a boulevard at night, and shots of Mona, sitting down smoking at the window of one of the bistros. Yet the two women will never actually meet. By creating such unfulfilled expectations, the

32 A transition between two shots that contain comparable graphic elements, like similar forms or shapes, or similar movements.

narrative structure creates a forceful evocation of the contradictory nature of urban life, where the solitude of the individual in the crowd belies the apparent multiplication of possibilities.

In spite of its fragmented, elusive plotline, *J'ai pas sommeil*'s arrangement of sequences generates a remarkable feeling of fluidity throughout, and the film's overall rhythm has been compared to a musical score by a number of critics:

> Le récit, inspiré en partie par un fait divers célèbre ... a ici une fonction climatique, rythmique, musicale, atmosphérique plutôt que narrative, la fiction est construite autour de foyers, de pôles d'aimantation décentrés plutôt qu'autour d'un centre unique. C'est ainsi que le scénario entrelace trois niveaux de récit, plus une poignée de micro-intrigues, qui alternent et se croisent tout au long d'une durée qui épouse un chemin plutôt sinueux.[33] (Jousse 1994: 20).

The strong sense of atmosphere that permeates the film certainly comes from Denis' ability, already mentioned with relation to her two first pictures, to impregnate the locations in which she films with a particular sense of presence, almost transforming them into a character in themselves. It is a particular vision of Paris that Denis proposes, one that plays with the capital's traditional image as 'la ville lumière' ('the city of lights')[34] to better explore its shady back stage: when she goes out at night to explore the neighbouring, brightly lit boulevards, Daïga, harassed by a stranger, ends up having to seek refuge in the darkness of a porn cinema. Paris emerges as a composite world, repellent and seductive, familiar and foreign. The soundtrack mingles languages (French, West Indian, Russian, English, Spanish, etc.), and types of music. Jazz-mambo tunes,[35] evocative of the film noir universe, cohabit with the music of the West Indies that inspires Théo's violin playing, and with the sickly beauty of the Tindersticks'

33 The story line, inspired by a real news events ... serves to create the mood, the rhythm, and takes on a musical and atmospheric function rather than a narrative one. The fiction is built around a series of de-centred sources rather than around a unique centre. The script thus intertwines three levels of narration and a handful of micro-plots that alternate and cross over throughout the film's rather sinuous duration.'
34 The expression dates back to the nineteenth-century transformation of Paris, which centre was largely rebuilt to be turned into the country's window, a centre for tourism and culture.
35 *Canción* (1950), played by Charlie Parker and the Orchestra de Machito.

ballads. The combination generates the atmosphere of an urban melting pot, but also a powerful feeling of nostalgia and exile that hints at many of the characters' hidden sense of alienation and longing. From the start, the film also includes long sequences of wandering, characters driving or walking through the streets, accompanied by slow, steady travelling shots. The wanderers' destination remains unknown, their goal is never directly reached. Deleuze's writing, already mentioned with relation to crucial aspects of Denis' film-making, again comes to mind: here, as in his description of the time-image, it is the moment of filming that counts and suffices in itself, creating pockets of pure cinematic experience. The singular effect of these instances is maybe best exemplified by one of the last sequences, that depicts Camille walking down a busy street just before his arrest. The nonchalance of his walk that seems almost shot in slow motion, the unravelling of colourful shop windows behind him, the brief glimpse at a tucked away, picturesque courtyard, the melancholy music of the Tindersticks, all the elements combined during this long travelling shot coalesce to create a moment of urban poetry. A certain ambiguity thus marks the presence of the policemen and the conclusion of the sequence, as if Camille's eventual arrest was but a disruption of the natural flow of the images to which the viewers had adhered. But the film ends again with characters in movement: Théo walking away from the police station, and Daïga driving away from Paris.

The postmodern character: artifice and lack

With its unstable point of view and kaleidoscopic format, *J'ai pas sommeil*'s narrative has been described as a collage (Jousse 1994: 20). Indeed, *J'ai pas sommeil* does not offer one dominant subjective entry into the story, does not invest one character as reference and anchorage. The camera accompanies a set of protagonists who remain elusive, fluctuating figures. As such, the film denies the viewer access to the superior knowledge and omniscient gaze that the opening sequence, with its uncouth guardian angels and their lingering laughter ironically evoked. Furthermore, it contradicts the customary identification process between spectator and character, arguably favouring, as suggested above, a kind of identification with the atmosphere and rhythm of the film instead. The characters themselves become postmodern figures, marked by uncertainty and

change, in a process that Thomas Docherty identifies as belonging
primarily to cinema:

> The spatial metaphor of surface and depth is replaced, after the
> influence of cinema, by temporal sequence and development: a figure
> in one scene or 'shot' can be thoroughly transfigured by the next, thus
> countering the notion of a transcendent 'self' lying 'behind' the
> surface 'apparitions' and disappearances. (Docherty 1996: 55)

Halfway through the film, for instance, the imperturbable Daïga,
who, beyond the linguistic barriers that isolate her, seems nonchalant
and aloof, suddenly explodes with rage and destroys the car of the
theatre director who lured her to Paris and failed to fulfil his promises.
The stern Théo, the model father, reacts with brutality to his companion Mona's vehement recriminations. The tiny Harry appears as
collected as a wise old man. As for the old women, *J'ai pas sommeil*
does not merely present them in the role of victims, but also, as in
Ira's case for instance, as highly resourceful and potentially egotistic
characters. The characterisation rests on a complex process of appearances and contradictions that becomes a source of ambiguity but also
a source of irony. Ninon, the hotel manager, is probably the most
earnest of all the protagonists, yet as a business woman, her warmth
never amounts to generosity. For all her apparent common sense and
experience, Ninon also voices the most mistaken judgement concern-
ing Raphaël and Camille. After advising Daïga to be careful when she
goes out by herself, Ninon exclaims, pointing at the two young men
who are crossing the hotel lobby, 'ils sont gentils, mais gentils!' ('such
nice, nice boys!').

Alternatively appearing as a reserved, soft-spoken young man and
as a profligate socialite and exhibitionist, as a tender lover and as a
bully, as an affectionate son and as a cold-blooded killer, Camille will
remain the most elusive of all the characters. Postmodern characters,
remarks Docherty, 'always dramatize their own "absence" from themselves' (Docherty 1996: 62). As a performer, Camille offers himself to
the gaze of an audience and of the camera, but it is the dimension of
the artifice that is played out. In his show at the night-club, Camille
merely mouths the lyrics sung by another. He dresses up, appears
clad in a long velvet dress and executes choreographed gestures so as
to enhance the gender ambivalence. Even as the camera lingers on the
body, nothing is disclosed: in many shots, the lens is too 'close', and

the young man's body (the 'body of evidence' as Denis puts it in one of her interviews) blocks out part of the frame, becoming obtrusive:

Dans les faits divers, même quand on lit les comptes-rendus de procès, l'opacité reste ... et c'est à travers ceux qui l'entourent qu'on parle le plus souvent du criminel, les témoins, les policiers, et surtout les membres de sa famille.[36] (Jousse 1994: 27)

Beyond the interplay of surface and artifice that crystallises around the character, the film does not reveal or explain, but merely hints at an existential void. In his 'looks' – from his hair and batman's hat to the necklaces and accessories he chooses to wear when he gets his photograph taken – Camille likes to play on overtones of darkness and evil. Furthermore, when he buys an expensive, tailor-made suit in a specialised shop, he regrets not being able to afford an outfit made of real leather: it is the costume, the appearance that yields authenticity and value. The propensity to take on guises, the transvestite perform-ances, and the obsessive narcissism (the portraits that fill his hotel room), all hint at the existence of a basic lack at the core of the character. In contrast with his brother who, through his music and his desire to raise his son in his country of origin, nurses a nostalgic, maybe illusory, connection with his cultural roots, Camille appears to have little interest in the past. After his arrest, his mother confronts him at the police station in his mother tongue, expressing her horror and inability to comprehend how her own flesh, the man who was once a small, gentle child, could have committed such horrendous crimes. But Camille answers in French, merely asking for his things (in French, his *effets*, a word which means both clothes and *effects*) to be brought to him. As in Denis' two first features, the postcolonial theme, the expression of the lingering effects of an internalised alienation, underpins *J'ai pas sommeil*, contrasted and reflected, in turn, through the parallel experiences of other characters. Camille's ability to deny the cultural and ethnic roots that his mother incarnates, and to 'identify' with the masks suggested by his environment recalls Frantz Fanon's analysis of the black man's neurosis in *Black Skin, White Masks*. In the psychoanalyst's study, the neurosis stems from the contradictory situation of the black man having to integrate into a

36 'Even when you read reports of the trial, in such cases, the opacity remains ... and it is through the bystanders – witnesses, policemen, and most importantly the family – that the criminal is discussed.'

white society which tends to define itself precisely in opposition with the Other, with the black man, with himself. In accordance with the contradictory logic of such an identification-alienation process, a character like Camille represents social 'integration' through crime, 'assimilation' by virtue of the dissolution of the self into the pre-conceived and the stereotypical.

> In Europe, the black man is the symbol of Evil. The torturer is the black man, Satan is black, one talks of shadows, when one is dirty, one is black – whether one is thinking of physical dirtiness or of moral dirtiness ... the Negro, without thinking, selects himself as an object capable of carrying the burden of original sin. The white man chooses the black man for this function, and the black man who is white also chooses the black man. The black Antillean is a slave to this cultural imposition. (Fanon 1986, 191–2)

As mentioned earlier, the portrayal of a serial killer operating within a society that appears largely corrupted and ineffectual neces-sarily calls to mind previous cinematic representations of psychotic alienation. But whereas the portrayal of the compulsive, tormented *M* and the *mise en scène* of his mock trial by the mob, for example, established a strongly ethical and humanistic message, the contem-porary, or postmodern, quality of Denis' film rests with its absence of direct moral judgement. *J'ai pas sommeil*'s criminal does not appear compelled to kill, neither does he seem tormented by remorse. Camille is not a tragic figure, and his crimes are difficult to deal with in a society 'dont l'appareil de répression est fondé sur l'idée qu'on doit donner du remords' ('whose apparatus of repression is founded on the principle of producing remorse') (Jousse 1994: 28).

J'ai pas sommeil's killer is not a rebellious figure either. Contrary to the deeds of Genet and Fassbinder's character, the beautiful traitor and murderer Querelle, for example, Camille's crimes are not acts of defiance. Dyer underlines how, through his character, Genet takes the stance of one who fully accepts his social designation and lives it out defiantly: 'You say this is what I am, OK, that is what I am, and I am going to be it to the hilt' (Dyer 1990: 75). Indeed, Dyer stresses, it is Genet's belief in the existing order of things that grants power to the provocation:

> The elements of evil, criminality and homosexuality are inextricably entwined in this tradition ... It is Genet's acceptance of the truth of the

Christian moral order that gives his work its special intensity. (Dyer 1990: 61)

Unlike Genet's heroes, Camille and Raphaël are not in revolt against the dominant system of value. Their killings do not bear a symbolic, subversive or nihilistic meaning. Rather, they seem like gruesome but logical expressions of a desire to participate fully in a materialistic system, of an overriding drive to conform. Camille may appear to play along with a game of self-prophecy, adopting as his one of the paths offered to him as a pauper, as a black man, as an HIV positive homosexual. But in contrast with a long tradition of transgression developed by trends of the French counter-literature to which Genet belongs, in this case, the fatalistic pursuit of evil does not amount to the celebration of a subversive, destabilising force, but is a sign of resignation. Denis remarked that crimes such as Camille's, 'ne peuvent venir que d'une forme de passivité, une acceptation presque morbide de l'état social où l'on est ... C'est pour ça que je parle de douceur, c'est une forme de soumission' ('can only come from a form of passivity, the almost morbid acceptation of one's social status ... That is why I talk of softness, of a form of submissiveness') (Jousse 1994: 28). A symptom of a wider social malaise, the psycho-killer of contemporary cinema is monstrous in the postmodern sense: behind a presence that evokes a lack, the representation of an absence, lurk disturbing forms of hyperconformity.

Postmodern narration: the return of the historical dimension

Like the characterisation and *mise en scène*, the narrative underlines the elusiveness of the serial killer's personality. Through its multi-faceted structure, however, it builds an impressionistic but meaningful picture of the context, describing it with unemphatic but suggestive precision, 'almost as if the fictional material was subjected to a documentary gaze' (Jousse 1994: 28). In her approach to the representation of contemporary evil, Denis thus appears to relate closely to the strategies of postmodern fiction:

> In short, postmodern characterisation seeks to return the dimension of history which earlier modes of characterisation, or the theoretical understanding of character as 'identity', deny ..., identifying change in the novel as something that always happens at the level of the

individual rather than in the wider sociopolitical formation itself
(Docherty 1996: 59).

Camille's first appears in a short, mostly silent scene, which shows
him having a violent altercation with his lover Raphaël. The motive of
the argument is never elucidated, but the setting and *mise en scène* are
significant. The scene takes place in the small hours, presumably at
the end of a night out, and is drowned by the sound of a refuse truck.
As the vehicle, with its black crew of early-morning workers, goes by
Camille, the national flag, hung on the facade of the local town hall,
flaps discreetly in the background. Thus, the composition briefly
comes together like a passing comment on Roland Barthes' analysis
of a *Paris Match* cover showing a black African soldier saluting the
French flag, and where the author unravels the discourse of colonial
propaganda that underpins the photograph's *mise en scène* (Barthes
1993: 189). In the postcolonial Paris of *J'ai pas sommeil*, the proud
soldier of the Republic is replaced by rubbish collectors. The racism
evoked in this film noir is not so much that of overt violence as that of
the hidden, institutional racism that permeates the language and
social structures. The presence of the criminal couple, Camille and
his white lover, renders tangible a malaise, the complexity of which
can only been suggested through the experiences of a multitude of
other characters. Camille conforms to the rules of a shady world into
which he can integrate, providing he can afford a way of life based on
expensive pleasures and appearance. But while he appears to lead an
idle life of relative luxury, his brother Théo, a musician, moonlights as
a furniture builder to make a living, and longs for his native country.
As for Daïga the actress, she ends up cleaning hotel rooms and
bathrooms in exchange for a roof. Her presence, like that of the small
community of Eastern immigrants crammed into her aunt's friend
Tolsty's (Ossip) tiny flat, is a reminder of the new flux of population
lured by the attractive lights of the Paris nebula. Simultaneously,
behind the constant hassle that the young woman faces, and the
precariousness of her situation (both Ninon and Ira comment on her
beauty as her means to social integration) lies the reality of what is
sometimes called the 'New Racisms' (Silverman 1999: 40). When
new borders became porous, new discourses of exclusion emerged,
this time upholding a difference less racial than cultural and economical, but represented as just as 'threatening'.

Hence, while *J'ai pas sommeil* destabilises the conventional process of identification and characterisation, attention is granted instead to the context and the historical dimension. Absence and lack are at the centre of the film's thematic, but are counterbalanced by an accumulation of clues – comments, often visual, often implied, on the social, psychological and physical environment of the characters – which are woven together to form the basis of the narration. At night, through the thin walls of Théo and Mona's high-rise flat, the cries of the neighbour's wife can be heard. Once, on the landing, Théo passes the middle-class-looking couple as they leave their flat in the company of two men and a dog. As in *S'en fout la mort*, the sight of a man with a guard dog suffices to suggest a sinister world of power and potential abuse. Beneath a seductive but shallow surface of cosmopolitanism, glittering night-lights and picturesque settings, *J'ai pas sommeil*'s Paris is also a place of alienation and non-communication, of routine intolerance, implicit racism and hidden domestic violence. Behind the urban 'buzz', it is a city inhabited by a crowd of isolated individuals, lonely old women and ineffectual prejudiced policemen, a place where bodies rather than souls are being exchanged and sold, and where churches are tourist attractions.

The 'return of the historical dimension' also amounts to a de-sublimation of evil. The depiction of the crimes eschews spectacular and aesthetic effects to become entwined within the subtle tapestry of daily ignominies, routine humiliations, and accepted violence that is drawn by the film. Since crime, in *J'ai pas sommeil*, is not an act of defiance against the moral order, its horror must come from its apparent banality, from its unbearable closeness. Dyer remarked that in *Querelle de Brest*, Genet had borrowed from 'the conventions of what is beautiful and sacred in order to make the criminal and male beautiful and sacred too' (Dyer 1990: 61–2). Fassbinder, in his adaptation, and with specific attention to the representation of killing, drew on religious imagery and Christian rituals to create a parody where sublime and kitsch mingle. Denis, on the other hand, adopts the most sparing of styles when dealing with the actual scenes of murder. The scenes are de-dramatised, consciously shot in a 'flat', detached manner, in medium, static shots and long takes, without particular effects of light, so as not to invite a voyeuristic gaze:

> Comme on ne peut pas échapper à ces scènes de meurtre, on ne peut pas non plus masquer les meurtres derrière une porte, sous une table,

dans un coin. Il faut qu'ils soient filmés en plein champ. En même temps, ces scènes interdisent le montage, il faut les filmer en un seul plan. Sinon, ou c'est dégueulasse, ou ce n'est pas très moral, on embellit le crime.[37] (Jousse 1994: 24)

Killing, in *J'ai pas sommeil*, bears no overtone of transcendence. At the end of the film, as the police inspector who interrogates him reads aloud the serial killer's list of crimes, it is the dull, seemingly endless repetition, which gives the content of the recitation its horrific quality.

White death

At the very beginning of the film, shots of Daïga's arrival in Paris are entwined with images of Camille going home at the end of a sleepless night, and with obscure shots of a dark interior filled with a buzzing sound. Slowly, from a close-up of a hand to a shot of a silhouette lying on the floor, in the shadow, the scene emerges as one of death. The body of the old woman who has been murdered is already sur-rounded by a cloud of flies: her disappearance has gone unnoticed for a week.

The choice of old women as the victims is doubly significant. Firstly, because it underlines the partial bankruptcy of a social system where the most vulnerable but also the least 'productive' of indivi-duals are marginalised and forgotten, but also because the body of the ageing woman bears symbolic overtones. Julia Kristeva has defined death as the ultimate expression of the abject. The self has been 'expelled' and the body remains, a process of decomposition and a sign of abjection for others (Kristeva 1982: 4). Her description finds its echo in Richard Dyer's analysis of the phenomenon of the 'White Death'. In *White*, his essay on race, Dyer examines the contradictory connections that link death and whiteness. On the one hand, the two terms can be associated to evoke beauty:

> Within Western Art, the dead white body has often been a sight of veneration, an object of beauty. While Christ on the cross may often be an image of agony, it is also one of beauty. In Victorian times, death –

37 'It was impossible to avoid the scenes of the murders, and you could not mask them, hide them behind a door, a table or in a corner; they had to be shot in full view. At the same time, they had to be shot in one take, otherwise it is disgusting, and not very moral: it would be embellishing violence.'

especially that of children, above all girls – was seen as a fit subject for painting and photography that had far more to do with beauty than with tragedy. (Dyer 1997: 208)

It is only at the condition of a 'deep conviction of the reality of transcendence, heaven or grace', Dyer stresses, that such an aesthetic idealisation of death becomes possible, however. And such belief in transcendental meaning has disappeared from the contemporary world depicted in *J'ai pas sommeil*. Here, 'the corpse, seen without God and outside of science, is the utmost of abjection' (Kristeva 1982: 4) and death is both sordid, banal, and absurd. While the radio broadcasts the cheerful tune of a song called 'Relax', it is the decomposition of a corpse beset by flies that allows for the discovery of an anonymous victim, later included in the long litany of names and addresses recited by a policeman. Later on, one brief shot shows a body laid out at the morgue. Static and devoid of all effect, the image has the chilling evidence of a preamble to an anatomy lesson. From beneath the cloth that covers the body, the face that emerges is that of an old person. The image of the corpse displayed in the anaesthetised whiteness of the morgue could be a visualisation of the hypothesis proposed by Dyer

> that the suspicion of nothingness and the death of whiteness is, as far as white identity goes, the cultural dominant of our times, that we really do feel we are played out. (Dyer 1997: 217)

As underlined earlier, the film does not reduce old women to the status of mere victims or to the function of symbolic elements, incarnating a society in decline. Yet as part of a metaphorical reading, the body of the old white woman becomes the iconic representation of an ossified postcolonial society on the defensive, haunted by its past and threatened by the multiple presence of the Other. Within this context, Camille's crimes, and his influence over his white lover, also take on a symbolic value. When Raphaël tentatively expresses his wish to leave him, Camille embraces him and covers him with his body. 'J'ai toujours été là pour toi ... Tu peux pas te débarrasser de moi. Tu le sais ça, tu peux pas.' ('I have always been here for you ... You can't get rid of me. You know that. You can't.') While Daïga and Théo choose to get away, Camille follows the logic of a materialistic system to its end. *J'ai pas sommeil*'s killer is not so much an immoral as an a-moral figure, who uses crime to participate fully in a system where wealth, appearance, and consumption have become ends in themselves. Thus, the malaise that besets occidental societies, the existential void that underlines the Godless postcapitalistic era, is reflected in the figure of the serial killer.

Considered in relation to a wider historical context – in this case, a contemporary France envisaged from the standpoint of a largely disenfranchised world – the meaning of the figure of the 'monster' thus goes back to etymological roots. (In latin, *monstro* is to show, *montrer* in French.) The monstrosity becomes a *sign* of a wider dysfunctionality. As such, the abnormality of the figure rests with its capacity to embody the logic of pre-existing discourses, and to *show* aspects that are generated and simultaneously denied by the society that he inhabits.

J'ai pas sommeil provoked the expected controversy. To some critics, the incorporation of the murders within the depiction of everyday life's ordinary crimes and cruelties resulted in presenting horrific killings in a relativistic light (Riou 1994: 114). The complexity of the narrative structure amounted to a 'subterfuge', 'une certaine lâcheté intellectuelle' ('a kind of intellectual cowardice'), allowing the filmmaker not to answer the questions set by her film, and 'de laisser à elle-même l'énigme qui unit le quidam et le criminel' ('to leave unresolved the enigma that binds any individual to the criminal') (Bourget 1994: 46).

On the contrary, for Denis to refuse to unravel the enigma, to avoid drawing a psychological portrait or propose answers to the mystery set by the fiction, is part of an ethical approach (Lifshitz 1995). Stepping aside from the conventions of the serial killer film that had become a popular sub-genre of American cinema in particular, *J'ai pas sommeil* attempts to avoid the easy path of simplistic moral judgements, and the escapism of voyeuristic, spectacular violence (Beugnet 2000). The denial of explanatory conclusions, like that of a voyeuristic demonstration of the killer at work, is key to an understanding of an approach where, as Denis puts it, 'le mal n'est jamais l'autre' ('evil is never the other') (Jousse 1994: 27). Familiar and integrated, evil can neither be safely confined to the figure of the Other or observed as a distanced, separate phenomenon, and made into an aesthetic object:

> Le film est le portrait d'un meurtrier, sans doute, mais également celui d'une ville, d'un monde dont la dérive tragique vers l'exclusion et

l'isolement rend plus présente à l'esprit de chacun l'imminence de la mort.[38] (Mérigeau 1994)

As in Kristeva's definition of abjection, the killer whose body the camera scrutinises in closeup is, like his crimes, 'abject'. The criminal and his actions are an intrinsic part of the very social body that seeks to expel them. They are part of the social fabric, yet need to be eradicated by the system because they threaten it and expose its vulnerability. To the policeman he faces after his arrest, Camille simply mumbles: 'Je suis un type facile. Personne n'a envie d'aller mal. C'est les choses qui déconnent.' ('I am an easy-going guy. Nobody wants to go wrong. Things get messed up.')

In the end, *J'ai pas sommeil* shuns certitudes and sends the viewer back to his or her own interrogations. In many ways, Denis' third feature could thus be described as a postmodern film noir, a film that prefigures the radical questioning of identity, truth, and representation that she later conducts in works like *Beau travail*.

> Film noir enables the possibility of a resistance to the omnivorous and homogenising power of a certain discourse … Criticism in cinema arises when the figural, in all its banal specificity, refuses to be subsumed under the discursive, with its drive to homogenisation and 'comprehension' (Docherty 1996: 268–9).

In the film noir Docherty adds, the body itself creates opacity. It stands in front of the light source, generating duplicitous shadows. Significantly, *J'ai pas sommeil*'s murderer never strikes alone: the white lover with the angelic name, the accomplice Raphaël, accompanies him to the end, mirroring Camille's movements like a white shadow.

Beau travail[39]

Beau travail originates from a commission by TV channel Arte for a series on the subject of foreignness entitled '*Terres étrangères*' ('Foreign lands'). Located, for the first time since *Chocolat*, in a foreign country

---

38 'The film is indeed the portrait of a murderer, but also the portrait of a city, of a world whose tragic downward spiral in exclusion and isolation outlines in everyone's mind the imminence of death.'

39 Part of the discussion on *Beau travail* is based on an article published in *Studies in French Cinema* (Sillars and Beugnet, 2001).

that she knew from her childhood,[40] *Beau travail* represents a kind of sum of her reflection on exile, alienation, and (post)colonialism. The film is a visually stunning work that combines a highly stylised vision with a thoughtful and complex working of its subject. It offers an interrogation of notions of collective identity – military, patriarchal, national, and colonial – and of their collapse into difference and obsolescence, evoked through the world of the elite military force of the foreign legion: 'Être étranger dans une terre, mais aussi être étranger à soi-même. L'idée de la légion est venue d'elle-même: c'est l'être étranger en soi' ('To be a foreigner in a land, but also to be a foreigner to oneself. The idea of the legion imposed itself upon me: to be as a foreigner in and to oneself ') (Lequeux 2000).

Aesthetically, the film is a hybrid. Privileging image and sound over dialogue, it borrows from dance, theatre, and opera, and composes a sensuous cinematic world. *Beau travail* weaves together a wealth of references that create a rich intertext and lays itself open to a variety of readings and approaches. Through its radical representation of the military and (post)colonial context, *Beau travail*'s tale of identity, desire and transgression is, like *J'ai pas sommeil*'s noir universe, haunted by the shadows of Genet and Fassbinder's homoerotic worlds.[41] As in the work of Genet and Fassbinder, in *Beau travail*, alienation and perversion are evoked through the aesthetics of the beautiful and the sublime.

The film gained wide critical acclaim and continues to generate a lot of interest and debate. At the centre of the discussions, the issue of political engagement, in particular, refers back to another one of Denis' main sources for this film: Jean-Luc Godard's *Petit soldat* (*The Little Soldier* 1960) (Dobson 2002). *Beau travail*'s affiliation to *Le Petit soldat* is rendered explicit through Michel Subor's presence as *Beau travail*'s commanding officer Forrestier. Thirty years before *Beau*

40 Formerly part of the French colonial empire, Djibouti is situated in the Horn of Africa, on the edge of the Red Sea, and at the confines of Ethiopia, Eritrea, and Somalia. It still houses the principal military bases of the French foreign legion. The region was granted the autonomous status of 'overseas territory' after the Second World War, and Djibouti became an independent republic in 1977.

41 Genet joined the legion at the age of nineteen but rapidly deserted. His only film work, *Chant d'Amour*, is a provocative representation of homosexuality and a subversive evocation of the military and carceral worlds. (*Chant d'Amour* (1950), b/w, 25 min, 16 mm). In addition, the name of the character played by Grégoire Colin recalls that of Genet's friend and writer François Sentein.

travail, in Godard's controversial evocation of the effect of the Algerian war, Subor played a French deserter, already called Bruno Forrestier, who is caught in a web of deception, betrayal and torture, where right-wing and left-wing factions use similar methods. Although it was censored at the time of its completion, *Le Petit soldat* was criticised for lacking a clear political engagement. Interestingly, a similar criticism has been levelled at Denis, whose stylised approach was interpreted as an embellishment of a colonial myth. Analysis of the film's complex *mise en scène*, however, shows that Denis' exploration of the myth of the legion, while it reveals its attraction, simultaneously unravels its colonial roots, and exposes the systematic negation of identity as difference and the denial of its own obsolescence that are necessary to its survival.

Beau travail is loosely based on the writings of nineteenth-century American novelist and poet Herman Melville. Inspired by the melancholy and nostalgia that permeates Melville's writing, by the force of the elements he depicts, and by the role played by the evil and the uncanny in his texts, Denis transposed one of his novellas, *Billy Budd, Sailor* (1891), to the world of the legion. The title of the film also refers to William Wellman's classic screen adaptation *Beau Geste* (1939), also about the legion, and close, in subject, to Melville's work.[42]

Like *Billy Budd*, *Beau travail* is the tale of an ambiguous triangular relationship set within a highly hierarchical and exclusively male universe. The story is told in retrospect by Galoup (Denis Lavant), a former sergeant in the legion's regiment in Djibouti, now living as an exile in Marseille. Galoup was once a perfect legionnaire and irreproachable officer, serving under the authority of his beloved commanding officer Forrestier (Michel Subor). But Galoup felt threatened by the arrival of a new recruit, the handsome and charismatic Sentain (Grégoire Colin). Immediately liked and admired by his comrades for his selfless nature and his courage, the young soldier was also noticed by Forrestier. Jealous, Galoup devised a plot to discredit him. Having come to the help of a comrade unfairly treated by Galoup, Sentain's punishment was to find his way alone through the desert. Given a faulty compass, Sentain narrowly escaped death and Galoup was expelled from the legion.

42 *Beau Geste* is based on a Percival Christopher Wrench story published in 1924.

The myth

By situating the film within the Foreign Legion, Denis draws on a persistent tradition of idealised masculinity. Constructed through image and story-telling, the legion is a body drenched in myth. Woven into France's literary patrimony,[43] its legendary history continued through a cinematic fashion of stars who donned the white uniform of the elite corps to feature in tales of faraway adventures, brotherly solidarity, and tragic loves.[44] Beyond the exoticism and romanticism, however, if the foreign legion came to occupy a unique place in the French collective imaginary and history, and if alternative representations of it have appeared so controversial, it is not only because it refers back to a conventional definition of the masculine, but also because the kind of discourse it embodies has been rooted in the country's definition of its national identity. In *Facing Postmodernity*, Max Silverman outlined how the pursuit of an ideal of unity and equality first established under the revolution ultimately gave way to the perverted forms of negation and normalisation which colonialism came to epitomise (Chapter 1):

> France was the quintessential modern nation state. Nowhere else did the star of equality, freedom and solidarity burn so bright ... On the one hand, French enlightenment philosophy provided the concepts for the pursuit of a higher form of humanity. The Revolution was the political blueprint for transforming those concepts into 'natural law'. The spirit of French Republicanism, embodied in the slogan 'the one and indivisible Republic' (*La République une et indivisible*), symbolised the persistence of this utopian dream of a shared humanity. (Silverman 1999: 3)

But this utopian dream, Silverman adds, rested on the successful construction and repression or assimilation of an 'other', a process

43 The destiny of some of France's cult literary figures and *poètes maudits* is linked to the colonies and to military bodies such as the legion. Arthur Rimbaud (1854–91), for instance, was involved in weapon trafficking in Africa and died in Marseille; a contemporary of Jean Genet, Blaise Cendrars (1887–1961) enrolled in the legion during the First World War.

44 In addition to *Beau Geste*, see for example: Josef von Sternberg's *Morocco* (1930) starring, like Wellman's *Beau Geste*, Gary Cooper, or Julien Duvivier's *La Bandera* (1935) with Jean Gabin. John Ford's *The Lost Patrol* (1934) has also been mentioned in relation with *Beau travail*.

that, again, he pinpoints as particularly central to the elaboration of French national identity:

> The homogenizing zeal of republicanism under the Third Republic ... the assimilation of diverse people around common goals, leading to a mad quest for uniformity in the name of equality ... did not have its direct equivalent elsewhere. (Silverman 1999: 4)

In the legion, this spirit found a superficial expression in a concept of belonging which offers individuals integration within its *corps d'élite*, apparently regardless of ethnicity, religion and nationality. But such integration is predicated on the unquestioning acceptance of the hierarchy and of the universal verity and validity of the laws of the legion, and, by extension, of the universality of the values of the French nation. Naomi Schor stressed how French colonialism has been represented 'as an act of generosity rather than of oppression, conferring upon its subjects the privilege of participating in France's defining universalism' (Schor 1985: 6). The demise of the Western colonial empires after the Second World War, and the affirmation of different sets of values – multi-culturalism, difference, the hybrid – rendered obsolete the principle of assimilation to a unique model. Yet as Denis' films remind us, the legacy of colonialism is not easily dismissed. 'The colonial is not after all dead but lies in its aftereffects', remarks Susan Hayward in her analysis of *Beau travail*. Denis' film, she adds, is an 'exploration in its many different forms, of the ravages of the '"post-colonial-body-as-the-aftereffects-of-colonialism"' (Hayward 2001: 161 159). The film's title, like the enthralling perfection of its images, the beauty of the landscapes and of the bodies, outlines the enduring force and seductiveness of the legion's ethos.

Part of the fascination exercised by the legion comes from its mode of recruitment. Specifically created to accommodate foreigners wishing to join the French army,[45] the legion offers to its recruit a new identity: those who join the legion are renamed. In principle, they leave their past behind. Their bodies are reshaped through training and identically clothed in uniforms. The film's visual address repeatedly plays to us this process of fusion that is able to metabolise even the marks of ethnicity. In the sequence where, at the beginning of the film, the soldiers, sitting in a boat, are portrayed in a series of

45 The legion was created in 1831. It is composed primarily of foreign soldiers. Its officers, however, are French.

close-ups set against the sky, tight framing of the figure is used in one of its most familiar functions – to create a sense of the epic and the heroic. At the same time, the close-up does not yield any of its classical narrative functions of clarification (to pick out *the* hero of a story from the crowd in particular), and if it isolates individual bodies, it is to better reinscribe them within the group. Strongly defined features, racial differences, and scars singularise the soldiers' faces, yet ultimately, as the close-ups follow one another, the repetition works to create a sequence of images linked primarily by a relation of contiguity and resemblance. In the likeness of figure movement and framing, it celebrates a particular ideal of belonging as a form of transcendence founded on the abandonment of the individual self: to transcend from mere man/soldier to elite warrior, the legionnaire abandons his individuality. This sequence, in particular, calls to mind Roland Barthes' text about propagandist imagery already mentioned in relation to *J'ai pas sommeil*. In his comment on a photograph representing a black African soldier saluting the French flag, Barthes summarised the underlining message as: 'France is a great empire … All her sons, without any colour discrimination, faithfully serve under her flag' (Barthes 1993: 116). In addition, these images of shaved heads, sculpted features and smooth, muscled physiques set against the sky offer a highly idealised vision of male bodies drawing on the ancient Greek notions of the alliance of beauty and valour. In the description of the legion's archaic yet still powerful model, Jane Sillars pointed out the importance of the classical substratum:

> Just as the modern French nation consciously modelled itself on some of the values and forms of the ancient republics, so the legion draws ideologically and iconographically on the models of classical antiquity. Its band of male warriors (a classical phalanx in the song of the legion) embody the ancient union of the beautiful and the good, their bravery and valour an expression of the manly virtues. (Sillars and Beugnet 2001: 168)

The dance sequences that punctuate the film also function to combine the epic dimension with a feeling of timeless osmosis. Denis collaborated with choreographer Bernardo Montet to include eight dances in parallel with the scenes of training. Set to the emphatic sound of a Benjamin Britten opera, also inspired by Melville's *Billy Budd*, these sequences recall the ancient links between dance and

war. Agnès Godard's camerawork functions as a relay to the movement created by the choreography. Via the editing, it creates an
alternation of brief shots of straining individual bodies and ensemble
shots where the unity of the group is recomposed and reaffirmed, the
singular subsuming behind the rule of discipline. At the same time,
Denis' use of music, dance and opera highlights the theatricality of
the confrontations dramatised in *Beau travail* and conveys a sense of
the inexorable, as if the fate of the protagonists, like that of the heroes
of ancient mythology, was already written. The circling dance of
Galoup and Sentain reveals them as set figures in a staged combat,
playing out their allotted roles. Sillars stressed how the visual imagery
of the net recurs in the film to evoke the deadly net of fate that
ensnares the three central characters. A net of shadows falls over
Forestier's features. A net pulls Sentain from the ocean. A net of
diamond mirrors close around Galoup's final dance. This overdeter-
mination is made most visible in Sentain's blow to Galoup which
seals his fate and sets his punishment: the gesture is played in slow
motion.

Before worldly passions permeate it, the universe of the legion
portrayed in the film has an aspect of paradise lost. Moving in
synchronicity against the timeless majesty of the landscape, the men,
rendered alike by youth and beauty, resemble a group of Endemyons.[46]
As they romp about in the sea under the benevolent gaze of their
commanding officer Forrestier, something childlike and innocent
emanates from the legionnaires' display of brotherly camaraderie.
The price for this apparent innocence is immobility and repression:
the legion's combination of strict hierarchy, of all-encompassing
routines, and rule of uniformity leaves little place for the expression of
yearnings and aspirations. The apparent perfection of this equi-
librium is necessarily upset by the intrusion of desire: the arrival of
Sentain, the actualisation of differences, and the emergence of envy
and lack. Throughout, however, Galoup's retrospective tale, haunted
by the memory of Forrestier, remains imbued with the desperate
nostalgia of the fallen son sent into exile.

The film's play with ancient classical references works to underline the archaism not only of the military structure but also of the

46 In classical mythology Endemyon was a son or grandson of Zeus. Offered a
 wish by the Gods, he asked to sleep forever so as to remain forever young.

concept of history it seems to embrace: one that denies man's historical being,[47] that conceives of time as cyclical and folding in on itself. Through its stylised aesthetics, the film portrays a body of men that creates and inhabit a space and time of its own, one that resists historical realities and relies on the exclusion of any 'other' that cannot be assimilated – the women, the people of Djibouti. *Beau travail*'s early sequences, for instance, emphasise close-up and tight framing in compositions that isolate the human figure individually or as a collective body. Removing it from its spatial background, they focus on the body and the movement of the body, downplaying the sense of location, as well as perspective and depth. As the film progresses, the same feeling of dis-location and stasis is reinstated in spite of the widening of the frame of action. The legionnaires inhabit a world devoid of the usual situating landmarks. The space they occupy appears constituted independently from the charting of the land by road and by railway tracks. Working alongside existing lines of communication, the legionnaires, watched by purposeful and curious Djiboutians, build roads to nowhere.

The sterility of the landscape that is revealed by the legion's move up country forms an obvious visual echo to the obsolescence of their own continuation, with Galoup describing the extinct volcanoes guarding their camp. As the *mise en scène* opens up the legion is revealed moving aimlessly through a misunderstood and barren landscape. Not quite synchronised to the speed of the travelling shot that pans across, the soldiers walk from right to left, creating a frieze effect. Parallel to the horizon, their movement eschews depth of field: theirs is not a journey of exploration. In many ways, the film echoes Frantz Fanon's description of the postcolonial subject as 'Individuals without anchors, without horizon, colourless, stateless, rootless – a race of angels' (Fanon 1963: 176).

'The force of time as change': disintegration of the myth

In her critical assessment of the 'logic that subtends French assimilationism', Schor underlines how 'an Arab woman, a black man, a Jew, can acquire French identity providing they relinquish all claims

47 As underlined in Chapter 1, man is understood as a 'historical being' when human existence is considered in relation to the complex and *changing* web of circumstances that determine it.

to their cultural (religious, linguistic) differences' (Schor 1985: 6). *Beau travail*'s dramatisation of the consequences of the breakdown of this contract of assimilation through the abandonment of difference is revealing. The film's murderous punishment is set in motion by the actions of Combé, the black Moslem legionnaire, who leaves his post to attend a local mosque during Ramadan. To provoke Sentain's anger, Galoup orders Combé to dig the rocky desert earth under the blazing sun. The harshness of the punishment is also a sign that the logic of it belongs to an obsolete structure, on the defensive.

First and foremost, *Beau travail* is an exploration of a body that has outlived the myth that founded it, of a form, 'shallow, impoverished, isolated' (Barthes 1993: 117) that persists after the ideal that created it has vanished. The continuing existence of a body like the legion thus depends on a double denial: the initial denial of a diverse history in favour of one hegemonic discourse, and the further denial of the demise of the grand narrative[48] of French imperialism. The blind dedication to an outdated ideal is established in the film's very first images. The credits open on a highly Platonic vision:[49] a travelling shot moves along a painting on a rock, showing the silhouettes of a group of legionnaires planting their flag on new land. The legion's song plays in the background, with its obsolete list of names of former colonies. There is no empire for the legion to conquer or even to protect anymore but, like a mechanism turning in neutral, it maintains its strict discipline, repeats the endless exercises and unchanging routines that have come to stand in the place of its function. The legionnaires do their daily training, but they also iron, bake birthday cakes, and argue over how many onions should go in the stew. While, together with the hierarchical structure and relinquishing of responsibility and past, this strange and quasi-familial domesticity emphasise

48 Grand narratives or metanarratives (Christianity, progress, capitalism, etc.) are terms coined by philosopher Jean-François Lyotard to designate those narrative discourses that justify the establishment and existence of political, social, and cultural systems. A grand narrative posits an origin (God or progress for instance) and a goal (universal knowledge, freedom). It claims to be universal and to explain all the other narratives that compose the historical process (see Chapter 1).

49 In the *Republic*, Plato (428–348 BC) uses the tale of the cavern (a group of men chained in a cavern from birth, can only contemplate the world as a shadow reflection on the rock. Freed from their chains, they refuse to turn away from this mere reflection to face the unknown) as an allegory for the process of learning to think for oneself.

the practically and emotionally autarchic dimension of military life, the film's insistence on the mundane undermines the mythology of hyper-masculinity, revealing the labour of construction which goes into its production (Sillars 2001). In the absence of an enemy, attacks are staged and conducted on empty buildings. Death occurs by accident, an explosion of red in the blue of the sea.

'I started from the myth and went through the mirror', Denis explained (Tinazzi 2000). In order to maintain its antiquated rule, the legion must fold onto itself, close itself to the wider world, to history and change. It must live in autarchy, conscious only of its own truth and seeing only its own reflection. The futility of the process, however, is suggested by the recurrent motif of the split mirror. The film's visual and narrative organisation works to undermine Galoup's idealised vision, progressively exposing the fragility of an illusory cohesiveness threatened from within and from without. The local and historical dimension is reinstated through the presence of the local people and, in a neat reversal of the colonial gaze, the group of men is constantly being watched, reduced, in the aimlessness of their detached existence, to the status of exotic spectacle. Parallels between the two worlds underline the stark contrast between the closed economy of the legion and the open exchange of the Djiboutians. The latter are shown engaged in trade and barter, buying rugs, procuring qat (the leaves of a hallucinogenic plant) for the commander, selling salt-encrusted curiosities. Their willingness to swap like for unlike reveals how the legion's stasis depends on its regime of similarity. The film does not rest on a strict, simplistic binary system of opposition: in effect, in its depiction of the relationship between Galoup and his Djibouti girlfriend Rahel, it suggests that another form of communication and exchange may still be possible for the legionnaire. But such overlap remains marginal to a military world dependent on the complete allegiance to an exclusive ideal. *Legio patria nostra*: as the motto recalls, the legionnaire's only home is the legion.

In the scene that opens the movie, the soldiers in uniforms and with shaven heads are contrasted with the local women, shown parading their difference – the hairstyles, the clothes with their diverse fabric and pattern, the varied dances – in front of the night-club's mirror. As Julia Dobson pointed out, this *mise en scène* appears to mimic the colonial male gaze (Chapter 1), yet the women's apparent self-awareness undermines the traditional process of objectification:

> The way in which Denis films the Djibouti women dancing inter-
> pellates a complex dynamic between spectacle and agency. We as
> spectators are acutely aware of the conventional function of the
> women as exotic spectacle both for the legionnaires and for conven-
> tional Western constructions of otherness. Yet they are seen sometimes
> reflected in mirrors sometimes immediately before the camera, an
> alternance which, combined with their apparent pleasure and agency
> in these scenes, prevents their objectification. (Dobson 2002)

This knowing and pleasurable combination of the subject and object
position, of the self in performance – the way the women dance, look
at themselves, and simultaneously invite the gaze of the soldiers and
of the spectators – suggests a fluidity of identity alien to the laws of the
legion. A further sign of slippage occurs with the de-synchronised
mouthing of a kiss – the beginning of a song sung by a man – by one
of the young women dancing in front of the mirror, a mimic repeated
by one of the soldiers at the end of the sequence. The playful gesture
can be read as a humorous reminder of the inescapably divided
nature of the human self – the impossibility for the inner self to
assimilate completely into an image, a gender identity, a uniform. It
draws an intriguing parallel with Forrestier's self-doubt and apparent
cynicism.

In the words of a disenchanted Forrestier, the outer elegance of the
legionnaire should reflect an inner elegance: becoming a soldier is to
become a unified being, leaving no gap between beliefs and attitude.
But the commanding officer himself is the very embodiment of the
impossibility of this perfect match between the being and its reflection. Just like Subor, as an actor, is connected to *Le Petit soldat*,
Forrestier, as a character, has a past (Dobson 2002). From his
performance in Godard's film, Subor keeps one crucial gesture:
standing in front of the mirror, he contemplates his face or hides it
behind his hands, while the camera changes its point of view from a
frontal to a side shot of his face. The gesture dramatises the split
between inner and outer being: Forrestier is a legionnaire without an
ideal, a man conscious of the absurdity of the military world he
belongs to. Commenting on Forrestier's presence as the embodiment
of disillusion and lucidity, Dobson quotes Deleuze's description of
the character in *Le Petit soldat* as a

> new type of character for a new cinema. It is because what happens to
> them does not belong to them and only half concerns them, because

they know how to extract from the event that part that cannot be reduced to what happens: that part of the inexhaustible possibility that constitutes the unbearable, the intolerable, the visionary's part. (Deleuze 1994: 19)

The soldiers' nocturnal outings to the local night-club, which they conduct together and in uniform, are a customary aspect of the legionnaire's life, assimilated to the lesser tasks they perform as part of their daily routines. In stark contrast with the sensual display of the opening sequence in the club, the ritualistic dances in the desert, choreographed on operatic music, are imbued with the detached grace of a gesture of transcendence. The camera records the perfect synchronicity of the legion's collective body in movement, gathering the men together in enveloping long takes. Yet ultimately the film does not so much stress the ideal cohesion of the group as portray the legion threatened by the very logic that governs it. The first shot of the soldiers dancing starts with their shadows, and Susan Hayward underlines how the choreography epitomises the legionnaires' disappearing selves, how their bodies, moving against a background of sand, leave no traces (Hayward 2001). But the relationship between bodies and earth also signals the constant pull of the organic, the suggestion that, in its negation of change and in its cultural amnesia, this collective body is being reclaimed by the natural world. In spite of the routines, always effected to perfection, in spite of the perfect folds of the uniform, the body of the legion appears at risk of merging with the plants and the rocks as the first dance, entitled the dance of the weeds, exemplifies: the machinery is already being colonised by the sand, and the legionnaires move in the wind like the weeds around them. Moreover, if initially the dances play out a rapturous but undifferentiated vision of physical sameness and choreographed movement, as the bounds of repression falter, they become more violent and more focused on Sentain, with images of clasping, contact, rescue and conflict foregrounded. In those moments, Agnès Godard's camera captures the men's physical presence in all its density, evoking the weight of the body as flesh (that is, the body in time, ageing) in a way that counterpoints the evanescence of the body as shadow. Similarly, in some of the training sequences, as the camera stays fixed, recording the passing of the men running or crawling, the bodies project themselves towards the camera, almost colliding with it, like a visualisation of the real about to burst through the borders of fiction and myth.

For all his dedication to the legion's system, Galoup himself is unable to achieve a perfect state of osmosis with his ideal. Within a world that celebrates valour, youth and beauty (the embodiment of a timeless military ideal), he is marked out from the start by his ugliness and his destructive passions: the introductory sequence, composed of the series of close-ups of the soldiers' faces, ends with an abrupt cut on the sergeant sitting at the bow of the boat, excluded from the group. Sentain's arrival thus functions to expose tensions that are already at work. Galoup projects his own sense of non-belonging on the young soldier. (Sentain sounds like *sans tain*, the term used in French to designate a two-way mirror.) In Galoup's eyes, Sentain's transgression is to fail in reflecting the legion's model and nothing more. The new recruit stands out from the collective. He is picked out of the lineout by the commanding officer and complimented for his exceptional qualities. Galoup's rage can be read as a measure of his repressed individual desire (the homosexual nature of his love for Forrestier and of his hate of Sentain), but also of his emotional invest-ment in a system of authority and control that has colonised his interiority. A tattoo of the legion's motto adorns Galoup's skin above the place of the heart. Like the motif of the chain – Forrestier's bracelet which Galoup may have stolen, the chain that he wears around his neck, or the chain that he leaves on the dance floor at the end of the film – it is a visual reminder of the extent to which Galoup is marked by his allegiance to the legion. The legion has taken charge of his past, present, and future, of his social, professional and emotional life. The price to pay was the relinquishing of choice and of individual desire. The process that 'frees' Galoup, by excluding him from the legion's system, is thus a violent and painful one. In his Marseille exile, Galoup is confronted with time and change (his body, he admits, is growing stiff). Like Forrestier in *Le Petit soldat*, whose concluding words are paraphrased in *Beau travail*'s voiceover narration (Dobson 2002), Galoup now has time to reflect, to take responsibility for his own existence and actions, and to face remorse. A sense of violent dislocation imbues the solo dance that closes the film. In contrast with the ethereal beauty of the desert dances and of their musical theme, the night-club where Galoup performs alone is only filled with the kitsch sound of disco music. Deprived of the ideal – even hollow and illusory – that had fashioned his existence, Galoup is confronted with the crudeness and solitude of an unfamiliar form of freedom.

> Galoup s'abandonne pour mieux se retenir, expérimentant par la gestuelle cette fragile et éphémère frontière où la liberté ne se délite pas en fuite, où la liberté n'est pas synonyme d'oubli de soi.[50] (Vassé 2000: 31)

Its reflection caught by the net of mirrors behind him, Galoup's body seems to express a painful oscillation, as if his being, riddled with the anxiety of its forced emancipation, could not disentangle itself from the mould that imprisons him. Hayward partly rejects Vassé's positive reading of the scene as a figuration of Galoup's liberation. For Hayward, the dance represents Galoup's 'postcolonial moment when he recognises in his own terms (dance) ... the futility of it all, of trying to be an a-priori unity of experiences'. In this reading, the end of Galoup's dance, as he scuttles away from the screen, simply shows how 'the dislocated postcolonial body disappears' (Hayward 2001: 166). In effect, the ambiguous juxtaposition of sequences that compose the end of the film opens a variety of interpretations of Galoup's fate. The sequence before last, shot in his Marseille bedsit, suggests that Galoup, 'unfit for life' is about to kill himself. The camera depicts his deliberate and minute preparations, the precise folding of the bed sheets on which he lies down, cradling a pistol. The camera, travelling along his torso in close-up, moves from the barrel of the gun to Galoup's tattoo, then to the fragile but forceful movement of a vein pulsing under the skin of his arm. From this image, however, the shot cuts into the scene of the solo dance. Though the previous sequence was clearly located in Marseille, the film now takes us back to the dance floor of the same seedy-looking night-club featured at the beginning, in the scene depicting the group of legionnaires mingling with Djibouti women. The multiplicity of readings that this enigmatic ending offers corresponds to the multiplicity of trajectories created by the disintegration of the legion's illusory system of unity as experienced by Galoup. The net of mirrors in front of which Galoup performs reflects and fragments both his body and its shadow – neither character nor story can now be reduced to a unique model.

---

50 'Galoup lets himself go then holds back again, testing, through his movements, this fragile and ephemeral frontier where freedom does not dissolve into flight, where freedom does not equate with self-negation.'

Contrary to the form of the true, which is unifying and strives for the identification of a character (its discovery or simply its coherence), the power of the false cannot be separated from the irreducible multiplicity. 'I is another' has replaced Ego equals Ego (Deleuze 1994: 133).

Narrative incertitude: the 'power of the false'[51]

As *Beau travail*'s equivocal ending illustrates, the impossibility of resisting and transcending the fluctuations of time and identity, dramatised at the level of the plot and characterisation, also impregnates the film's narrative space. The kind of grand narratives and systems of beliefs of which a body like the legion is a by-product rest on discourses of truth which present themselves as universal and unchanging. Theorists interested in the connection between cinema and ideology have been quick to point out the parallel between this form of discourse and the cinema of the continuity system.[52] In mainstream cinema, the continuity principles are applied so as to create, through a continuum of time and space, the illusion of a stable, truthful vision. Deleuze contrasts this classical mode of description, which he calls 'organic', with a 'crystalline' regime where the narration

> ceases to be truthful, that is, to claim to be true, and becomes fundamentally falsifying. This is not at all a case of 'each has his own truth', a variability of content. It is a power of the false which replaces and supersedes the form of the true, because it poses the simultaneity

51 The expression, inspired by Nietzsche's writing, is used by Deleuze. It is important to stress the relevance of Deleuze's sources in the context of *Beau travail*, considering, in particular, the beginning (the painted shadows on the rock) and the end (Galoup's dance) sequences of Denis' film. Deleuze's elaboration of the concept of the time-image stems largely from a contrast between the Platonic search for a transcendental truth and Nieztsche's advocacy of the 'power of the false', that is, the acceptance of the illusory nature of transcendence et the recognisance of the changing and subjective nature of existence.

52 The continuity system generally applied in mainstream film – such as the chronological ordering of events and sequences, the clear localisation of the actions in the space, the consistency of the camera's point of view – ensures that the story world, the behaviour of the characters, their actions and movements appear coherent, 'truthful'. See also chapter and notes on *Nénette et Boni*.

of incompossible presents, or the coexistence of not-necessarily true pasts. (Deleuze 1994: 131)[53]

As we have seen in the previous chapters, although she always starts from the real, Denis' filmmaking has consistently eschewed the rules of strict logic and cause-and-effect in order to evoke a reality that is never entirely unified and knowable. Of all her films, it is in *Beau travail* that her approach to the narrative form arguably comes closest to a crystalline mode. In *Beau travail*, two modes of discourse initially coexist and contradict each other: one expresses itself through the unifying ethos and finite world of the legion and the other through the historical, changing reality of the Djiboutians or of the life that Galoup re-enters as a civilian. The uncertain and often contradictory relationship between movement, time, and space, and between the voiceover narration and the images, work to underline the illusory nature of the first mode, creating a

> combined circuit where the real and the imaginary, the actual and the virtual, chase after each other, exchange their roles and become indiscernible. It is here that we may speak the most precisely of crystal image: the coalescence of an actual image and of its virtual image ... (Deleuze 1994: 127)

Denis and scriptwriter Jean-Pol Fargeau wrote Galoup's diary first, and constructed the script proper on this basis, with a voiceover running through the film. Even though Galoup holds the role of narrator, however, his comments do not function primarily to generate the sense of coherence and (chrono)logic that the voiceover conventionally aims to create. Rather, the flow of his spoken words forms a kind of melodic line that combines with Denis and Nelly Quettier's symphonic editing to pattern the rhythm and framework of a primarily sensual vision:

> Cet abandon du rythme et des responsabilités militaires se coule dans les méandres de la voix-off, qui guide les images sans les diriger, qui concentre toute la présence verbale du film pour mieux détacher les

53 Godard is one of the filmmakers that Deleuze mentions in this context. Deleuze talks about *Le Petit soldat*, but also cites a short called *Le Grand Escroc* (part of a collective film called *Les Plus belles escroqueries du monde*, 1964) which, interestingly, was inspired by a Herman Melville novel based on a self-referential narrative and entitled *The Confidence Man: His Masquerade* (1957).

personnages du dialogue et faire jaillir les corps à l'état brut.[54] (Vassé 2000: 30)

Galoup's voiceover provides limited factual information. In a wandering episodic fashion, punctuated by long silences and the murmur of his voice singing the legion's hymn, it describes his state of mind, his nostalgia and feelings of threat. Impressionistic views of Marseille portray the Mediterranean city as a cold and grey place of exile, marked by the passing of the seasons, but, although in this instance the voice indicates the place and time ('Marseille, late February'), there is no clear indication of the lapse of time that separates the events from their retelling. Moreover, in his introductory remarks, the narrator himself admits the subjectivity and unreliability of his tale as he remarks, yoking the martial and the cinematic: 'Les choses dépendent du point de vue. De l'angle d'attaque' ('Things depend on the viewpoint, the angles of attack'). In effect, the images rarely match the actual words and the camerawork and editing never securely establish a visual point of view: who, for instance, manipulates the objects that belong to Forrestier – the photograph, the bracelet –, the commanding officer himself or Galoup?

The first visual manifestation of the narrator's presence outlines the nature of the process of retelling. The screen is first filled with the blue, oscillating surface of the sea. The image of Galoup's hand, writing on a notebook, fades in under the first image. In this superimposition, past and present, subjective memory and myth seem to overlap: the writing takes place against a fluctuating backdrop, a symbol of the changing character of memory and a direct visual manifestation of the work of time on subjectivity. Like her character's tale, Denis' filmmaking evokes a form of palimpsest. As mentioned before, *Beau travail* weaves together a rich and diverse intertext that adds layers to Galoup's narrative and hints at the existence of a multitude of other, virtual, stories. In the process, the frontier between character and actor in particular becomes blurred. Some of the actors carry with them their cinematic persona, for instance, evoking through their gestures (Subor/Forrestier) and dance routines (Lavant/Galoup)

54 'The effect of abandoning the military rhythm and responsibilities moulds itself in the meandering of a voice that guides the images without directing them. The verbal presence of the film is concentrated in this voice, allowing the characters to detach themselves from the dialogue and project themselves as bodies, raw matter.'

the shadows of past incarnations.[55] At the same time, the characters they embody bring with them their own history: the rumours that surround Forrestier's enigmatic figure in *Beau travail* suggests an involvement in France's 'dirty war' – the Algerian conflict – the hidden war depicted in *Le Petit soldat*. The film thus suggests that both at the individual and at the wider historical level, a process of repression of the past is at work, the denial of an inglorious dimension of the nation's history that directly threatens the fundaments on which a structure like the legion bases its existence and ethos.

These elements mingle with the echoes of the myth of the legion, and with Galoup's own recollections. His reflections form a mix of interrupted scenarios, descriptive scenes of his past and present, and poetic visions, never safely identifiable as dreams or as memories. They filter through the film's unstable ordering of sequences and disorientating spatial treatment. Yet, for most of the critics, far from working towards a difficult, frustrating viewing experience, the combination creates an enthralling feeling of narrative depth, which Jean-Michel Frodon attempts to define by stressing three aspects of the filmmaking:

> Un: la beauté intérieure, évidente et inexplicable, de chaque plan, chaque instant capté comme pour lui-même, son élégance formelle et sa mélancolie à chaque image différente.
>
> Deux: ça ne raconte rien, et pourtant entre ces petits blocs d'images et de sons si précis, si poignants, se faufilent mille histoires. Des histoires qui viennent des légendes, de l'histoire, de la littérature, de la peinture, du théâtre, de la musique, de la danse, du cinéma. Et voilà que cet assemblage 'non-narratif' bruisse de récits murmurés, aux marges de l'écran et de la mémoire.
>
> Trois: 1+1=3, précisément. Ces additions de petites scènes ... loin de composer des binômes simplistes, produisent un troisième espace. La simplicité des lignes et la convocation des récits se combinent pour fabriquer autre chose – un mystère, magnifique et terrifiant.[56] (Frodon 2000)

55 Denis Lavant came to fame through his roles in Léos Carax's films. In *Mauvais Sang* (*Bad Blood*, 1987), and in *Les Amants du Pont-Neuf* (*The Lovers of the Bridge*, 1991), he performs remarkable acrobatic dance routines. Grégoire Colin, as we know, is one of Denis' fetish actors and held the main role in *Nénette et Boni*, shot in Marseille (Chapter 3).

56 'One: the internal beauty, obvious yet inexplicable, of each shot, as if each

The opening sequences, for instance, till the first desert dance that introduces the group of soldiers as a whole, fail to provide a sense of the general organisation of the space (the layout of the camp or its situation with relation to the city for instance). They function like a patchwork, a series of impressions of worlds that barely overlap, of fragments that betray the existence of parallel and dissimilar realities and stories. In the early sequences, in particular, the perception of a changing time and space offered by the harmonious accumulation of visual details, colours, textures, movements, and diegetic sounds in the scenes portraying local people, emphasises, by contrast, the feeling of osmosis, sameness, and suspended time evoked by the legion's world.

The film's opening images, the travelling shot on the rock painting accompanied by the song of the legion, cuts abruptly into the scene of the night-club filled with the crude sounds and lyrics of dance music. After an insert of the title (*Beau travail*), the film cuts into an image of a man (an employee from a telecommunications' office?) trying to establish contact with Djibouti (as we have seen, the failed or incomprehensible telephone conversation is a familiar motif in Denis' films). Cut. A long take shows the mountainous desert landscape seen through the window of a train, moving from *right to left*. Cut. A long take depicts the inside of the carriage crowded with passengers. Cut. The shot frames a window again, with women looking out. This time, the landscape unfolds from *left to right*. Cut. A succession of still shots show a dusty wind blowing over an expanse of desert. One still shot shows the carcass of a tank abandoned in the desert (sound of rusty metal fragments swinging in the wind) and cuts into the same image with a tighter framing. Cut. A medium close-up focuses on

instant was captured for itself, its formal elegance and its melancholy different in each image.

Two: it does not actually recount anything, yet between these small blocks of images and sounds, so precise and poignant, a thousand stories filter in. Stories that come from the legends, from history, from literature, from painting, from theatre, from music, from dance, from cinema. And this 'non-narrative' combination is filled with the murmur of tales from the margins of the screen and of the memory.

Three: 1+1 = 3, precisely. This addition of small scenes ... far from composing simplistic binaries, produces a third space. The simplicity of the signs and the evocation of the stories combine to build something else – a magnificent and terrifying mystery.'

weeds blown by the wind on the surface of the desert earth. Cut. Still directed towards the ground, the camera pans slowly to reveal the outline of a first shadow, then of several more. The sound of Britten's music progressively swells up. The camera pans up to reveal the body of Combé, then of the other soldiers, standing with their arms extended above their heads.

This succession of sequences is exemplary of the film's overall narrative and spatial organisation. Rather than presenting a unified and immediately apprehensible reality, the filmmaking works to blur distinctions between objective and internal reality, exteriority and interiority, memory and dreams. The certainties of place and time dissolve in jarring cuts, superimpositions and backwash movements reminiscent of Deleuze's definition of the crystalline narration. The sense of stasis that characterises the legion's life is thus ruptured by the resurfacing of fragments of other temporal and spatial planes. The fleeting image of the shepherdess that appears later on in the film for instance, although inserted between two shots of Galoup resting, remains disconnected, suspended (like a Deleuzian crystal image) between the virtual and the actual.[57]

The fragmentation and dis-location that has characterised the charting of space and time by the camera and the editing ultimately invades the diegetic dimension proper as Sentain finally gets lost. Having taken the defence of Combé, Sentain is condemned to a solitary walk through miles of deserted land. It is impossible to grasp with any precision the spatial and causal relation between the various shots that compose the elliptically edited sequence that depicts and follows his being driven out and left to find his way back. Sentain's solitary meanderings and the shots of a passing train, for instance, or of Galoup at the barracks, cannot be related precisely in terms of distance, closeness, simultaneity of time, or in terms of the characters' perception and point of view. When the exhausted Sentain finally stops, the picture of the salt-ridden beach where he has lain down literally fills the screen, its whiteness and sameness denying the possiblity of finding any secure orientation.

Sentain's near-death, his 'crystallisation' on the bed of blindingly white salt that eats at his skin echoes, in visual terms, two contrasted

57 A crystal image can neither be reduced to the visualisation of a present or of a past situation, of an immediate reality, a dream, or a recollection, but coalesces all of these possible interpretations together.

notions of foreignness. On the one hand, it can be read in terms of the pull of the organic evoked in the context of the dance of the weeds: nature seems to reclaim the legionnaire's body, to absorb it as if it was mere, undifferentiated matter. As such, the sequence works as a visual metaphor for the legion's anachronistic ideal of self-effacement, which removes the subject from a changing reality, traps and fossilises the subject in the static space of myth. Sentain, however, is discovered and rescued by a caravan of local travellers: 'perdu' ('lost'), he murmurs, as he regains consciousness, possibly a sign that the experience has forced him to face his non-belonging, his foreignness. In this way, the images of his ordeal invoke more positive interpretations, similar to Kristeva's reading of Rimbaud in *Strangers to Ourselves*:

> Rimbaud's 'I is an other' was not only the avowal of the psychotic phantom that haunts poetry. The word announced exile, the possibility or the necessity of being foreign and of living in the foreigner's country, thus prefiguring the art of living in a modern era, the cosmopolitanism of the excoriated (écorchés). (Kristeva 1994: 25)

The space of myth – free-floating, unanchored in space and time, cyclical, and repetitive – is reframed through the film's visual form into the space of history – situated, local and specific. Yet, the shadow of colonisation does not simply evaporate in the desert air. In *Beau travail*, the two dimensions coexist, and interpenetrate through the film's ability to hold in tension the ghosts and echoes of its various source texts. In its poetic portrayal of colonial obsolescence, *Beau travail* shows the appeal of the myth of oneness and sameness while it simultaneously moves away from an 'organic narration' to suggest its impossibility. Dismantling the apparent coherence and fixity of the time and space that the legion inhabits, the film conjures up the pull of the historical dimension, riddled by the anxiety of time passing but opening up possibilities of creative transformation.

If, as one of the title's interpretations suggests, *Beau travail* is a work of/on beauty (un travail du beau), its aesthetic approach and stylisation do not evacuate the film's analytical dimension or diminish its critical vision. On the contrary, *Beau travail*'s compelling evocation of the legion as myth is coextensive with the denunciation[58] of its dream of fusion and of its colonial ethos:

58 As such, it is poles apart from Leni Riefenstahl's filmmaking, to which *Beau travail* has been compared on the grounds of its portrayal of a certain male

Quand je filme ces visages de guerriers, ça a moins à voir avec la beauté qu'avec l'image qui émane de la légion elle-même, le symbole de l'homme mythique. La beauté est ailleurs: dans les splendides visages solaires des Djiboutiens.[59] (Lequeux 2000)

Conclusion

From the start, Denis' investigation of the theme of exile, of the issues of alienation and dis-location in the postcolonial world, was coextensive with an exploration of the powers of cinema. Already in *S'en fout la mort*, even more so than in *Chocolat* or in any of the shorts and documentaries shot by Denis, it was the act of filming itself that mattered. *S'en fout la mort* thus initiated a filmmaking where image, movement, and narration, freed from the determining precepts of the screenplay, become inseparable. Her contemplation of the possibility of different forms of narrative destabilisation continues to materialise through the stylistic and narrative explorations she conducts in later films,[60] where closeness to the body and tactile camerawork are combined with a complex play on scale and *mise en scène* in space. Denis' cinema of exile is not merely the depiction of situations of estrangement, it is, in itself, a fertile cinematic experience of de-familiarisation – one that challenges the gaze, the perception, and the imagination of the viewer.

---

beauty. Riefenstahl's propaganda films, and in particular *Triumph of the Will* (1934), are still the object of raging controversies: they are artistically remarkable, but they were made on behalf of the Third Reich, prefiguring aspects of the Nazi system.

59 'When I film these warriors' faces, it has less to do with beauty than with the image that emanates from the legion itself, the symbol of a mythical man. Beauty is elsewhere: in the splendid solar faces of the people of Djibouti.'

60 Deleuze stressed how the 'non-distancing of the moving body' was one of the techniques of a cinema that seeks to carry out 'a direct presentation of time by reversing the relationship of subordination that time maintains with normal movement' (Deleuze, 1994: 37). Yet, in her critical assessment of *S'en fout la mort*, Denis, quoting the critic Serge Daney, remarks that with this film she had remained within 'the eye of the storm' (Lifshitz, 1995).

References

Audé, Françoise (1990), 'S'en fout la vie', *Positif* 356, 71–2.

Barthes, Roland (1993), *Mythologies*, Paris, Seuil, 1957, reprinted in London, Vintage, trans. Annette Lavers.

Beaver, Harold (1967), Introduction, *Billy Budd, Sailor and Other Stories*, London, Penguin English Library.

Beugnet, Martine (2000), *Sexualité, marginalité, contrôle: cinéma français contemporain*, Paris, L'Harmattan.

Beugnet, Martine (2001), 'Negociating Conformity: Tales of Ordinary Evil', in E. Ezra and S. Harris (eds), *France in Focus*, Oxford and New York, Berg, pp. 195–207.

Blum, Sylvie (1996), 'Returning to Indochina', *Jump Cut* 41, 59–66

Bourget, Jean-Louis (1994), *'J'ai pas sommeil'*, *Positif* 401–2, 46.

Bouzet, Ange-Dominique (1990), *'S'en fout la mort'*, *Libération*, 5 September.

Buss, Robin (2001), *French Film Noir*, London: Marion Boyars.

Deleuze, Gilles (1994), *Cinéma 2: L'Image-temps*, Paris, Editions de minuit, 1985, reprinted as *Cinema 2: The Time-Image*, trans. H. Thomlinson and R. Galeta, London, The Athlone Press, reprinted in 1994.

Dobson, Julia (2002) 'Sequels of Engagment: From *Le Petit soldat* to *Beau travail*', unpublished paper presented at the conference 'Cinéma et engagement', Nottingham Trent University, 12 September 2002.

Doane, Mary-Anne (1991), *Femmes Fatales*, New York and London, Routledge.

Docherty, Thomas (1996), *Alterities: History, Criticism, Representation*, Oxford, Clarendon Press.

Dyer, Richard (1990), *Now You See It: Studies on Lesbian and Gay Films*, London and New York, Routledge.

Dyer, Richard (1997), *White*, London and New York, Routledge.

Fanon, Frantz (1963), *Les Damnés de la terre*, Paris, Gallimard, 1961. Reprinted as *The Wretched of the Earth*, London, Pluto Press.

Fanon, Frantz (1986), *Peau noire, masques blancs*, Paris, Editions du Seuil, 1952, reprinted as *Black Skin, White Masks*, London, Pluto Press.

Frodon, Jean-Michel (1988), 'Claire Denis: une enfance africaine', *Le Point*, 9 May.

Frodon, Jean-Michel (1991), 'Contre l'oubli, écrire, filmer', *Le Monde*, 11 December.

Frodon, Jean-Michel (2000), 'Beau travail: la danse du soleil et des armes sous la caméra de Claire Denis', *Le Monde*, 3 May.

Gili, Jean (1988), 'Entretien avec Claire Denis sur *Chocolat*', *Film* 1, 14–16.

Hayward, Susan (2001), 'Claire Denis' Films and the Postcolonial Body', *Studies in French Cinema* 1:3, 159–65.

Jousse, Thierry (1988), 'Jeux africains', *Cahiers du cinéma* 407–8, 132–3.

Jousse, Thierry (1994), 'Les Insomniaques', *Cahiers du cinéma* 479, 22–6.

Kaganski, Serge and Bonnaud, Frédéric, 'Leçons de ténèbre', *Les Inrockuptibles* 297, 30–4.

Kristeva, Julia (1982), *The Powers of Horror: An essay on Abjection*, trans. Léon S. Roudiez, New York, Columbia University Press.

Kristeva, Julia (1994) *Strangers to Ourselves*, trans. Leon S. Roudiez, New York, Columbia University Press.

Lefort, Gérard (1988), 'Claire d'Afrique', *Libération*, 17 May.

Lefort, Gérard (1990), 'Le Cercle noir', *Libération*, 5 September.

Lequeux, Emmanuelle (2000), '*Beau travail*', *Le Monde*, 3 May.

Lifshitz, Sébastien (1995), *Claire Denis, la Vagabonde*, 48 minute documentary, colour, prod. La Fémis.

Marker, Cynthia (1999), 'Sleepless in Paris: *J'ai pas sommeil*', in *French Cinema in the 1990s*, ed. Phil Powrie, Oxford, Oxford University Press, pp. 137–47.

Mazabrard, Colette (1989), *Cahiers du cinéma* 424, 53–4.

Mérigeau, Pascal (1994), 'Les Inconnus dans la maison', *Le Monde*, 18 May.

Pascal, Michel (1994), 'Camille le Maudit', *Le Point* 1131, p. 32.

Riou, Alain (1994), 'Erreurs d'aiguillage', *Le Nouvel Observateur*, 26 May, p. 114.

Rodowick, David (1997a) *Gilles Deleuze's Time Machine*, Durham, Duke University Press.

Rodowick, David (1997b) 'La Critique ou la vérité en crise', *Iris* 23, 3–25.

Sartirano, Claude (1990), 'Combat de Coq', *L'Humanité Dimanche* 25, 7 September.

Schor, Naomi (1985) *Bad Objects*, Durham and London, Duke University Press.

Sillars, Jane and Beugnet, Martine (2001), '*Beau travail*: Time, Space and Myths of Identity', *Studies in French Cinema* 1:3, 166–73.

Silverman, Max (1999) *Facing Postmodernity – Contemporary French Thought on Culture and Society*, London and New York, Routledge.

Strauss, Frédéric (1990a), 'Féminin colonial', *Cahiers du cinéma* 434, 28–33

Strauss, Frédéric (1990b), 'Combat de nègres et de coqs', *Cahiers du cinéma* 435, 64–5.

Tarr, Carrie and Rollet, Brigitte (2001), *Cinema and the Second Sex: Women's Filmmaking in France in the 1980s and the 1990s*, New York and London, Continuum.

Tinazzi, Noël (2000), '*Beau travail*', *La Tribune*, 3 May.

Tranchant, Marie-Noëlle (1988), '*Chocolat*', *Le Figaro*, 16 May.

Turim, Maureen (1989), *Flashbacks in Film: Memory and History*, New York and London, Routledge.

Turim, Maureen (2001), 'The Trauma of History: Flashbacks Upon Flashbacks', *Screen* 42:2, 205–10.

Vassé, Claire (2000), '*Beau travail*: Liberté du corps', *Positif* 471, 30–1.

Young, Lola (1986) *Fear of the Dark: Gender, Race, Sexuality in British Cinema*, London, Routledge.

1 *Chocolat* (1988) Isaach de Bankolé (Protée), Cécile Ducasse (France)

2 *Chocolat* (1988) Mireille Perrier (France as an adult)

3 *J' ai pas sommeil* (1993) Richard Courcet, Laurent Grévill (Camille, le Docteur)

4 *J' ai pas sommeil* (1993) Line Renaud (Ninon)

5 *US Go Home* (1994) Alice Houri, Jessica Tharaud (Martine et Marlène)

6 *Nénette et Boni* (1996) Alice Houri (Nénette)

7 *Beau Travail* (2000) Denis Lavant (Galoup)

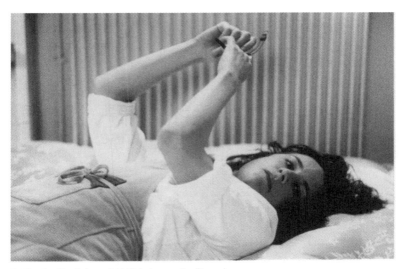

8 *Vendredi soir* (2002) Valérie Lemercier (Laure)

9 *Vendredi soir* (2002) Vincent Lindon (Jean) and Claire Denis

3

The *mise en scène* of desire:
towards a cinema of the senses

Love, desire and sexuality, as depicted in the world of Denis' films, elude the conventional romantic framework that defines and binds them together in mainstream fiction. From *Chocolat* to *Vendredi soir*, the sexual and emotional dimension emerges with the contradictions and uncertainty inherent in its complexity, and while they are shown in a melancholy, tentative and sometimes morbid light, Denis' approach to these themes remains nevertheless profoundly sensual. The representation of desire, explored in its emotional, sexual and subversive aspects, is indissociable from the director's elaboration of a 'cinema of the senses': a cinema that relies, first and foremost, on the sensuous apprehension of the real, on a vivid and tactile combination of sounds and images that expands cinema's primarily visual powers of evocation.

In its *mise en scène* of desire, Denis' filmmaking not only creates correspondences between the senses, but, as we will see, it also confuses the traditional process of identification and point of view. Desire thus emerges in its ambivalence and diversity, as inherently linked to transgression. It affects individuals regardless of their gender, race or nationality, and as such, challenges the taboos and hierarchies erected by social orders that attempt to tame desire by designating its legitimate objects. It threatens the integrity of the body and of the self, and reveals the fragility of the human mind and flesh, beset by a sense of loss and lack and always at risk of dissolving into desire, to be 'consumed' by it. Ultimately, transgression takes place at the level of the representation itself, when the boundaries between fantasy (where everything is still possible) and actualisation (the reality of the consummation) are erased.

The thematic of desire runs through all of Denis' work. As we have seen, in her cinema of exile, it is entwined with the representation of the (colonial) Other and the experience of displacement. In her other works, it is foregrounded as a theme in itself. In some of her short films, the two dimensions are combined and their symbolic relation played out.

Duo and A propos d'une déclaration

Denis' two short art films (2 min and 2.35 min respectively) were filmed and produced with her usual team of collaborators, and their formal and thematic outlook is close to that of her feature fiction films. A hint of the surrealistic permeates the images of these works. They fragment the body (the female body in particular is decapitated in both films), play on the encounter of opposites (the softness of the flesh and the sharpness of the razor in A propos for instance), and present controversial representations of desire, with a mingling of black humour and eroticism that sits uneasily with familiar notions of political correctness.

Duo was commissioned by the BBC, as part of a series in which a number of directors were asked to confront painting with their filmmaking. Claire Denis chose a work by her contemporary Jacques de Loustal (1956), known for the bold figures and tropical mood of his paintings. Her 2 min video film is based on a slow, uninterrupted travelling shot which goes back and forth, exploring the content of the painting, as well as the space that lies around its edges. In a similar overlap, the soundtrack mingles the sound of jazz-mambo music (*Tin Tin Deo* interpreted by the Roy Nathanson Quartet, 1990) together with the distant echoes of urban traffic (the sound of a passing ambulance for instance). The opening image is a close-up on the face of the painting's main figure: a black man wearing a white hat. The figure's sharp profile is brought out with a thick outline, and he is depicted looking towards the left edge of the frame. The gaze of the camera moves slowly down, along the man's body, dressed in a suit and sitting in a stiff pose, before revealing the object of his gaze: a white female figure, naked, lying on her belly, the body cut off at the waist by the edge of the painting. Moving back along the bottom of the picture, the camera reaches the right edge of the painting, and, beyond it, the dark patterns of a man's shirt, then the face of actor Alex Descas (*S'en fout la mort, Trouble Every day*). Descas steadily returns the gaze of the camera before drawing on a cigar and filling the screen with smoke. The travelling movement starts anew to finally reveal the painting in its entirety. The film thus combines the study of the painting with those features that are specific to cinema: movement, fragmentation, the denial and simultaneous reinstatement of the frame, the combination of sound and image. It brings out the components – details of shapes, patterns, and colours – before showing the composition as a whole. It places in a relation of direct contiguity the world depicted by the painting, and, by including diegetic sounds as well as a live figure, that of the film. The second may look more 'realistic', but it is just as posed, constructed, and over-determined. The painting, which could be the depiction of a scene in a brothel, stages, and, at the same time, offsets the conventional *mise en scène* of the male gaze/female object, by exacerbating binary differences: the male figure fully dressed and rigidly posed, the female figure naked and on display, one black, the other white.[1] The composition brings to mind Frantz Fanon's 1960s writing on the stereotypes that determine cross-racial sexuality: the cliché of the black man as a sexual animal feared by the white man and desired by the white woman, and, conversely, the myth of the possession of the white woman as the ultimate door towards integration (Fanon 1986: Chapters 2 and 3). The film's crossing over the edge of the painting adds an additional facet to the *mise en scène* and questioning of these myths. The camera, carried by a white camerawoman in a film directed by a white woman director, scrutinises closely a black man's face in a sequence of images saturated by the stereotypical.

A propos d'une déclaration was also the result of a commission, proposed by the contemporary art institute Fondation Cartier. Each of the artists and filmmakers contacted was asked to create a work for an exhibition on the theme of love. As in *Duo*, *A propos d'une déclaration* uses the close-up to fragment the body, to instrument mysterious relations between its protagonists, and, possibly, to conceal the personal

1 *Duo* and *A Propos* could also be read with reference to Gustave Courbet's famous and controversial work *L'Origine du monde* (1866) (an important reference to the work of the surrealists). The racial dimension would thus be brought into the familiar questioning on the mystery of creation evoked through the representation of the female body and sexual organs.

dimension of the work. *A propos d'une déclaration* could be read as the impressionistic tale of a brief encounter, captured, as the grainy quality of the DV image also suggests, secretly and in haste. It starts in a plane, with still pictures of a black man's hands outlined against the blue of the sky seen through a plane porthole. It cuts to images of a hotel bathroom where black and red female underwear are hung, then to a brief shot of the man asleep on his belly (his face will never be shown) in the adjoining room. The next shot shows a woman undressing. Her body is decapitated by the frame, and, like that of the man, her face will never be seen. The images then show her getting into a bath. Shot from the neck down, that is, from the point of view of the protagonist herself, the gaze of the camera glides and shifts along the body as if following the movements of the water. In a touch of surrealistic humour, a plastic fish appears and floats in between the woman's legs. She grabs a razor and holds it against her pale skin before she starts shaving her pubic hair. Throughout, the soundtrack includes the distant sound of a wolf howling: merging with the humorous undertone, an obscure sense of threat and magic imbues this enigmatic portrait of a contemporary mermaid. In both films, the symbolic references outline the web of conventions and myths that still surround and determine the existence of desire: some of these myths are undeniably attractive, they evoke the part of the archaic and mysterious in human desire. But they also need to be kept in check, debunked by humour, for instance, for their roots, as illustrated in Denis' early feature fiction films, lie in a historical framework of inequalities and taboos. Hence, in *Chocolat* and in *S'en fout la mort*, the lingering inheritance of the colonial past still poisons and precludes the emergence of desire, and the impossibility of its realisation finds its expression through the director's privileging of the unsaid and the unfinished.

The moment of transgression

Between *Chocolat*'s Protée and Aimée, *S'en fout la mort*'s Jocelyn and Toni, *J'ai pas sommeil*'s Daïga and Camille, desire is a tangible presence that creates a sense of grace and desperation because it remains unspoken and hypothetical: unblemished, but unfulfilled. The exchange of looks and the caressing wistful gaze of the camera may betray the attraction, but nothing is said and bodies hardly touch. The intense physicality of *Beau travail* is channelled through the rituals of the training and of the dance, and repressed desire becomes the vector for a struggle between power and identity. The films are infused with sensuality, yet sex is impossible, indefinitely delayed, or kept off-frame. From the start, Denis thus appears acutely aware of the aesthetic (narrative, visual) impact and of the affect of unrealised desire: the viewer, like the characters, remains in suspense; situations and people retain all their potentialities; fantasy is preserved:

> Je suis intéréssée par les prémices des choses. Par exemple, je suis intéréssée par le désir. La montée du désir. Et puis quelque-chose fait que j'en reste là ... Il y a quelque-chose qui fait que le désir se suffit à lui-même, et que souvent il est suivi d'une frustration. Parce qu'il est si fort, que ce qui vient, pour répondre au désir, n'est pas assez fort pour le combler ... Je crois que je serais une vraie pessimiste si j'allais au-delà de ça et que je me disais, au fond, une fois l'extase passée, finalement, c'est pas mieux qu'avant. Mais je n'ai jamais emmené mes films jusque-là. Même dans *US Go Home* ... l'image d'après, c'est l'après.[2] (Lifshitz 1995)

The treatment of time and the importance of the unsaid are thus closely related to the representation of desire in Denis' work. As we have seen, her filmmaking shuns narrative constructions that reduce time to the stages of a plot – to the series of time slots necessary for the depiction of precise actions leading to a conclusion. Independently of the plot, as in Deleuze's definition of a time-cinema, time can become the time of diffused fear, of waiting and expectation, of boredom, of alienation. In a similar way the depiction of desire between people does not merely premise sex. Privileging the mystery of the beginnings, desire's promises, rather than its consummation, corresponds to Denis' approach in general. In this, as for the other aspects of the films' content, she prefers to allude rather than expose and explain. In addition, as the director puts it, 'desire is sufficient in

2 'I am interested in the beginnings of things. For instance, I am interested in desire – desire rising. And then something happens and I don't go further ... For some reason desire is sufficient in itself, and often it is followed by frustration. Because desire is so powerful that what comes as a response is not enough to fulfil it. This is something I can see in my work ... I think I'd be a real pessimist if I went beyond and then told myself that, finally, once the ecstasy has gone, it is no better than before. But I have never taken my films to this point. Even in *US Go Home* ... the picture is a picture of the afterwards.'

itself: in some ways, her films take the form of an extended courtship where minute rituals are pleasurable in and for themselves. Yet, in her 1995 interview, she also admits to a growing need to 'go beyond', to show the consummation of desire:

> Le moment de la transgression peut être hors-champ, ou sous la barre du cadre ... mais c'est ce moment-là, où quelque-chose s'abandonne au film, et que je n'ai jamais filmé encore ... Peut-être moi, il faudrait que je fasse un travail là-dessus, sentir ça, comment je peux amener le désir vers une résolution ...[3] (Lifshitz 1995)

In effect, physical love has progressively become a more central motif of Denis' filmmaking. The director has dedicated four feature fiction films to the exploration of desire and sexual awakening. *US Go Home* and *Nénette et Boni* are coming-of-age films, where sexuality remains tentative, fantasised, or rejected as abject. In *Trouble Every Day*, the first of her films to include sex scenes, desire is deathly, and the notion of pleasure and fulfilment subsumed in the horrific nature of the killing. Leaving the realm of the monstrous, with *Vendredi soir*, she shot the first of her pictures to present a story of fulfilled sexual desire. Throughout, one crucial aspect of Denis' narrative and formal approach is the non-normalising role of desire and sexuality. Desire is not subsumed to narrative or moral imperatives: it is neither a means to include the obligatory sex scene as in mainstream cinema, nor to bring back deviant characters, via love, towards acceptable cultural and social standards. Similarly, the representation of the body shuns voyeuristic and exploitative aims: bodies are not displayed merely in order to be 'consumed' visually by the spectators. Denis' concern does not seem to be, however, of the order of (self-)censorship. She investigates alternative strategies that depart from those contemporary discourses and practices through which sexuality's growing visibility has become another means to control and normalise.[4] Indeed, in

3 'The moment of transgression can be off-field, below the frame ... But it is that moment, where something gives in to the film, and that I have never filmed yet ... Maybe I should try to work on this, try to feel and find a way, how to take desire to its resolution ...'

4 In his seminal writing on sexuality, philosopher Michel Foucault stressed how the contemporary obsession with sexuality resulted from it being included in a discourse of knowledge and power. The drive to expose and reveal, he warned, presented as a rebellion against regressive laws of censorship, was in fact not necessarily a sign of liberalisation. In some ways (as demonstrated by some of

cinema in particular, while sexuality has become a dominant theme, the representation of desire and love, as well as the *mise en scène* of sex scenes, remain extremely codified. Conversely, in Denis' filmmaking, sexuality is thematically as well as aesthetically linked to the crossing over into the unknown, and, as we will see, its film representation allows for an experimental move towards a cinema of the senses.

For her teenage characters, sexuality is necessarily enmeshed with a form of transgression. In their story world, symbolic and cultural figures of authority, such as fathers, are represented as irrelevant or weak, kept at a distance or absent from the diegesis. Yet, the taboo remains; sexuality belongs to the order of the mysterious and daunting. Accordingly, while the director's formal strategy privileges the sensual, the approach is not about exposing. Inanimate objects, textures, surfaces and colours as well as bodies are described in detail through camerawork that plays on the defamiliarising effect of scale as well as on framing. As we will see, the filmmaking thus undermines the traditional process of 'positioning' whereby the spectator-observer is encouraged to adopt a predefined point of view. In *US Go Home* and even more so in *Nénette et Boni*, *Trouble Every Day* and *Vendredi soir*, the mise en scène of desire is the premise for an exploration of cinema as a 'tactile, sensory experience' that works to unsettle the relation between viewer and image.

US Go Home

In the 1990s, French channel Arte launched a television series entitled '*Tous les garçons et les filles de leur âge*' ('All the boys and girls of their age'), borrowing its heading from the lyrics of a famous teen pop song of the 1960s (Françoise Hardy 1962). The aim was to present semi-autobiographical chronicles of adolescence that would evoke specific epochs of the recent French past. Nine prominent French directors were asked to draw on their memories and to reconstitute, in an hour-long film featuring a dance, a visual, and musical portrayal of the

---

the applications of psychoanalysis, and, in the extreme, by the strategies of pornographic exploitation), the obsessive focusing on sexuality allowed for a greater standardising control. Foucault also insisted, however, that pleasure is derived from the process of revealing and unveiling the intimate. (*Histoire de la sexualité I: la volonté de savoir*, Paris, Gallimard, 1976).

period corresponding to their own teens. *US Go Home* rose to the challenge on all counts. The film catches the spirit of the epoch it depicts through a detailed reconstitution that grants attention to those small but significant markers of a time likely to bring back memories to viewers that experienced it. Particularly evocative, the extensive list of cult songs that constitute the soundtrack is also a reminder of Denis' own love of music, and of the crucial role it plays in her work (Denorme and Douin 2001: 26).

US Go Home is set in the mid 1960s, and its central characters have roughly the age that Denis reached in the years following her return from Africa. The location precisely matches Denis' memory of *la banlieue* (the suburbs of Paris) where her family settled. It also represents a particular moment of the country's urban history: the last years of the American presence in the post-Second World War military bases, the beginning of the accelerated programme of housing development, and the birth of the large estates that completely transformed the areas around large cities:

> Quand je suis rentrée d'Afrique, je suis arrivée en banlieue, je suis rentrée dans un immeuble que j'avais vu se construire. Tout autour, il y avait de la gadoue. Cétait le début des grands travaux. Ce qui faisait que les gens qui se retrouvaient, c'était sur des terrains vagues, des zones entre les villes ... Là où j'habitais, il y avait un verger de pruniers et puis les terrains vagues. C'est là que les adolescents se retrouvaient, que les choses se passaient. Quand j'ai fait *US Go Home* ... j'ai voulu montrer à l'équipe les lieux où j'avais été adolescente. Mais ces lieux là n'étaient pas réutilisables.'[5] (Denorme and Douin 2001: 26)

Beyond its autobiographical and historical basis, the film also takes its place and significance within the context of Denis' concerns as a filmmaker. Not only do *US Go Home*'s central themes, its photography, and its treatment of narration and space all relate to the director's body of work as a whole, but most of *US Go Home*'s actors

5 'When I came back from Africa, I settled in the suburbs, in a building that I had seen being built. It was muddy all around. It was the beginning of the *Grand travaux* (i.e. the state's general programme for urban development). As a result, people met each other on wastelands, in the in-between zones separating towns ... Where I lived, there was an orchard with plum trees, then stretches of wasteland. That's where the youths met, where things happened. When I did *US Go Home*, I wanted to show the crew the place where I lived as a teenager. But that particular location could not be used anymore.'

and crew members appear in other films by Denis. One notable exception is that of the co-writer Anne Wiazemsky who became known as an actress and scriptwriter in the 1960s, in particular as Jean-Luc Godard's collaborator. Wiazemsky's presence thus creates a link with the period concerned, with its cinema, and more precisely with other film depictions of suburban life in the 1960s. Some of Godard's films come to mind, for the New Wave director shot seminal portraits of an 'Americanised' French society (*Masculin-Féminin*, 1965, *Made in USA*, 1966) and of French Parisian suburbia. In *Deux ou trois choses que je sais d'elle* (1966), his exposition of the double mutation – urban and consumerist – that affected the French way of life is embodied in the character of Juliette (Marina Vlady), a housewife who works as a prostitute to pay her bills. In *US Go Home*, the figure of the mother, although she is only glimpsed, as well as Martine and Alain's argument about prostitution as a profession, can be read as an implicit homage to Godard's heroines, Juliette as well as Nana, the prostitute of *Vivre sa vie* (1962). Yet, *US Go Home* does not draw a bleak picture of the suburbs. As such, it contrasts not only with earlier, dystopian visions such as Godard's, but also with most 1990s films about the Parisian *cités* or housing estates. *US Go Home* is about being at the margins, but in spite of the social observations woven into its narrative and the presence of the outsider (the American soldier), it is not primarily and overtly about marginality as social exclusion. It shows life as an adolescent and as an inhabitant of the newly built *cités*, as a borderline state – a state of undefined expectation. It is in its use of the location as more than a mere backdrop that *US Go Home* fits into a French tradition of cinema *de banlieues* where 'banlieues et faubourgs sont au cinéma depuis toujours, plus qu'un décor, un territoire, un acteur à part entière de la narration, donnant dès les premières images sens à l'action qui s'y déroule'[6] (Cadé 1999: 173).

Set in the outer suburbs of Paris, *US Go Home* chronicles a day and a night in the life of three young people. Martine (Alice Houri), her older brother Alain (Grégoire Colin), and her best friend Marlene (Jessica Tharaud) prepare to go out to the customary weekend parties. Martine has decided that by the end of the night she will not be a virgin anymore. Alain initially refuses to take his younger sister and

6 'the city's suburbs and outskirts are, from the beginning, more than a set, a territory, an actor within the narration, giving a sense to the action that unfolds from the very first images.'

her friend along, but the three teenagers nevertheless eventually end up in the same house. Alain attempts to have sex with Marlene who resists, while Martine also fails to find a suitable partner and wanders aimlessly through the house. Brother and sister leave together, and the young girl hitches a ride with an American from the local military base. Her brother chooses to set off home on foot, but Martine decides to spend the rest of the night with the soldier.

The undefined space

The opening credits, which unfold to the sound of a radio broadcasting in English, are directly followed by a sequence in long take of Alain sitting on his bed, reading. Behind him, record sleeves of British bands – the Yardbirds, the Animals, the Kinks ... have been pasted across the geometrical pattern of the 1960s wallpaper. The nature and content of the young man's book provide a humorous contrast to the direct surrounds and to the theme of the film. Dressed in a white T-shirt, facing the camera, the young man reads aloud from *On the Brevity of Life*,[7] an extract that stresses the Stoic's ideal of restraining human passions and excesses, and condemns in particular the penchant for sex and alcohol. The seemingly uncompromising, puritanical attitude of Alain's character, echoed later on in his disparaging comments about girls, is offset by a later sequence, also shot in his bedroom. The scene is filmed in long take, and included as an audaciously extended sequence. It shows the youth dancing and singing along to a song, by The Animals, which evokes a world of sexual desire, speed, and consumerism. The young man moves back and forth in front of the fixed camera, progressively letting his energy flow, and eventually jumping in and out of frame. In these two sequences, the character thus embodies the dynamic turmoil of the adolescent state. Alain's contradictory desires, his lust for purity and for sex, his love and hate of America are matched by the two teenage girls' mix of curiosity, daringness, and fear. In turn, the characters' confused aspirations, expressed in the restricted but safe haven of the teenager's sanctuary – the bedroom – appear simultaneously exacerbated and quenched by the world that surrounds them.

7 The philosophical writings of Seneca (4BC–65AD), Roman thinker, writer, and politician, including *On the Brevity of Life*, provide the basis of the Stoic school of thought.

Following the opening sequence of the young man reading, a long panoramic shot sets the geographical context. The images move from a green, slightly hilly countryside, dotted with a series of characterless houses, to a view of a highway alongside concrete housing units in construction. As in an old-fashioned documentary, Martine's voiceover comments the scene:

> C'est ça le bassin parisien. Une cuvette. Derrière la brume, là-bas au fond, y'a Paris. On voit rien, mais c'est Paris. Par temps clair, on dirait que Paris est tout près. Mais pour y aller, c'est toute une expédition: alors on y va pas. On vit là. Au bord de la cuvette. Au grand air. Les immeubles poussent partout. Dans les prés, les champs, les vergers ...[8]

This early sequence seems at first destined to fulfil the role of the conventional establishing shot,[9] yet it establishes nothing but a nondescript zone still in the making, and, in this sense, it encapsulates the vision of adolescence vividly evoked by *US Go Home*. Denis resorts to the familiar concept of adolescence as the incarnation of a suspended moment between childhood and adulthood, yet it is not merely their age, but also the place where they live – close yet not close enough to the capital – and even their nationality, that keep *US Go Home*'s characters in the margins, in a kind of no-man's-land. They surround themselves with the signs of a culture, and, first and foremost, a musical culture, that is the defining marker of youth in the 1960s, yet only reaches them as a distant echo from the other side of the Atlantic. The depiction of their living space thus superimposes a set of contrasting or contradictory visual and aural signifiers where the familiar and the banal clash with the exotic and unfamiliar.

Paradoxically, in spite of their ordinary, middle-class feel, in their incompleteness, the suburbs where the teenagers live constitute a suitable space for the *mise en scène* of adolescent existence: a *terrain vague* (wasteland) in the literal sense of the French expression – an indefinable space. Unfinished, it combines building sites with open fields, stands close to the highway yet not far from a forest. The

8 'This is where Paris is located. A basin. Behind the mist, out there, is Paris. You can't see anything, but it is Paris. On a clear day, you'd think Paris is very close. But to get there, it is quite a trip. So we don't go. We live here. In the open air. Buildings are sprouting everywhere. In the meadows, the fields, the orchards ...'

9 The establishing shot often takes the form of a long shot that opens the film, providing basic information and orientation to the viewer (a general view, situating and describing the environment the protagonist(s) inhabit(s)).

editing, the camerawork and the soundtrack emphasise the hybrid nature of the place. The initial slow panoramic shot abruptly gives way to a montage of eclectic images: concrete buildings, a group of colourfully dressed schoolgirls standing at a bus stop, American flags, an American car parked in a forest clearing, a building site, fields, a passing train ... The images of buildings themselves, for all they herald the future defacement of the green belt, take on a kind of bucolic dimension. Shot in long takes in the changing light, they seem to merge into the landscape like natural landmarks. The soundtrack is equally heterogeneous, combining the sounds of engines, of birds singing, the tune of a Yardbirds song (*Good Morning Little School Girl*), phrases of schoolbook Russian, military drills shouted in English, Martine's voiceover ...

Martine's comments are full of the name Paris, yet the capital never materialises. Hidden in the haze, tantalisingly close yet unreachable, the metropolis retains its fantasy aura, the promise of 'real' life amidst the urban bustle. Equally evocative of a fantasy 'elsewhere' is the music. As a montage of fixed-frame and slow panoramic shots captures the reassuring banality of budding French suburbia, the soundtrack swells with the well-known sounds of a culture that resonates with the echoes of youth rebellion. Of this fascinating world, the French youths merely get a glimpse via the broadcasts of British Radio Caroline and the images displayed on record sleeves.

The sequence ends with shots of a series of newly planted road signs. Beyond the humorous note (these markers are set to provide directions in a zone that is still, for the better part, an uncharted wasteland), these images are also a suitable metaphor for the adolescent state. Behind the profusion of signs which extends to clothes and accessories, hides an indefinable sense of wanting and anxiety. The security provided by a sense of belonging – to a place, even if it is still being built, to a family and a group of friends – is offset by the implicit attraction and fear of the unknown – adulthood, sexuality, foreignness.

In its choice of locations, the composition of the images and the focus on inanimate objects and empty spaces, *US Go Home* foregrounds *Trouble Every Day*. In common with *Trouble Every Day*, *US Go Home* also demonstrates Denis' ability to recreate a set of highly contrasting atmospheres within the same film: in effect, the spatial organisation determines the narrative structure of the film. Martine and Marlene's journey to the perfect party takes them from the lower middle-class flat to the middle-class semi-detached house to the large stone villa of the *fils à papa* (rich daddy's boy) standing in its own ground. As in traditional coming-of-age tales, the progression, marked by a change of mood as well as of space and environment, leads to the return of a more experienced heroine, yet the film retains the open ending typical of Denis' style.

From suburbia to fairy-tale

With their shiny, depthless surface, the images of the new suburban home lack the mystery and sensuality that the textured obscurity and the fairy-tale dimension of the later episodes evoke. The family flat is a protective but limiting space, where exiguity and lack of intimacy is underlined by the use of medium close-ups. The parents remain absent or marginal within this essentially adolescent vision of home. Alain and Martine's mother appears briefly, shot in the kitchen, surrounded by the artefacts of the budding consumerist society and locked in the routine of the domestic economy: she is either doing the washing-up or dealing with the bills. Here Denis played the card of the *rétro* genre, dotting the images with all the signifiers of the 1960s, creating a representation of a past recent enough to be simultaneously familiar and unfamiliar. Calling on the viewers' memories with an affectionate reconstitution of the period's interior decoration and habits, the humorous combination of evocative details thus counterpoints the feeling of entrapment generated by the space and the camerawork. The flat's walls are covered with the lurid wallpaper in vogue in lower middle-class homes at the time: endlessly repeated geometric motifs in strong shades of browns and oranges. The stripes of Martine's top and her mother's flower-patterned pinafore add to the overabundance of this oppressive backdrop. The claustrophobic quality of the space is underlined by Alain's yearning for solitude. 'J'peux jamais être seul' ('I can never be alone') he protests at the end of the dance sequence, as the shot cuts into a counter-shot, revealing that the door to his bedroom opens onto the living room, and that his sister has been observing him. From the kitchen where Martine and her mother converse across a packet of *Ricoré* instant drink, to Marlene's bedroom where the two friends dress up and exchange confidences, the home provides a safe but confined space from which music offers a ready escape. In spite of the sunny weather, the girls

decide to don bright plastic raincoats, for which Martine will repeatedly attempt to find a safe place during the party which the girls finally
attend. In effect (and though television, a nascent phenomenon at the
time, is absent from the diegetic space), the first part of the film
seems to evoke the shiny flatness of plastic, of the televised image or
of colourful magazine photographs. If a sense of vague anxiety seeps
into some of these shots, it is their apparent shallowness and lack of
mystery that create it. In contrast, the images shot at the villa or in the
forest are imbued with the tactile depth more readily associated with
the cinematic image.

Invited to a party organised by one of their peers, the girls merely
observe it from behind the garden hedge. Shot in bright light and
populated by overdressed youngsters, the event does not deserve to be
attended: the parents are present, the father is even dancing in
amongst the crowd of youths. A narrative ellipsis takes the girls to a
shaded park, in front of a stone villa: the atmosphere has switched
from the sitcom to a modern version of *Le Grand Meaulnes*,[10] with
expensive sports cars replacing the novel's horse-drawn carriages.
The girls climb a large staircase, and pass a beautiful solitary girl
before they reach the dance floor. The colours have become subdued.
The camera turns into a wandering presence, moving between the
dancing couples in long travelling shots. In the darkness, its tactile,
preying gaze seems to draw out silhouettes sculpted by the shadowy
light. One of Martine's dancing partners drags her aside and starts to
kiss her. But the young man plays the tough guy, and his affected
attitude gives the young girl the giggles. From then on, the mysterious
house turns into a haven of snobbish indifference. For the rest of the
evening, surrounded by couples (as in an echo of the Hardy song that
gave the series its title), Martine wanders alone, bored, until she
opens a door and discovers Marlene and Alain together. Poised and lit
in painterly fashion, the couple form a strange, frozen tableau.
Attracted by the older boy, Marlene has let herself be undressed. In a
era where the pill is still a novelty, however, she is beset with
conflicting pressures. Naked, but frozen by fear, and on the brink of
tears, she obstinately keeps her legs clenched. Leaving her behind,
Alain drowns his selfishness and uncomprehending anger in an

10 In French literature, Alain-Fournier's (1886–1914) *Le Grand Meaulnes* (1913) is
the epitome of the romantic coming-of-age novel. Told by a fifteen-year-old
narrator, its story centres on a mysterious castle and a masked ball.

equivocal embrace with his sister. Their dance forms a long sequence in elliptical editing, a moment of suspended time preceding the last chapter of Martine's story.

The feeling of frozen time bleeds into the sequence of the two teenagers walking home. Shot in long takes, its movement is edited in a series of contradictory directions. Lost on a deserted road at night, at the edge of a forest, the couple walk past the parked car of an American soldier who offers them his last bottles of Coca-Cola. In an intriguing combination, the fairy-tale element thus becomes indistinguishable from a set of love-and-hate stereotypes about America. Alain's stubborn hostility is true to the spirit of the time, marked by the Vietnam protest and the rise of the communist ideal. At the same time, throughout their dialogue of the deaf, Vincent Gallo's performance as the soldier is reminiscent of the improvised style of acting that first emerged in the independent American cinema of the 1960s and 1970s. The light in these sequences is brightly contrasted, as if emanating from a full moon or from the technique of the *nuit Américaine* (an 'American night', that is, a scene shot in daylight and later manipulated at the developing stage to recreate the effect of a nocturnal shot). As the young girl and the soldier drive further into the forest, the dream-like atmosphere deepens. The characters' lovemaking is not shown. The couple walk away from the camera. The following shot, however, which shows the young woman resting her head on the soldier's lap while he drives, is imbued with tenderness.

In the car, the soundtrack had briefly made space for the sound of Ska[11] rhythms, a music emblematic of the mingling of influences that foretells the dawning of a new era of musical, cultural and racial mix. Yet the final scene is one of exclusion. Shot in a bright morning light, it shows Martine joining her brother and friend, who are waiting for her at the edge of a deserted plaza. The young girl sits with her back to the American, as he drives off, revealing the *US Go home* graffiti that adorns the wall behind his car. The symbol of the crossing-over, the wall, is still present, but as the three teenagers sit silently in a highly composed, static *mise en scène* reminiscent of still photography, the moment seems both frozen in time and exclusive. Denis' portrayal of adolescence thus balances closeness and distance. The period preceding adulthood is a fleeting moment, and in the end, like its soundtrack,

11 Originally from Jamaica, Ska music first came to prominence in the 1960s. Revived in the 1980s, it is associated with the emergence of mixed-race bands.

US Go Home's evocation of a vanishing era is permeated by a sense of melancholy nostalgia.

US Go Home draws subtle and changing patterns of affiliation and opposition. Between brother and sister, amongst a same age group, between youths of a common country, social circle and district, bonds are alternatively stressed, undone and re-established. The empathy that seems inconceivable between a girl and a boy of a similar age and social and cultural background (Alain and Marlene) becomes possible between a young girl and a perfect stranger, a man and a foreigner. Sexuality is not necessarily connected to love, and in that sense, Denis' depiction of a teenage girl bears similarities to the portrayal found in the work of her contemporaries like Claire Breillat. Difference and closeness, attraction and rejection combine and overlap. Such fluidity, however, as the last images suggest, may only belong to an elusive, undefined space, such as the time of adolescence that *US Go Home* evokes.

Nénette et Boni

Resolved to work again with the lead actors of *US Go Home*, Alice Houri and Grégoire Colin, Denis continued her exploration of coming-of-age themes in her following feature.[12] Most crucially, by focusing on the brother-sister theme that was already prominent in *US Go Home*, *Nénette et Boni* investigates a facet of cross-gender relations that is rarely addressed in film. Loosely inspired by a song from the *Tindersticks II* album, the enigmatic and gloomy *My Sister*, the film also echoes the work of directors such as Catherine Breillat and Christine Pascal[13] in its evocation of the complex and troubled dimension of blood ties and sisterly love. A bitter-sweet comment on communication is woven into the film's narrative backdrop. In the opening sequence, a glib crook attempts to sell a set of doctored telephone cards to a group of immigrants. The film is punctuated by brief

12 Certain elements, such as the title, which humorously evokes the 1960s cult rebel figures of Bonnie and Clyde, and the presence of Vincent Gallo, cast as an American sailor, also create a loose web of connections with the previous film.

13 Pascal's dark exploration of feminine sexuality and childhood in *Félicité* (1978) in particular, is echoed in *Nénette et Boni* (the scene where Nénette prepares food and spoonfeeds her brother for instance).

inserts depicting strangers calling abroad, and discussions on incomprehensible phone bills. In this way, the effect of the card trafficking emerges sporadically throughout the film like a benign virus, eventually disrupting what should have been a crucial discussion between Nénette and a medical worker. Meanwhile, however, in order to repair their severed bond, Nénette and Boni's means of communicating follows its own obscure path.

Eighteen-year-old Boni lives in the decrepit home of his deceased mother where he also houses a small gang of friends. Thanks to his take-away van, Boni scratches a living as a pizza maker and spends much of his time fantasising about the local baker woman (Valéria Bruni-Tedeschi). One day, his sister Nénette, whom he has not seen for years, appears on his doorstep. Pregnant from a man she refuses to name, the young girl has escaped from her boarding school. Sister and brother reject their estranged father's (Jacques Nolot) offers of reconciliation, and while Nénette's pregnancy draws towards its term, they develop a tumultuous relationship. Nénette decides to give the baby away at birth, but Boni steals the new-born from the hospital.

The real as raw matter

Denis and Fargeau wrote the scenario in the latter's home town, Marseille, and ended up setting the story in one of the city's popular districts, Le Canet. Denis stressed the importance of filming this location, and, in an interview about the film, she compared the writing stage to turning oneself into blotting paper, 'de s'imprégner de parcelles du monde' ('to becoming impregnated with fragments of the world') (Guilloux 1997). Indeed, and even though there is always an effect of de-familiarisation and sometimes an element of the supernatural in her films, Denis' filmmaking starts from specific locations and real situations. Over and above the script, it is the actual contact with a living environment that provides the basis of the shooting. In effect, since *Nénette et Boni*, Denis has increasingly described her work as first and foremost a physical process in which the real is the raw matter to be shaped into a film. *Nénette et Boni* contains a genial scene of pizza making that Denis humorously suggested as a metaphor for the kind of filmmaking practice that she sought: Boni, shot in close-up, expresses his erotic fantasies while furiously kneading a soft ball of dough in which he eventually buries his face.

Le cinéma a pour matériau le monde dans lequel il est tourné ... il
fallait travailler sur la matière, que le film prenne corps, et donc
inventer une manière différente de travailler, proche de celui de la pâte
à pizza ...[14] (Guilloux 1997)

For Denis, to use the real as raw matter is not equated with construct-
ing a 'realistic' representation. The final work presents a vision imbued
with fantasies and fashioned by the filmmaking process. Denis'
cinema thus continues to eschew 'realism' in the two traditional
senses of the term. It shuns the highly scripted mainstream model
that reconstructs situations (in the studio, if necessary), following the
determined set of codes that gives the storytelling a 'realistic' feel.[15]
On the other hand, it does not attempt to capture reality and to
represent it to the viewers with as little intervention as possible in
accordance with Bazinian[16] principles. For Denis, the real as perceived
by the filmmaker is a raw matter that has to be worked through –
recorded and put into images that are framed and shot in particular
angles and organised by the editing – so that it eventually gives form
to the body of the film.

In a short film called *Nice, Very Nice* (1995), her contribution to the
collective venture *A propos de Nice, la suite*,[17] Denis had already presented an unusual facet of a Mediterranean French city. *Nice, Very
Nice* is a silent thriller that follows the wanderings of a young man

14 'Cinéma's raw matter is the world in which it is filmed ... it was necessary to
   work on this matter, so that the film took shape (*prenne corps*, that is literally,
   'took body'), to create a new way of making film, similar to the making of pizza
   dough.'
15 Although it reconstructs an idealised or fantasised reality, by applying the rules
   of the continuity system, mainstream cinema meets the expectations of the
   spectator used to certain conventions, and renders the actual filmmaking
   process invisible, creating an impression of realism.
16 André Bazin (1918–58) one of the most influential of film theorists, developed a
   definition of realism that, in opposition with the studio-based reconstructions of
   the dominant Hollywood system, celebrated cinema's ability to capture and
   represent reality with the minimum of alteration. Italian néorealism provided
   one of Bazin's models.
17 *A propos de Nice, la suite*, includes a series of shorts commissioned as a homage
   to Jean Vigo's (1905–34) celebrated *A propos de Nice* (1934), a 21 min documentary that drew a biting portrait of the city of the *douceur de vivre*. The 1995
   sequel, however, received little critical approval in spite of its impressive list of
   contributors (Abbas Kiarostami and Paviz Kimiavi, Catherine Breillat,
   Raymond Depardon, Pavel Longuine, Claire Denis, Costa Gavras, Raul Ruiz).

(Grégoire Colin), who has been contracted to commit a murder. The film is set during the Nice carnival, yet it is an exploration of the darker areas of the tourist haven, the underbelly of a city that lives under the shadow of the mafia. In its choice of place and types of characters, *Nénette et Boni* also eludes certain expectations and in this way fits into the definition of the new realist trend that emerged in the French cinema of the 1990s (Beugnet 2001). As in the films of her contemporary, the Marseille director Robert Guédiguian, although it plays on Marseille's cinematic myths, Denis' film makes no attempt at visually exploiting the city's traditional picturesque assets, past and present (Blüher 2001: 12).[18] Well into the film, the first general view merely shows the silhouette of Marseille's famous Notre-Dame de la Garde in the background of a shot taken from the train station. Policemen, passers-by, and homeless people mingle in the front of the station where Nénette sits down briefly to share a burger with a hungry stranger (Richard Courcet). Most of the story takes place in one house and a few streets of the popular area where Boni lives. The location is provincial, the characters are ordinary locals, and great attention is granted to the atmosphere of a specific district. But the privileging of the local does not preclude the universal dimension. On the contrary, the specificity imbues the characters and, by extension, their story, with an authenticity that arguably provides a basis for the exploration of universal values: on the veracity of *Nénette et Boni*'s depiction of a small-time pizza maker's world, depends the value of the film's existential questioning (Blüher 2001: 12).

Nénette et Boni constructs a vivid portrait of a popular Marseille, but, rather than through establishing shots and picturesque views, it does so in an impressionistic fashion, by collecting and putting together sound and visual touches: the accents; the banter of a small-time crook; the group of illegal immigrants and the ethnic mix; the macho behaviour and sexist throwaway comments; images of parking lots, dirty walls and torn wire fencing; scenes of nocturnal trafficking where, in the orange glow of the lamps, the silhouettes of the security staff mingle with those of the thieves; close-ups on the faces of laughing youths; exiguous flats where stolen goods are hidden under children's beds; sailors' uniforms; the contrast between blue sky, dazzling colours and the pervasive signs of ordinary misery ... Instead of recording

18 *Beau travail* also provides an unusual impression of Marseille in the winter time.

an external, pre-organised view, the film is composed of glimpses so as to form an internal vision of the world it represents. Moreover, in place of the long shots, medium shots and shot/counter-shot combinations that would aim at informing and orienting a viewer-observer, the filmmaking consistently privileges close-ups and medium close-ups, developing a kind of intimacy with both the space and its inhabitants. Yet the absence of physical distance should not be equated with an absence of critical distance, with a passive, merely empathetic viewing. On the contrary, the stylistic stance appears to call for an active viewing, arguably comparable to the kind of reading required from poetry.

To each of the main characters or groups of characters is associated a particular universe, evoked in sequences characterised by a specific range of sounds, colours, lights, and textures. (The gang of boys, for instance, connected to urban sounds and settings, are characterised by a strong feeling of osmosis, a physical closeness reinforced by the sound of their on-going chit-chat and the comfortable darkness that surrounds them while they sleep at the house). Rather than linking these sequences in terms of the development of plot and action, the editing, often based on abrupt ruptures, collates or opposes blocks of images – a structuring principle that seems closer to poetry than to conventional narrative. The editing spurs comparisons, creates oppositions (the most obvious one being the opposition between Boni and Nénette's worlds), and questions certain signs. As we will see, clichés and gender assumptions, in particular, are progressively undermined by the alternation of sequences, and, as the film unfolds, by an overlapping of initially opposite universes. The transformation that the main characters undergo in the course of the film remains largely unspoken. Similarly, where the film raises wider issues – about gender, sexuality, representation, and social and cultural norms – it does so implicitly. Ultimately, the spectator has to draw his or her own conclusions not only from the film's play on a rich intertext, but, first and foremost, from the web of suggestions and interconnections that it generates. Between vision, hearing, and the other senses, as well as between images, concepts and emotions, the filmmaking creates a set of Baudelairian correspondences (Chapter I) that extend cinema's primarily audio-visual vocation:

Ce qui serait vraiment surprenant, c'est que le son ne pût pas suggérer la couleur, que les couleurs ne pussent pas donner l'idée d'une mélodie, et que le son et la couleur fussent impropres à traduire des idées; les choses s'étant toujours exprimées par une analogie récipro-que, depuis le jour où Dieu a proféré le monde comme une complexe et indivisible totalité.[19] (Baudelaire 1976: 784)

A cinema of the senses

The exploration of Boni's universe 'plunges the spectator into the field of the sensual' (Garbarz 1997: 38). Sensations are evoked either directly (by showing the actual act of looking, smelling, touching ...) or indirectly, through shots of objects and textures, through shades of colours and light that establish correspondences between the differ-ent senses. Boni's acute sensitivity and alertness, signalled by the piercing intensity of the gaze that he occasionally directs at the camera itself, is stressed by the vividness of the colours that fill the frame when the image represents his point of view. A heightened set of bright candy hues surround the object of his desire, the baker woman. Blocks or touches of strong colours – the deep blue of the kitchen walls, the yellow of a bottle of oil on top of the refrigerator – brighten the inside of the dilapidated house. In the scenes of the pizza kneading and with the small brioches that Boni voluptuously crushes in his hands, the sense of touch comes to the fore. The feelings of softness and warmth are evoked through the camera's caressing close-ups of the woman's and of the boy's body. One sequence of contrasting textures and colours starts with a frame entirely filled with the flowery folds of a bed cover. The gaze of the camera travels over the colourful surface of the fabric then lingers on Boni's naked back as the young man masturbates on his bed. Later, the refraction of a sunbeam through glass, followed by a shot of Boni, his eyes closed and face turned towards the light, suffice to evoke a sensation of heat and sleepiness. The sight of the golden croissants and baguettes at the bakery and the sound of Boni's coffee machine (a humorous counter-point to Boni's erotic daydreaming) are evocative of comforting

19 'What would be really surprising is that sound should be unable to suggest colour, that colours should be incapable of inspiring melody, and that sound and colour should be unsuited to the translation of ideas; given that things have always expressed themselves by means of a reciprocal analogy, since the day when God called forth the world as a complex and indivisible whole.' (Trans Mary Breatnach)

morning rituals, and bring about an array of pleasant odours, tastes, and sensations. Woken up by the noisy machine, Boni looks at it tenderly and leans forward to stroke it.

All kinds of playful metaphoric and metonymic figures (the baker woman's opulent figure surrounded by freshly baked buns and breads) serve to evoke Boni's erotic obsession, and his sensual daydreaming. But there is also something of the oxymoron[20] in this representation of Boni's perception of his environment – a melancholy at the heart of the liveliness. At first, the usual hierarchies of taste and the sense of penury appear to fade away. A shopping mall is imbued with a magical feel, an unkempt house is transformed into a haven of colourful sensations, and bad taste, banality and dilapidation seem to merge into the expression of sensual pleasure. Yet, as the wistful tone of the Tindersticks' musical score suggests, if Boni gives himself up to daydreaming, it is because his largely aimless life is marked by a painful absence. The figure of the dead mother, whose room Boni has left untouched, haunts the whole film, impregnating Boni's fantasies, and generating its own set of signs and metaphors to signify the unspoken disarray created by the loss. The reappearance of Boni's sister revives these buried feelings and brings them to the fore.

Eros and Thanatos

Initially, Nénette and Boni represent two opposites: Eros and Thanatos, the life and death principles. Boni's existence appears entirely sensual. Open to a world of sensations and fantasies, it revolves around a fantasy figure of Woman. A cross between pin-up and mother, be-tween the sexual and the biological, through the prism of Boni's vivid but restricted imagination, the baker woman's ample figure incarnates the most stereotypical of feminine representations. Nénette, by comparison, is a figure of refusal. Closed against the world, she denies, as much as possible, her own physical existence, and appears to surround herself with a wall of negation.

The arrival of Nénette at Boni's place is a striking illustration of the clash between the two worlds, but also of the way Nénette's presence threatens Boni's dreamworld, and the feminine stereotypes that fills

20 A figure of style that designates the contradictory association of two words: a 'melancholy liveliness' for instance.

it. Boni's first sight of his sister is from his window. A shot reveals her face, barely showing on the top of the stone wall behind which she stands and which fills most of the frame. Boni does not acknowledge his sister's presence, and she watches him drive off in his pizza van. Later on, as the young woman asks for a cigarette from one of Boni's friends who stayed at the house, she again barely emerges from behind a stone wall, topped, this time, with iron bars and spikes. In between these two takes of Nénette is inserted one of the longest erotic variations on the baker woman. To the hardness of the stone surface and the feeling of entrapment associated with Nénette, that sequence opposes all the nuances of softness, roundness, and warmth. It starts with an extreme close-up on a layer of fresh cream, moves along the white textured swirls of cream in a slow pan till the frame is filled with a bright pink mass of candy sugar. The sequence cuts on to a close-up shot of sugary brioches, then a medium shot that shows the baker woman's breasts appearing in the low cut neckline of her pink blouse. The camera remains fixated on her breasts as the young woman leans over, revealing more flesh. Her face enters the frame, made up in pastel colours and framed by blonde hair. The next shot focuses on her fingers delicately picking a raffle ticket from the top of a cream cake. A cut moves the scene inside the bakery, and shows one of the bread-making machines. The soft shapes of uncooked baguettes fall limply on the conveyor belt.

In this playful emulation of the erotic genre, the figure of the baker woman activates all the trappings of the conventional sexist representation. Her body is doubly objectified, fragmented, and fetishised by the gaze of the camera, and compared to other elements of the surroundings: in Boni's fantasies, she becomes a piece of dough, to be literally and metaphorically kneaded and shaped. She is depersonalised and nameless: she is Woman. As she bends over to rearrange her cakes, or moves along the rhythm of a sentimental Beach Boys' song, offering herself to the gaze of a sailor – and, by the same token, to the gaze of the viewers – she seems a perfect example of Laura Mulvey's 'to-be-looked-at-ness', of femininity constructed as passive object of desire and as spectacle.[21] And, indeed, her unthreatening

21 Laura Mulvey's seminal article, *Visual Pleasures*, is one of the founding texts of modern film theory. Using psychoanalysis as a framework, Mulvey pointed out some of the mechanisms through which cinema constructs and directs the gaze so as to fulfil the expectations and desires of a male audience. By 'to-be-looked-

appearance and pliable figure seem to literally 'fascinate' the male observers: both Boni and the American sailor contemplate her, dumbfounded, with eyes filled with wonder. Moreover, the character recalls a tradition of feminine myths[22] typical of French cinema, and even more specifically of Marseille's cinematic past. From the literary and 1930s film legacy of Marcel Pagnol,[23] in particular, familiar settings including bars and bakeries make up the city's mythical landscape. Amongst its set of colourful southern archetypes, heroines including bakers' wives and young women in love with sailors become the tragic objects of men's desires.

> Le fantasme de Boni – pas moins typique que son objet de désir: une boulangère à l'accent chantant – se dessine sur un univers presque aussi traditionnel: trafics en tous genres dans la ville où le trafic fait partie du folklore local, Marseille, comédie humaine aux personnages éternels, et comédie tout court: le mari de la boulangère est un Américain aux airs de rocker, mais il était naguère, quand elle travaillait dans un bar, un marin du port.[24] (Strauss 1997: 65)

The female character thus appears prisoner of a double framework of preconceived representations of Woman. But the stereotyping is debunked from the start by the parodic nature of the images. The editing and the excess of a playful *mise en scène* clearly place this representation within the context of Boni's fantasies and humorously lay bare the simple mechanisms that attempt to reduce femininity to a cliché – to a sexualised and motherly body. The candyfloss world in which the character of the baker woman appears recalls the stylised

---

at-ness' she designates the reduction of the female character and body, in the narrative and in the *mise en scène*, to passive object of male desire and gaze. ('Visual Pleasure and Narrative Cinema', *Screen* 16:3, Autumn 1975, 6–18.)

22 Cinema, as we have seen, has greatly contributed to the constructions of certain myths relating to racial, but also to gender definitions. Woman as mystery, or women as dependent and passive (objects of desire) for instance, are amongst the myths discussed early on by feminist film theorists.

23 Writer and director Marcel Pagnol (1895-1974) is famous for his Provençal tales, shot on location in and around Marseille.

24 'Boni's fantasy – no less typical then the object of his desire: a baker woman with a singsong accent – emerges within a universe that is almost as traditional, made up of all kinds of traffics in a city where trafficking is part of the local folklore. Marseille is a human comedy with eternal archetypes, and just a comedy: the baker woman's husband is an American who looks like a rocker but who was, in the past, when she worked in a bar, a sailor from the harbour.'

atmosphere not only of musicals,[25] but also of the erotic cinema of the 1970s. The camerawork, with its fetishistic close-ups, refers to a clichéd set of filming techniques, and even the music, with its slow, synthesised xylophone chords, evokes the mannerism of the erotic genre. At the same time, the humorous associations generated by the editing undermine even the threatening macho element that Boni's fantasies contain. Boni's unrefined comments and daydreams, 'chargés d'images qui ne peuvent débrider que l'imaginaire d'un puceau' ('charged with images that would only stir the imagination of a virgin boy') (Strauss 1997: 64), are punctuated by unheroic images of limp baguettes, and one of his wildest dreams vanishes in the loud gurgling of his coffee machine. In effect, in the *mise en scène* of his sensual fantasies, it is Boni's body, as much as that of the object of his desire, that is displayed in front of the camera.

> L'œil de Claire Denis, plus curieux, moins désabusé que d'autres, trouve matière à un peu de mystère (le corps de Boni, drôle de zèbre à la fois virginal et sensuel, scruté comme une page blanche et un parchemin) et matière à fiction.[26] (Strauss 1997: 65)
>
> Boni est essentiellement un être physique dont l'existence est pour ainsi dire réduite à celle de son corps, que la cinéaste filme à chaque instant de la journée et qu'elle nous montre littéralement souffrir, jouir, se gonfler, se vider, s'épanouir, s'épancher ... On ne peut, dans ces moments d'extrême intimité, qu'être frappé par la complicité totale, et rare, qui lie la réalisatrice à son jeune comédien.[27] (Garbarz 1997: 39)

Ultimately, the fantasy itself escapes its master. Progressively, sequences showing the baker woman's own sensual world extend and exceed the sequences depicting Boni's dreams. Scenes of tender intimacy with

25 In this regard, *Nénette et Boni* recalls the universe of Jacques Demy's films, and in particular *Lola* (1961), in which a young woman who works in a bar is courted by an American sailor.
26 'Claire Denis' eye, more curious, less disenchanted than others', finds an element of mystery (Boni's body, a strange hybrid, both virginal and sensual, and scrutinised like a blank page and a parchment) and raw matter for her fiction.'
27 'Boni is an essentially physical being whose existence is, so to speak, reduced to a body that the director films at every moment of the day. She shows a body in pain or in ecstasy, a body expanding, pouring out, literally emptying itself ... In these moments of extreme intimacy, the total and rare complicity that links the director to the young actor is striking.'

her husband show her as a desiring figure, taking pleasure in his as well as in her own sensuality. Boni's fevered imagination eventually catches up with him when, in a shopping mall, the baker woman recognises and approaches him. During the scene at the café she comes across as an earthly figure, a friendly, engaging neighbour who talks about sensations and attraction between people with a disarming combination of enthusiasm and embarrassment.

But, first and foremost, it is the disruption created by Nénette's presence that threatens to shatter Boni's perceptions. Landing in the midst of her brother's small macho world like a call from reality, Nénette introduces into her brother's fantasised vision a darker dimension of physicality, sexuality, and gendered self-abuse, self-disgust, morbidity. While Boni's and the baker woman's face and body are repeatedly offered to the gaze, Nénette remains an elusive presence, and the camera often only captures her averted profile. Boni is connected with bright colours and appetising smells and images and, like the baker woman, he likes the scent of his own skin. His sister is associated with a more subdued range of hues, with darkness and sleepless nights. The smell of her brother's unwashed clothes disgusts her, as does the presence of the unborn intruder inside her pregnant body. In her attempt to provoke an abortion, she calls on an abject combination of substances and emanations: in the suffocating atmosphere of the steamed-up bathroom, she drinks vinegar and immerses herself in a mixture of hot water and mustard.

The first shot of Nénette shows her floating on the surface of a swimming pool. In this chlorine-filled version of the amniotic liquid, her body appears enveloped within a wide blood-red T-shirt: 'a strong image of this negation of the life that she carries'[28] (Strauss 1997: 65). As her belly grows, the shots tend to split her body in two, concentrating mainly on the upper part, with occasional shots of her legs emerging from oversize shirts. Nénette decides to 'cross out' her pregnancy by giving an 'accouchement sous X' (literally in French an 'X' birth, that is, the birth of a baby who is immediately given away for adoption) and goes to the maternity clinic clad in combat trousers. The scenes that immediately follow the birth are unsettling because they eschew the expected narrative turnabout. Asked whether she wants to hold the child, Nénette answers no, refusing to even look at

28 'Cette négation de la vie qu'elle porte, c'est aussi une image forte'.

the newborn. The same scene in a traditional melodrama would celebrate the ultimate victory of the maternal instinct. But in *Nénette et Boni*, such reactions do not appear spontaneous or bound to a particular biological category. Evoked briefly in connection with the baker woman, who is seen with a very young child in one of the dream sequences, the maternal eschews Nénette, but emerges in Boni. Whether at the gynaecologist's (played by Alex Descas) or in the hospital during the sequence of the birth, the frame focuses on Nénette's face, impassive or in pain. It is her brother who takes the Polaroid picture of her womb after the scan. Later, a downward shot, taken as from Nénette's point of view, shows the round shape of her belly distorted by the movements of the unborn child. The moving belly seems like an alien presence, alive and detached from her. Boni, however, after his sister's attempted abortion, touches her stomach with wonder and puts his ear against the skin to listen to the baby's movements.

As ever, from an ethical and political point of view, Denis' treatment of sensitive issues proves controversial and challenging. Behind the apparently liberating (non essentialist) turnabout of gender roles, the shift that the desire for a baby appears to create between Nénette and Boni raises the familiar question of an effacement of the feminine. In particular, it reactivates the arguments spurred by the successful release of Coline Serreau's *Trois hommes et un couffin* (1986) and its American remake, Leonard Nimoy's *Three Men and a Baby* (1987), which portrayed three men acting as surrogate parents following the desertion of a new-born child's mother. Serreau's film, it was argued, promoted 'men as superior "mothers" to women, vilifying or degrading the women, and even fantasizing the biological assumption of the maternal function' (Fisher 1991, quoted in Powrie 1997: 149).

The name of the father

With relation to the representation of the maternal principle, the sequences that directly precede Boni's kidnapping of the baby at the hospital contain some intriguing details. Before he goes off to fetch his shotgun – the phallic symbol par excellence – there is a brief shot of Boni taking off the white apron that frames his belly as if to counterpoint the previous shot of Nénette's pregnant body. While Nénette appears to withdraw completely (not only do the shots that follow the birth underline her own childlike appearance, but the young woman subsequently refuses to wake up), the feminine and the masculine thus seem to be combined and collapsed into the one character of the brother. Boni is troubled at the idea of the baby not bearing 'a name'. Contrary to his sister, he thus appears willing to uphold the traditional patriarchal notions of identity and family lineage. At the same time, the final shots of the young man show him holding the child as in a variation of a Madonna pose. In tune with Tania Modleski's assessment of Nimoy's film, *Nénette et Boni* can thus be read as one of those representations that 'simply give men more options than they already have in patriarchy: they can be real fathers, "imaginary" fathers, godfathers, *and*, in the older sense of the term, surrogate mothers' (Modleski 1988: 80, quoted in Powrie 1997: 149).

But *Nénette et Boni*'s striking visual treatment, combined with the choice of context and characters, suggests a different interpretation. Mainstream comedies such as Serreau's or Nimoy's mobilise a set of narrative and formal conventions in order to convey and justify a specific message – in these cases a (regressive) vision of changing gender roles – as convincingly as possible. By promoting identification or acquiescence with a particular character, a point of view or a story line, the film assigns a specific 'position' to the spectator.[29] In some ways, the *mise en scène* of Boni's macho fantasies, where Boni's comments complement a set of images that are saturated with familiar gender clichés, could be read as a mock, condensed version of a traditional narrative strategy or *récit*.[30] Yet, as we have seen, even this fantasy world seems to slip away from easy generalisations. In effect, *Nénette et Boni* consistently eludes the narrative and formal

29 Certain devices, such as the point of view shot (the camera seemingly relaying what a particular character sees), the shot/reverse-shot (two complementary shots that work almost like a question and answer: showing a character looking and then what is being looked at for instance), the voiceover commentary, etc., 'inscribe' the (theoretical) spectator into the text and facilitate the assimilation of the values it promotes. In other words, the way in which the story world is conveyed, that is, the form of the *récit*, contributes to the *positioning* of the spectator. See for instance Nick Brown, *The Rhetoric of Film Narration*, Ann Harbor: University of Michigan Press, 1982.

30 'The *récit* is the signifier, statement, narrative text itself, i.e. the verbal or cinematic discourse that conveys the story to the spectator' (*New Vocabularies in Film Semiotics*, p. 95). As such, the *récit* is distinguished from the story itself (the *content* of the *récit*), and the narration, that is, the *act* of recounting.

framework aimed at guiding a viewer's understanding and judgement. Thanks to its elusive narrative structure, and in spite of the
intimacy created by the camerawork, the characters retain their
mystery, and the spectator is left to ponder on the meaning of their
reactions. Through its sensual approach to its material, the film also
undermines the traditional power of the all-seeing gaze[31] and the
process of spectatorial positioning. By inviting the viewer into a close,
tactile relation with the characters and their world, the filmmaking
privileges an empathetic experience. In the prevailing of the close-up
mode, the actual point of view – who sees or feels – loses its importance, and through the correspondences that the film establishes
between the senses, and the near-abstract quality of some of the
images, the boundaries between subject and object loosen. Entry into
the story world may take place at the level of the felt instead of as an
all-knowing observer or through a particular character's vision.
Within this environment, the changes that the characters undergo are
described in an organic rather than psychological way. Boni's reluct-
ance at letting his sister enter his world, and his initial violence, could
be compared to the reaction of a body being grafted with a new part.
Yet progressively, even the fantasy world of the young macho boy
becomes impregnated with a pathos that would seem alien to it.

Neither the stylised, phenomenological approach nor the focali-
sing effect of the close-up implies the consignment of the off-field
(the wider context) to non-existence. however. The presence of the
frame is often heightened in long static shots where the characters
move in and out of its boundaries, as with the first shot of Nénette
floating in the pool, for instance. By explicitly limiting the scope of
vision, the frame simultaneously reminds us of the existence of an
off-field. Furthermore, as we have seen, the film collects details,
impressions that contribute to the composition of a vivid picture of
Boni's environment and of his way of life. *Nénette et Boni*'s trajectory
thus remains inscribed in the story's particular social and economic
context. Critic Fréderic Strauss pointed out the significance of the
social comment that underpins *Nénette et Boni*:

31 Through a privileged observer's point of view the spectator can have access to
   more information than the character in the story for instance. The controlling,
   defining power of the gaze has been studied by feminist film theorists in
   relation to the maintaining of certain (patriarchal) norms (see above note 21 on
   L. Mulvey).

Denis se tient à distance de la peinture sociale, sans pourtant rester sur le quant-à-soi d'un langage visuel éthéré: sociologiquement, *Nénette et Boni* a son mot à dire, et parle avec justesse de cette génération qu'on a baptisé parfois la 'génération X', celle de l'avenir obstrué ...[32] (Strauss 1997: 65).

Not only does the precarious existence of the central protagonists of *Nénette et Boni* reveal a lack of emotional as well as practical experience, but they are too young to fit into the categories of 'father' and 'mother'. Formally as well as in narrative content, rather than exposing a shift in gender roles, and an appropriation of the feminine by the masculine, the film appears to map out the absence or irrelevance of such models. There are undoubtedly Oedipal[33] overtones to the depiction of *Nénette et Boni's* dysfunctional family, but less familiar alternatives have to take the place of the fading traditional models. The conventional gender and social roles are either non-existent or unacceptable, and in the absence of this defining framework, relationships and communication are complicated. By default (the pregnant Nénette presumably comes to her brother because she has no-one else) the blood ties still come into play, but in less defined, more haphazard combinations. The two young people do not completely reject the old bond. Rather, as with their names, it survives in an altered form: not the old-fashioned Antoinette and Boniface, but simply Nénette and Boni.

32 'Denis keeps her distance from the social genre, without hiding behind a removed visual language: sociologically, *Nénette et Boni* has a lot to say and gives a truthful depiction of this young generation sometimes designated as the 'Generation X' – the generation with a blocked-up future ...'

33 In the original Greek legend, the tragic hero Oedipus, who had been abandoned at birth, meets his father as an adult, kills him, and ends up marrying his own mother. Through the writings of Sigmund Freud (1856-1939), the myth became a central element of psychoanalysis. According to his theory of the oedipal triangle, the father and mother figures provide the models in comparison with and against which the child will develop his or her own personality. In this set of symbolic (rather than real) positions, the father figure stands in the way of the little boy's love and desire for his mother. By overcoming his aggressiveness towards his father, and by accepting the impossibility of his incestuous drive towards his mother, the little boy learns to transcend his desires. By the same token, the child enters the dimension of the symbolic, where the world is not merely felt and absorbed, but understood through and structured by language. The process is implicitly challenged in *Nénette et Boni*, both at the level of the story itself, and in the formal approach that privileges the sensual over the spoken word.

'In Claire Denis' film, the death of the mother is truly the matrix of other, equally dreadful desertions, that fixate the characters in a morbid isolation and preclude them from opening up', stresses Garbarz (Garbarz 1997: 38). While the mother's disappearance has left a gaping hole which Boni hides behind fantasies, and Nénette behind rejection, the father, a small-time trafficker, is given an ineffectual, superfluous presence. Initially, he appears little more than a weak representative of the old patriarchal order of values. Yet an ill-defined malaise, evoked in an enigmatic flashback, surrounds the family history. Spurred by the memory of the mother, the sequence starts like old family footage of an outing at the beach, but concludes with a shot of two divers coming out of the sea, one carrying the limp body of an octopus in his belt. The vision remains unexplained, as does the father's reproachful comments about his deceased wife's preference for her son. But behind Nénette's escape away from her father's sphere of authority, and her refusal to name the father of the child she bears, looms the murky shadow of incest. As such, Nénette also comes to embody a hidden side of the tradition of family melodrama which is associated with Marseille, and evoked, as we have seen, by the figure of the baker woman. Ginette Vincendeau has pointed out how, in the classical tradition of French cinema exemplified by Pagnol's classics (*Marius*, 1931, *Fanny*, 1932, *César*, 1935, *La Femme du boulanger* (*The Baker's Wife*), 1938), so as to protect the social order and to provide names for their fatherless unborn children, the young heroines end up with much older, father-like figures. The subtext of such films, Vincendeau argued, functioned as metaphors for paternal power and as travesties for incestuous relationship (Vincendeau 1988: 78). On the other hand, in *Nénette et Boni*, the erasure of the father figure is coextensive with Boni's attempt at reconstructing a unit. By drawing a cross over her pregnancy, Nénette also crosses out the mark of her (patri)lineage, the father's name, and declines to take her place within the kind of value system it implies. Given Boni's hatred of his father, one can wonder at whether the name the young man bears and wishes to pass on to the baby is that of his father or that of his mother. In any case, the denial of the father, as actual and symbolic figure, is confirmed by his physical erasure. The scene of his assassination by anonymous Mafiosi is framed by a scene where Boni listens to the movements of the baby in his sister's belly, and a scene showing the young man cleaning his mother's room to turn it into a nursery. The film thus evokes a cycle of transformation where death and life, like Nénette and Boni, complement each other:

> La fabrication du pain et le travail de la pâte à pizza illustrent physiquement cette *transformation de la matière* qui est au cœur du film: tout comme la farine et l'eau produisent le pain, la réunion de Nénette et Boni a rétabli le lien du sang, constitutif de l'abandon originel.[34](Garbarz 1997: 39)

The conclusion of the film remains open. It does not attempt to depict the actual functioning of the precariously reconstituted unit. However, the utopian element of pre-Oedipal[35] communion that the sequence of Boni holding the baby evokes, is humorously kept in check. While the camera greedily records the feelings of softness and warmth evoked by the new-born's body, and the attractive-repulsive sound of his gurgling noises, Boni appears to be in a state of grace. But the symbolic weightiness of the scene is debunked by an impervious manifestation of the real: the baby urinates on Boni. Moreover, the film does not conclude with Boni and the baby but with Nénette. The setting is the garden of Boni's house, covered in snow. Echoing earlier shots of Boni's hand holding the baby's, a close-up shows Nénette's fingers searching for a smoke amongst the dead cigarette butts that fill an ashtray. The final image frames the young girl's face as she casts a quizzical, enigmatic gaze at her surroundings.

Nénette et Boni represents a significant move in Denis' exploration of a cinema of the senses. An intriguing parallel is thus drawn between the characters' trajectory and the evolution of the director's work. Nénette and Boni reconstitute a bond, but the process is concomitant with the effacement of the figure of the father, and of the spent system of values he might have represented. At the same time, Denis' filmmaking moves further away from dominant cinematic lineages. Though the intertext of a film like *Nénette and Boni* incorporates a rich set of traditional representations, its formal approach to its subject sets it against some of the most established

---

34 'The making of the bread and the kneading of the pizza dough are the physical illustration of this *transformation of the raw matter* that is at the heart of the film: just like flour and water produce bread, the reunion of Nénette and Boni reestablishes the blood tie – the founding element of the original abandonment.'

35 That is, the idealised moment of osmosis between mother (Boni in this case) and child before the baby realises that it has a separate body.

models, not only of mainstream cinema, but of a long tradition of French film:

> *Nénette et Boni* est un film qui affronte la fatalité du cinéma français, où s'engager dans la fiction, c'est d'abord hériter de pas mal d'inertie – poids mort du scénario, atavisme de la psychologie, carcan de la sociologie. Un linéage un peu exsangue, comme celui de Nénette et Boni, et qui, comme leur père, appelle moins le rejet haineux, qu'une envie de dépassement, un besoin de raviver ce qui compose le paysage cinématographique ou l'horizon familial, au nom du plaisir, tout simplement.[36] (Strauss 1997: 64)

Trouble Every Day

In *Trouble Every Day*, the elaboration of a cinema of the senses started in *Nénette et Boni* continues, but the approach works towards an evocation of desire in its connection to terror. Here, the effect of the correspondences and of the sensuous camerawork, and the effective destabilising of the conventional strategies of perception and point of view, result in the construction of a pregnant atmosphere of anxiety. Indeed, monstrosity, the opaque centre of *J'ai pas sommeil*, is also at the heart of *Trouble Every* Day, an evil shadow that seems to haunt the nocturnal Paris of Denis' films, as in a contemporary evocation of Le Comte de Lautréamont's *Maldoror*.[37] But in *Trouble Every Day*, as in *J'ai pas sommeil*, Denis' heroes are not rebellious figures wilfully set to offend God and the social order. In the Godless worlds of her films, evil, drained of its transcendental or subversive overtones, comes closer to conformity and ordinariness. As in *J'ai pas sommeil*, the

36 '*Nénette and Boni* is a confrontation, where to engage oneself in fiction means to inherit a load of inertia – dead weight of the official script, atavism of the psychology, sociological shackles. A rather exhausted lineage, like that of Nénette and Boni, and which, like their father, provokes less a hateful rejection than a wish to surpass, to revive that which composes the cinematic landscape or the family horizon, simply in the name of pleasure.'

37 Isidore Ducasse (1846–70) lived in the district of Montmartre, where he wrote the *Chants de Maldoror* under the pen name of Le Comte de Lautréamont. First published in 1869, this narrative prose poem, celebrated for its lyricism, has become a cult text of underground literature. The *Chants* evoke the horrific exploits of Maldoror, a lost soul and vampiric figure dedicated to offending God through the systematic exploration and enactment of sin, crime, and blasphemy, in their most abhorrent forms.

strangeness of the monstrous portrayed in *Trouble Every Day* feeds on the banal. Irremediably enmeshed within the familiar realities and spaces of ordinary life, it embodies two sides of the same contemporary malaise: the sense of meaninglessness that besets Western societies left devoid of any other values than the ones of a late capitalistic era, and the primeval fears and taboos that social systems attempt to repress. Just as the media, the family, the police, and judicial system were powerless at identifying or eradicating the source of evil in the first film, religion in *Trouble Every Day* is but a tourist attraction, and science fails to elucidate or cure the social and moral 'illness' incarnated in the monster. The films thus evoke the abject in two complementary forms: from the inside, as the threat to the integrity of the body of society, and from the outside, as the threat to the integrity of the individual body. But whereas in *J'ai pas sommeil*, the monstrous and the criminal ultimately emerged as disturbing forms of hyperconformity, in *Trouble Every Day*, the transgressor is a tragic figure, beset by irrepressible cravings, but tormented by the horrifying nature of his or her desires.

The work was first envisaged as part of a series of short films commissioned by an American producer, then as a trilogy of supernatural stories taking place in a hotel, with Atom Egoyan and Olivier Assayas[38] as co-directors (Frodon 2001). From the start, Denis drew inspiration from Gothic literature, and the short stories of nineteenth-century Irish writer Sheridan le Fanu in particular. Having already worked with Vincent Gallo, then an up-and-coming figure in independent American cinema, she had also planned to cast the actor as the main character. The initial projects were abandoned but Denis and scriptwriter Fargeau decided to rework them into a feature film, with a role for Vincent Gallo, but also for Alex Descas and Béatrice Dalle. The principle of Anglo-Saxon Gothic literature as an inspiration was retained, as well as the idea of staging the story at least partly in a hotel. The result is an unusual mix of genres and atmospheres, ranging from the thriller to classic Gothic novels and to gore.

The main plot lines follow the destinies of two couples, one French the other American. Doctor Léo Sémeneau (Alex Descas) was once an up-and-coming researcher, specialised in the study of the effect on the human brain of substances extracted from tropical plants. His wife

---

38 Assayas eventually made *Irma Vep* (1999), partly created as a homage to director Louis Feuillade (see following footnote).

Coré (Béatrice Dalle) suffers from a horrific illness that may be linked to Sémeneau's mysterious professional disgrace. Beset by uncontrollable and deadly sexual urges, she regularly escapes the suburban house where Léo locks her up, to hunt for human prey that she ultimately devours. The ambitious scientist Shane Brown (Vincent Gallo), once interested in Sémeneau's work, possibly misused the findings of the latter, and now suffers from the same illness as Coré. Shane has brought his newly wedded wife June (Tricia Vessey) to honeymoon in Paris where he also intends to seek help from Léo. Tormented by his murderous cravings, he sets out to visit the laboratories where Sémeneau once worked. Left behind at their luxurious hotel, an anxious June tries to find out the reasons for her loving husband's irrational behaviour.

New territories: at the frontiers of genres

The narrative features of *Trouble Every Day* correspond to those elements by now characteristic of Denis' style. Like that of *J'ai pas sommeil*, its plot is based on the simultaneous unfolding of several story lines which the parallel editing, and the loose mingling of a multitude of individual trajectories, allow to unfold in an elliptical fashion. For instance, whereas the film presents some of the characters of a scientific thriller, ultimately, very few pieces of information emerge to clarify the relationship between Léo's work and the illness suffered by the two main protagonists. Similarly, although it is suggested that betrayal, professional as well as emotional, has taken place, the past relationship between Shane, Coré, and Léo remains largely unexplained. Equally typical of Denis' approach is the sparse use of dialogue which contributes to the denial of an explanatory mode, and, by the same token, reasserts the significance and the effect of the visuals and of the soundtrack in themselves. The music of the Tindersticks sets the film's equivocal, melancholy tone. The results of the continuing collaboration of Denis and Godard was also praised by the critics, who stressed the evocative quality of *Trouble Every Day*'s lavish photography, and described the film's images as sumptuous and compelling. But beyond the perfecting of an already established stylistic approach, *Trouble Every Day* also signalled the director's investigation of new territories: the film sets out to explore deep into the meaning and effect of transgression and tackles its subject with a savageness so far unmatched in her filmmaking. In doing so, Denis ventures into cinematic territories that are usually occupied by popular genres such as horror and gore. The very nature of these genres, based on techniques designed to generate physical reactions of fear and disgust through the unrestrained visual exposition of abject violence and bodily destruction, make the association with Denis' reputation as a director of the elusive and the implicit somewhat surprising. In addition, and although such cinematic genres find early sources in examples of popular literature such as *Fantômas* and *Belphégor*,[39] and some of their roots in the French nineteenth-century *Grand guignol* theatre,[40] horror and gore do not occupy a prominent place in French film production. The contemporary preoccupation with the body and the abject recently inspired a series of films that experiment thematically and formally with themes that are close to those of horror cinema (the work of directors like Gaspard Noé, Philippe Grandieux, Marina de Van for instance).[41] But like Denis' films, the work of these filmmakers sidesteps genre conventions and remains marginal within national production. Amongst French film directors of previous generations, masters of the horror genre such as Georges Franju (1912–87), director of *Les Yeux sans visage* (1960) and Jacques Tourneur (1904–77) have been mentioned in connection with *Trouble Every Day*. There are, for instance, unmistakable similarities between the main female character of *Cat People* (1942) and the character of Coré (Kaganski and Bonnaud 2001: 34). The main references to horror cinema, however, come from the other side of the Atlantic (in fact, Tourneur's career, for instance, was based mainly in the USA), though they are linked to eccentric approaches to the horror genre or to vampire stories. Many critics compared the film

39 The stories of Fantômas and Belphégor both focus on arch-criminals, making a sophisticated use of mystery and terror. Fantômas was created by Pierre Souvestre and Marcel Alain in 1911–13. Belphégor was written by Arthur Bernède in 1927. First released in newspaper instalments, the novels almost immediately followed by film adaptations: Louis Feuillade's *Fantômas* in 1913–14, and Henri Desfontaines's *Belphégor* in 1927.

40 Popular in the late nineteenth and early twentieth century, in particular, *Grand guignol* designates both a place (a theatre that closed in 1962) and a theatrical genre. The original 'shock theatre', *Grand guignol* presented its audience with shows based on an accumulation of graphic violence designed to horrify and disgust.

41 See section on 'A Cinema of Abjection' in Martine Beugnet (2000).

to the work of independent filmmakers like David Lynch and David Cronenberg. In her interviews, Denis herself cites Abel Ferrara (*The Addiction*, 1995), De Palma (*Dressed to Kill*, 1980) and Stanley Kubrick (*The Shining*, 1980, in particular, comes to mind), though she is prone to mentioning them alongside Jean Renoir's classic social melodrama *La Bête humaine* (1938).[42] In addition, through some of its characters and settings, and through its connection to the thriller and its feeling of diffuse anxiety, Denis' film cannot fail to evoke aspects of the Hitchcockian inheritance. First and foremost, however, *Trouble Every Day* is a hybrid, a film with a rich intertext that crosses the boundaries between historical periods as well as visual and literary art forms. From children's tales to German expressionism, to Anglo-Saxon Gothic literature, and to the contemporary photography of a Jeff Wall, the film's atmosphere and impact feed on immemorial fears that emerge in diverse forms and spaces;

> Quelque chose de profondément amphibie caractérise le cinéma de Claire Denis. Il est à la fois fait du point de vue des femmes et des hommes, des prédateurs et des proies, d'ici (la France, ses pavillons de banlieue en pierre de taille, le Paris de Fantômas et de Belphégor,) et d'ailleurs (l'international, Abel Ferrara, Hong Kong). Il traverse le genre (gore, horreur, fantastique), les genres (homme/femme, animal/ humain) et ne s'installe pas.[43] (Lalanne 2001)

Un film d'effroi

Even before its release, the rumour that, for her latest movie, Denis had ventured into the gore genre and that the film contained two graphic scenes of gruesome murders, was enough to create a small scandal at

42 *La Bête humaine* (The Human Beast) is an adaptation of an Emile Zola novel. Jean Gabin plays a train mechanic beset by murderous impulses that eventually drive him to kill his lover. Denis talked of the metaphors for the fatalistic drive that moves the hero (the framing, the image of the train engine and so on), as important elements of inspiration during the making of *Trouble Every Day*.

43 'Something profoundly amphibious characterises Denis' cinema. It is shot from the point of view of women as well as of men, from the point of view of the predators as well as from that of the prey, from here (France, with its freestone suburban villas, the Paris of Fantômas and Belphégor) et from elsewhere (the international dimension, Abel Ferrara, Hong Kong). It crosses genre (gore, horror, fantasy), genders (man/woman, animal/human), and does not settle anywhere.'

the Cannes festival. In fact, *Trouble Every Day* was not presented as part of the festival's official selection, and was premiered at a late-night screening during which a section of the audience walked out. Yet the unmatched daringness of the film does not lie primarily with its scenes of graphic violence. As in her previous features, much is implied in *Trouble Every Day*, and, expectedly, the work does not resort to spectacular gory effects as an aim in themselves.

Narratively and formally, the film constructs a reality that is impregnated with a diffuse, yet prevalent and deeply affecting anxiety: camerawoman Godard stressed how *Trouble Every Day* was not so much a horror film as a *film d'effroi* – 'a film of terror'. The feeling of dread seeps in insinuating, like the sound of the dripping water in the basement of the hotel, the apprehension carried by the few musical chords that occasionally break the silence of the deserted corridors. In the image of the endless circular movement of the flask rotors in the laboratories, the film appears to set in motion a fatal, deathly cycle that cannot be averted. The director and the camerawoman both cite the work of Canadian photographer Jeff Wall as a crucial source of inspiration. Wall's large pictures, usually presented in light boxes, always play on a feeling of lack and expectation. Human figures and objects set in suburban wasteland or in deserted streets and office spaces appear to be waiting, surrounded by an indefinable sense of threat. Denis arguably comes close to the gore style in the bold, graphic approach to the murder scenes, and in the privileging of the visual over dialogue. But where *Trouble Every Day* radically departs from the genre's main convention – 'le bannissement du hors cadres ('the banishment of the off-frame') (Godin 1999: 10), i.e.: showing everything – is in the crucial role that is granted to that which lies at the borders of the frame, and the constant feeling that something is happening, or about to happen, just outside or at the limits of the image. The camera work plays on what Pascal Bonitzer called *décadrage* effects: de-familiarising angles and framing. Often, it focuses on empty spaces or inanimate objects and creates, in the centre of the image, a void that destabilises the gaze (Bonitzer 2001: 126. See Chapter 1). In long and medium shots, the human figure tends to remain off-centre and surrounded by large areas of emptiness. Closer up, it is often captured through intriguingly high or low angle shots, or sectioned by extreme close-ups that transform the human body into that of prey. The young chambermaid (Florence Loiret-Caille), although mostly seen alone, seems to be constantly observed. Almost nothing happens until the end of the film, yet she appears beset by an invisible presence that, as the unspoken attraction exercised by Shane grows stronger, becomes, by virtue of the images' suggestive power, progressively more threatening. As she pushes her trolley through the long, windowless corridors of the hotel, the camera follows closely, often focusing in close-up on the back of her head. Reminiscent of the long drives through hotel corridors in Kubrick's *Shining*, the sound of the trolley's wheels, the long travelling shots through endless rows of identical doors, and the close-up on the young couple's room number build up the apprehension, creating a feeling of inexorable process. In the basement where the hotel staff prepare for their shifts, the carpeted upper floors with their muffled atmosphere are replaced by resonating concrete corridors and a maze of metallic lockers. The immobility and silence is only offset by the sparse, intriguing return of the music mingling with the sound of trickling water. While the young woman undresses and looks vulnerable, surrounded by the cold surfaces of the iron cupboards and sinks, a predatory camera seems to observe her from behind nearby doorframes and piles of laundry. The slow rhythm of the film is not dictated by the unravelling of a plot: its tempo is that of anxiety. The sequences are interspersed with shots of inanimate objects, thus endowed with a strange presence: still lifes of pill bottles, of laboratory flasks and samples, a close-up on the petty spoils that the chambermaid hides in her locker – images that imbue the atmosphere with an uncanny immobility.

The sense of dread appears to travel between images, but also between spaces. The choice of locations and the manner in which the editing interconnects them are crucial elements of the film's construct. Jean-Sébastien Chauvin draws a parallel between Denis' ability to create a multiplicity of atmospheres and the hybrid quality of the film in terms of genre:

> Le genre, chez Claire Denis, tient de la déambulation-infiltration, tend moins à pervertir une modernité cinématographique qu'il ne la dote d'un horizon élargi ... *Trouble Every Day* étonne par la liberté de circulation de tous ces éléments et la facilité avec laquelle Claire Denis passe d'un lieu à l'autre.[44] (Chauvin 2001: 77)

44 'Genre, in Claire Denis, resembles a wandering-infiltrating process. It has less to do with the perverting of a cinematic modernity than with providing it with an

Each of the spaces that the camera visits undergoes a process of defamiliarisation both through the *mise en scène*, the heightened sound effects, the mingling of languages, and through the editing that draws links between worlds that are usually dissociated, geographically, culturally, and historically. The credit sequence already plays on this process by endowing stereotypical views of Paris with a Gothic quality that is more readily associated with Victorian London. Following a shot of an anonymous couple kissing in a car, the first image of the Seine is of dark, moving waters on which floats the yellowish reflection of lamplight. Behind a row of vaulted bridges, a twilight glow fills the cloudy sky and surrounds the cityscape with poisonous colours. The credits appear in trembling letters, like reflections on water. These shots of Paris are, at one and the same time, familiar and uncanny. In content, they could be compared to Robert Doisneau's[45] Paris. However, the music, the lingering shots, the light and colours, the menacing obscurity, create instead the feeling of insidious trouble that will permeate the whole film and transform Paris, the city of lights, into a Gothic city of dark shadows. Certain details and images associated with the characters also hint at this Gothic affiliation: an early shot of Coré shows her arms extended under her coat in a bat-like fashion. Similar connotations imbue the sequence of Shane walking away in the streets of Paris at night, long-haired and un-shaven, clad in his leather jacket, his face gaunt and haunted. As June sets off on her husband's trail, with her gloved hands and her neat pastel coloured suits, she resembles a contemporary reincarnation of a Hitchcock heroine. Shots of the young American woman's fragile demeanour, of her delicate face resting on white sheets or framed by a black hood, also underline her Victorian style of beauty, however.

The sequence of the opening credits cuts to a shot of a wasteland at the edge of the city. In the cold, low light, Coré is waiting next to her parked van. A truck pulls up, his driver climbs out and walks towards her. The scene could be the start of a social drama, the depiction, in realistic style, of a scene of prostitution. But this is offset by the close-

---

wider horizon ... In *Trouble Every Day* the freedom with which all the elements circulate, and the ability with which Denis goes from one space to another, is striking.'

45 Photographer Robert Doisneau (1912–94) has produced some of the most famous series of black-and-white images of Paris, including the popular shots of young lovers kissing in the streets.

up on Coré's face, showing her feverish, rapacious gaze. The meeting between the young woman and her prey is not shown: the next scene is shot at night. As Léo appears in search of his wife, the truck driver lies dead and the wasteland is transfigured. In the orange glow of the road lamps, the tall grass drips with blood, and Coré is shown crouching on the ground like a wild animal, still chewing on raw human flesh: save for the distant murmur of the traffic, the Parisian periphery could be a piece of African savannah. From the vision of Léo and Coré clutching each other in the middle of disaster, the film cuts directly to a staple of the romantic film: a shot of Shane and June, cameo-framed, looking through the porthole of a plane. But horror irrupts even at the heart of romance. Through the preying gaze of the camera and its sectioning close-ups, anxiety insinuates itself into the midst of the couple's tender embraces. Soon, the raw colours and savageness of Shane's visions contrast with the subdued, cool colours and the feeling of comfort that imbues the images of the inside of the plane with its sleeping passengers. The trip had started with a flight over the city of Denver and ends with a shot of a traditional Parisian suburb.

The main internal spaces all generate their own uncanny atmosphere. From behind its wrought-iron gate, surrounded by a tall wall, Léo and Coré's sleepy stone pavilion looks mysterious and daunting, standing as a reminder, as Jean-Marc Lalanne remarked, of the Paris of Fantômas, rather than as a fine example of the charming suburban architecture of the beginning of the twentieth century.[46] The hotel's comfortable but impersonal surroundings generate a stifling impression of emptiness and impending disaster. In contrast with the dark, intriguing pictures of the open lab in the Guyane forest that briefly appear on the screen of Shane's computer, the sterile environment of the neurological laboratory, bathed in glaring neon light, should embody unchallenged scientific knowledge and control. Yet, as the camera moves through its sparsely occupied rooms, from neat rows of test tubes and flasks to brain samples neatly sliced, horror filters in, triggered by the void created by the systematic order that rules over the space. Through editing, the world of the laboratory is constantly connected to the unknown that Shane and Coré incarnate and that science must deny. The film's only flashback depicts a confrontation

---

46 Intriguingly, the villa was a former delinquent centre, partly burned down, and closed for refurbishment at the time of the shooting.

between Léo and the director of the laboratory (José Garcia), where the latter refuses Léo the support he seeks because it does not fit in with the official lines of research: *'Ça ne cadre pas'* (literally: 'it does not fit *in the frame'*). A direct cut then shows Coré, after the savage murder of a young man, drenched in blood, standing in front of what looks like a bloody, dripping blood-mural.

As terror infiltrates each of the spaces that the story traverses, it also subordinates the shielding devices offered by culture, religion or science against the power of the unknown. Here, love, marriage and scientific knowledge can neither cure, nor protect. In this in particular, the timeless music of the Tindersticks plays a crucial role. Like a benevolent, knowing presence, even in the midst of the horror, it brings out the sense of melancholy and primeval feeling of fatality that surrounds the characters.

Devouring desire

If the association of desire and sexuality with death and horror is a somewhat hackneyed topic in cinema, *Trouble Every Day* nevertheless manages to imbue its subject with a particular poignancy. In terms of narrative form, Denis remains unconcerned with traditional genre features, and in particular the conventional plot trappings of suspense and climaxes, but she also avoids the element of derision and the endless play on imitation that dominates contemporary Horror and Gore. *Trouble Every Day*'s rich intertext does not pertain to pastiche, it refers to the constancy, through the ages, of the collective anxieties that the film evokes:

> Les morsures, avant le cinéma, déjà dans la littérature, appartiennent presque au patrimoine collectif de l'inconscient. J'ai donc abordé le genre sans ironie, parce que l'ironie et le pastiche, je suis incapable d'en faire.[47] (Morice 2001). Le film est l'héritier des contes, de la mytho-logie, de la littérature fantastique et romantique, c'est une porte vers l'indicible, vers une autre part de nous-mêmes, vers des états douloureux, des métamorphoses qui sont peut-être l'expression d'une angoisse. S'il fallait parler de genre, je parlerais de film autobiographique, d'une

47 'Before cinema, already in literature, biting almost belonged to the collective patrimony of the unconscious. I approached the genre without irony, because I am incapable of irony and pastiche.'

remontée aux racines de ce qui fait frémir quand on est enfant, les vampires, les loups-garous, les Barbe-Bleue, Dracula, Docteur Jekyll et Mister Hyde ... Partout ressurgit la crainte de l'homme d'être encore un peu animal.[48] (Tinazzi 2001)

Preceding the credits, and unravelling on the melancholy music of the title song, the film's first sequence is of dark, bluish images, showing a couple kissing in a car. The gaze of the hand-held camera, hovering over the intimacy of the scene in close-up, seems vaguely predatory. Soon, however, it is the embrace itself, offset by the cold light, the darkness that surrounds the two silhouettes, and by the soundtrack's haunting tune and lyrics, that becomes menacing. The woman reclines while the man leans over her in a long and rapacious kiss. As the darkness deepens and progressively engulfs the lovers' silhouettes, the camera moves to show the man's fingers caressing the woman's exposed throat. The screen fades to black, then fills with twilight images of the Seine's troubled waters. The lovers that briefly feature in the opening sequence will not reappear: independent of narrative links proper, the images encapsulate the film's thematic, the focus on the dark overtones of desire, on the vulnerability of the body exposed to it.[49] In its evocation of territories that belong to the most repressed areas of human thought, the film thus calls to mind a long tradition of horror cinema:

'Passé le pont, les fantômes vinrent à sa rencontre.' Par cette petite phrase inscrite sur un carton du *Nosferatu* de Murnau, le cinéma trouva la formule inaugurale pour entrer dans sa plus belle nuit, celle des histoires qui font peur et des cauchemars pour adultes. Avec *Trouble Every Day*, Claire Denis elle aussi passe le pont ... Le film rejoint l'autre rive du désir, celle des amours monstres et des passions

48 'This film is an heir of the fairy-tale, of mythology, of the Gothic and romantic novel. It is a door towards the inexpressible, towards another dimension of ourselves, towards states of suffering and metamorphosis that are perhaps the expression of an anxiety. If I had to talk of genre, I would talk of autobiographic film, of going back to the roots of childhood fears – vampires, werewolves, Bluebeard, Dracula, Dr Jekyll and Mr Hyde ... Everywhere, man's fear of still being part animal resurfaces.'

49 According to Deleuze's descriptions, such a sequence would be composed of '*lectosignes*', of images to be read as well as seen. They form the visual actuali- sation of a theme, just as the still lifes of objects that punctuate *Trouble Every Day* constitute both an 'inventory' and a series of 'time images', direct images of time as the time of fear. (*The Time-Image*, 1989: 23).

cannibales, là où les baisers profonds n'ont plus rien à voir avec la tendresse.[50] (Lalanne 2001)

In Lalanne's comments, the adjective cannibalistic is only relevant in connection with the term passion: Denis repeatedly refuted comparisons with cannibalism as a ritual, preferring to speak of desire, in its most unlawful expression:

> Moi, je parle du désir de manger l'autre, de la 'dévoration' dont il est question dans les romans, de ces moments de trouble dans la passion amoureuse où se révèle une force brute (et non brutale) qu'on appelle la libido.[51] (Tinazzi 2001)

Hence, at the heart of the film is an exploration of desire at its most compelling and dangerous. Sexual desire is shown in its ambiguity, as the impulse that is associated with love, and yet which brings us close to the animal and to death. The impact of *Trouble Every day* thus grows from its capacity to unravel and put into images a well of repressed fears and taboos connected to the nature of being human. As such, the film draws on all the discourses that have been generated in order to express and ward off, or to elucidate and to control such fundamental fears: psychoanalysis and science, religion, but also literature, cinema and the other arts.

In the tradition of rational thought that has remained so central to French culture, each human being has the potential to know him or herself fully. Each individual can assert him or herself as a unified, coherent whole, a conscious persona owning a body and mind that are consistent in time. By pointing out the part played in our lives by the unconscious and by uncontrollable impulses, however, psychoanalysis revealed a frailty in these certitudes.

> This illusion of unity, in which a human being is always looking forward to self-mastery, entails a constant danger of sliding back into the chaos

50 '"Once the bridge was crossed, the ghosts came to meet him". With this brief sentence from one of the intertitles in Murnau's *Nosferatu*, cinema found the initial formula that opened the door on the most beautiful of nights – the night of frightening stories, of nightmares for grown-ups. With *Trouble Every Day*, Claire Denis also crosses the bridge ... The film crosses over to the other side of desire, that of monstrous loves and cannibalistic passions, where deep kisses have nothing to do with tenderness.'

51 'I am talking of the desire to eat the other, of the 'devouring' described in the novels, in those confused moments where passion and love reveal a brute (and not brutal) force called libido.'

from which he started; it hangs over the abyss of a dizzy assent in which one can perhaps see the very essence of Anxiety. (Lacan 1953: 15)

Quoting Lacan and Kristeva, Barbara Creed stresses, in one of her seminal articles on horror cinema, how the genre draws on this anxiety. By staging, in graphic detail, the metamorphosis and annihilation of the body, horror films play on this obscure feeling that we are never in full control of our own selves, that the sense of being a unified, self-knowing individual is but an illusion. However, before psychoanalysis exposed it, and before horror cinema, using film's capability to mimic the real, took hold of it, the question of the fragility of the human self had already been sensed and played out in those long-standing literary and art genres from which Denis drew inspiration. Fairy-tales and folk traditions, horror stories and Gothic literature, have constantly revisited the dark, unknown territories of human existence. Their heroes are often at risk of being devoured, drained of their blood by vampires, reclaimed by the animal world. Their monsters incarnate unacceptable, repressed facets of human nature. But as embodiments of the fragile border between normality and abnormality, these creatures often carry both the characteristics of the human and of the inhuman. In *Trouble Every Day*, Coré and Shane, like contemporary Jekyll and Hyde figures, are inhabited by contradictory impulses, torn between their love for their respective companions and their urge to devour the objects of their desires. In one of her rare lines, Coré, unable to live with the horrific reality of her own self, expresses her desire to die. Shane and Coré are beset by murderous cravings that bring them close to those predatory animal instincts that are usually dormant in human beings. But, as the Tindersticks' wistful tunes ceaselessly recall, they are nonetheless human, conscious of their own mortality and that of their lovers, and tormented by guilt. In effect, it is the humanity of these characters that endows their desire with a desperate but irrepressible force. In the words of surrealist writer Georges Bataille:

C'est au contraire du fait que nous sommes humains, et que nous vivons dans la sombre perspective de la mort, que nous connaissons la violence exaspérée, la violence désespérée de l'érotisme.[52] (Bataille 1961: 22)

52 'It is precisely because we are human, because we live under the sombre prospect of death that we know the exacerbation of violence, the desperate violence of eroticism.'

Human sexuality is always, directly or metaphorically, central to reflections on the ambiguity of the human condition. Akin to death, the sexual act implies both an invasion or a penetration of another's body, and the (momentary) loss of individual consciousness (in French, the orgasm is commonly called *la petite mort*) ('little death'). As the opening sequence of *Trouble Every Day* suggests, kissing is close to biting, just as the sexual act bears a similarity to the act of killing. It is this tenuous border between what is deemed normal and acceptable, and that threatening, repressed part of human desire, that Denis is interested in portraying. By blurring the frontier between genres, but also by looking at the human being on the brink of annihilation, the film constantly treads on the edge of transgression. Godard's precise camerawork and lighting are thus used to explore the vulnerability of the self, of the body, and of the flesh exposed to unbridled desire.

> Le vampire doit boire du sang pour renaître, avec cette idée que le corps est mystérieux avec tous ses fluides. La morsure est un moyen d'entrer en contact avec cette intériorité. C'est une façon poétique, belle et douloureuse, de parler de l'acte sexuel, entrer dans le corps de l'autre ... Les scènes sanglantes, je les ai abordées comme des scènes sexuelles.[53] (Péron 2001)

In line with Denis' own comments, in describing *Trouble Every Day*'s two scenes of murder, critic Louis Guichard quotes Truffaut's famous remark about violence in Hitchcock's cinema: 'Toutes les scènes de meurtre sont filmées comme des scènes d'amour et vice-versa' ('All the scenes of murder are filmed like love scenes and vice versa') (Guichard 2001, p.36). In the first scene of killing, the difficulty was to show the moment of transgression, the invasion of the other's body not only through penetration but through the bite, and the exposure of the flesh under the skin, while retaining the ambiguity of the embrace. To the Hollywood approach to violence as 'montée, agencée, fragmentée, masquée non pas par le folklore mais par une vague idée que c'est le bien qui va surmonter le mal' ('edited, constructed, fragmented, concealed, less because of the folklore, than of the principle according to which good will win over evil') (Frois 2001), Denis and

---

53 'The vampire must drink blood to come back to life, with this idea that the body, with all its fluids, is mysterious. The bite is a means to reach into this interiority. It is a poetic, beautiful, and painful way to talk about the sex act, to enter into the body of the other ... I addressed the bloody scenes as if they were sex scenes.'

Godard thus opposed the slow pace of lingering close-ups and long takes.

Coré's ultimate prey is a young man (Nicolas Duvauchelle) who lives across the street. The obsessive quality of the boy's fascination, not shared by the frightened friend who spies on Coré and Léo with him, hints at his status as prey and victim. The image of the human figure at the window, the visual metaphor of human yearning, is used in his case as well as in Coré's and Shane's. Like the victims of the classical vampire stories, without even knowing its source, the youth cannot resist the force that draws him towards his death. Early on, a sequence showing a failed attempt to break into the house serves as a preamble to the eventual meeting between the victim and his killer, and reveals the link that binds them. The youth is shown observing, with mounting curiosity, the mysterious, closed-up house where he senses a presence. More than any of the other parallel story lines, the episodes centred on the young man – his curiosity, the surrounds, the props – are evocative of the world of childhood and of fairy-tales. After Léo's departure, the youth and his friend climb over the wall into the overgrown garden. The small pavilion, its shutters closed and its doors barricaded, evokes the mysterious houses of fairy-tales and Gothic novels. In contrast with the cold light of the winter morning, the inside of Coré's bedroom is dark and richly coloured. A painterly shot of the young woman lying among the folds of her purple bed cover shows her waiting, as if aware of the presence of the youths. While they explore the means of access to the house, Coré finds a key, and struggles frantically to open the bars. The boys eventually leave under the watchful gaze of the young woman who remains imprisoned upstairs, an intriguing presence that the trespassers themselves sense without seeing. In a later sequence, the two youths finally enter by breaking into the basement of the house. They first go through Léo's laboratory, where even the discovery of a refrigerated brain in amongst the strange collection of test-tubes and plants cannot deter the intruders.[54] Throughout their exploration of the house, the camera adopts an objective point of view and unfamiliar angles that add to the daunting effect of the dilapidated surroundings. In typical horror style, the camerawork thus creates a growing sense of entrapment

54 In fact, as if in a nightmarish version of *Alice in Wonderland*, the characters taste some of the displays before they continue their exploration.

and expectation, the feeling that the house itself has a gaze. It is the intriguing sight of a door roughly barred with thick wooden planks that greets the youth who reaches the landing in front of Coré's room. The sequence cuts from one side of the barricade to the other as the two, 'recognising' each other, mingle their fingers and eventually start kissing through the interstices. Shot in extreme close-up, the images become almost abstract, a visual metaphor of the force of the attraction that unites the lovers. As the young man destroys the barrier, Coré lifts her dress to show her sex. The next shot is an extreme close-up of skin, and recalls the techniques that Godard would have first experimented with on the shooting of Agnès Varda's *Jacquot de Nantes* (1990) (Chapter 1). Throughout the following long take, the camera slowly travels along the young man's torso, from the armpit to the nipple and the belly button, capturing each magnified feature of his pale flesh as in a detailed landscape shot. A close-up of his ecstatic face is followed by shots of Coré's hands caressing his body. A cut to the other youth, who has remained downstairs, only offers an illusory reprieve. The film's melancholy tune has started to rise, signalling the beginning of the fatal, irrepressible process of annihilation. The remaining part of the sequence, shot in close-up and in long takes, creates obscure but suggestive textured patterns, where the uncertain images of torn flesh are offset by the descriptive soundtrack. As Coré's kisses turn into bites, the young man's cries turn from begging her to stop, into an unarticulated howl that mingles with his killer's moans. Coré's attacks retain, all along, the ambiguity of a frantic embrace: she kisses, bites, and assaults her prey's body with both fury and tenderness.

The sequence draws its forceful impact from an unsettling of the spectator's position. Through the framing and scale of the images, the light and the heightened sound effects, it creates a viewing experience where the spectator loses his or her status of mere observer, by challenging the familiar patterns of orientation, the sense of a definite, superior point of view. In the filming of the body, Denis and camerawoman Godard's concerns closely relate to those of a director like Claire Breillat, described by Emma Wilson in terms that could equally apply here. Her work Wilson explains,

> disrupts the relations of distance and control, on which viewing has been seen to depend, by her emphasis on the tactile. She refuses merely to offer us images of the body's surface, of its integrity and wholeness. She is concerned ... to make the viewer question the

relation between inside and outside, to make us feel, as much as see, the images displayed. (Wilson 2001: 151)

As such, the first killing sequence, like that of the murder later perpetrated by Shane, also precisely recall the definition, proposed by Creed, of the source of horror cinema's effect:

> The horror film puts the viewing subject's sense of a unified self into crisis, specifically in those moments when the image on the screen becomes too threatening or horrific to watch, when the abject threatens to draw the viewing subject to the place where 'meaning collapses', the place of death. (Creed 1986: 65)

Trouble Every Day's portrayal of the darker territories of human sexuality bears unmistakable echoes of the literary currents that emerged in the margins of the French rational school of thought. In its exploration of the transgression of essential borders (in the above sequence, the invasion of the prey's consciousness, and the breaking into the house that announce the severing of the skin and the tearing up of the body), it necessarily calls to mind the writings of Julia Kristeva on the abject. It also evokes Georges Bataille's dark surrealism, and his writings on eroticism in particular ('L'amant ne désagrège pas moins la femme aimée que le sacrificateur l'homme ou l'animal immolé.') ('The lover disintegrates the loved woman no less than the sacrificer disintegrates the man or animal he slays') (Bataille 1957: 100). Bataille was interested in that part of the human psyche that remains inherently opposed to the rules imposed by social and religious systems. Whereas society attempts to coax the individual into controlling his or her own desires in order to become a productive member of a community, sexuality brings the human back towards a state of 'consummation' rather than of organised consumption. In sex, the human being can rediscover the free, unproductive expenditure of energy and let individual consciousness (and with it, responsibility, planning, fear, and self-protection ...) be engulfed in the powerful hold of undifferentiated pleasure. Barbara Creed remarks that, like Bataille, 'Kristeva emphasises the attraction, as well as the horror, of the "undifferenciated" (Creed 1986: 48). It is a similar confusion of fascination and repulsion to that evoked in Bataille and Kristeva's writing that is portrayed in *Trouble Every Day*'s scenes of 'consummation' and is carried through the performances, *mise en scène,* and camerawork:

> Abjection itself is a composite of judgement and affect, of condemna-
> tion and yearning, of signs and drives. Abjection preserves what existed
> in the archaism of pre-objectal relationship ... (Kristeva 1982: 9-10)

Bataille's reflections, like the work of Jean Genet mentioned in
connection with *J'ai pas sommeil*, remain based on the critique of
Christian thought still powerful at the time. In *Trouble Every Day* as in
J'ai pas sommeil, however, religion has become but a mere trace,
inscribed in the architecture that forms Paris's main tourist attractions, and recuperated by popular imagery.[55] Shane's crude mime as a
monster, destined to amuse his wife during a visit to Notre Dame
cathedral, is offset by the poetic image of the young woman's green
scarf floating away in the Parisian sky. Ultimately, however, for all the
impressive beauty of its facade, of its statuesque and evocative gar-
goyles, the site appears to bear only a superficial symbolic significance
and no power of redemption in the face of the malediction that
threatens to destroy the newly married couple. *Trouble Every Day* is set
in the age of rational thinking, where belief in science has replaced
the belief in the power of God to eradicate evil, and where perceptions
of the unknown, of death, are recast, and exorcised in terms of the
process of discovering and mastering through scientific knowledge
(Foucault 1982: 136).

Yet the world of science, represented by the laboratories that
Shane visits, and by Léo's relentless and ultimately doomed quest for
a cure, is helpless in the face of Coré's and Shane's mysterious, deadly
impulses. In effect, as indicated by the director of the laboratory's
refusal to invest in Léo's research, the existence of such 'illness' cannot even be taken into account. Incarnated in the sterilised environment where lab workers operate clad in white and in blinding neon
light, the scientific world upholds a moral discourse that, as in former
religious systems of thought, relies on binary oppositions and the
clear differentiation between good and bad, rational and irrational.
Shane's and Léo's confrontations with the director of the laboratory
are filmed in series of shot/counter-shot, as in a duel. In *Trouble Every
Day*, Denis reiterates her rejection of such a perception of reality both
thematically, by showing the failure of the scientific response, and,

55 To many a tourist, *Notre Dame* does not so much represent a powerful medieval
   testimony of Christian worship as the set of a Victor Hugo novel that inspired a
   Disney adaptation.

formally, even in the murder scenes, by stressing the ambiguous nature of the addiction suffered by her characters.

> Le cinéma américain montre une civilisation très avancée où les savants, les politiques détiennent la vérité. La violence, dans les films américains, est toujours le fait des mauvais, des autres. Leur violence est horrible et pernicieuse mais soi-disant morale, parce que les méchants perdent à la fin. Je trouve cette morale simpliste proprement dégueulasse.[56] (Morice 2001)

That the illness should originate from the research led by Léo in French Guyana[57] gives it an additional significance and creates a connection with the postcolonial theme so central to Denis' work.[58] *Trouble Every Day*'s sub-plot recalls the attempt, to largely destructive results, to regulate colonial territories so as to exploit their natural and human resources. In Denis' films, the ghost of the colonial wreck continues to haunt former colonial countries. In *Trouble Every Day*, Shane and Coré are contemporary vampires, creatures of a post-colonial era tormented by a curse brought back from a former colony. Shane in particular is apparently punished as a result of his contribution to the scientific tampering with a nature that remains largely mysterious – a risk he took because of greed and ambition.

The film's title, borrowed from the title song written for it, refers to the endless return of those dark fears and drives that are inherent in human nature. The emergence of the repressed and the unacceptable in one form or another is unavoidable, and the struggle to master it starts anew every day. And in the contemporary world inhabited by Denis' creatures, there are few redeeming forces at work. The vanishing of the Christian culture of death (death as a form of transcendence),

---

56 'American cinema shows a very advanced civilisation where the truth belongs to scientists and politicians. Violence in American movies is always due to the bad ones, to the others. Their violence is horrific and pernicious yet depicted as moral because the bad guys always lose in the end. I find this simplistc moral absolutely revolting.'

57 Situated in the North-East of South America, French Guyana is a former penitentiary colony, now a French *Département*. Its troubled history generated a wealth of myths and a rich tradition of literary fiction.

58 *Trouble Every Day* bears faraway echoes of Jean Rouch's thought-provoking indictment of colonial culture, *Les Maîtres-fous* (1956), a powerful documentary shot amongst Sahelian immigrants in the African Gold Coast. The film focuses on a group of workers who meet in secret to perform a kind of exorcism of the colonial order that surrounds them.

and the limitations of a scientific world that attempts to clean it up and make it invisible, have given death all its raw powers of horror back. Devoid of its metaphysical or scientific aura, death as portrayed in *Trouble Every Day* becomes again the ultimate abject, the unavoidable pull of the void. In the words of historian Philippe Ariès: 'The belief in evil was necessary to the taming of death; the disappearance of the belief has restored death to its savage state' (Ariès 1983: 614, quoted by Boss 1986: 20).

To critic Frédéric Bonnaud, *Trouble Every Day* is an 'acte de foi' ('an act of faith') in the powers of cinema (Bonnaud 2001: 39). In effect, to those who loved it, *Trouble Every Day* testifies to a belief in the cinematic image's continuing power to fascinate its viewer (like a distant echo of the fascination exercised by the vampire hunters on his prey). Based on a different genre genealogy, *Trouble Every Day* nevertheless continues the thematic and aesthetic exploration started in *J'ai pas sommeil* and *Nénette et Boni*. In effect, as the plot line and dialogue are progressively reduced to an essential but minimal outline, Denis appears to rely more and more on the sensual dimension of film, and on the suggestive impact of the unspoken. As Godard puts it: 'de croire en la capacité de suggestion des images, ça peut donner des ailes' ('To believe in the images' ability to suggest can give you wings') (Péron 2001). The denial of the dialogue and narrative as expository tools also becomes a crucial part in the elaboration of the film's infectious atmosphere of diffuse anxiety. The lack of explanatory discourse feeds the apprehension generated by the slow, compelling unravelling of the characters' trajectory. As with the increasingly unintelligible cries of Coré's victim, the film as a whole evokes unspoken fears and a horror that are 'beyond words'.

At the same time, the hybrid quality of Denis' filmmaking, at the crossroads between genres and art forms, between realism and nightmare, signals a renewed questioning of the nature of reality and of representation that hints at the fragility of our perception of the real. With *Trouble Every Day*, Denis arguably goes back to one of cinema's essential powers: the power to infuse magic into reality, to give it back a part of its mystery by hinting at the hidden dimension that lies behind its surface.

Vendredi soir

During the development of the scenario of *Trouble Every Day*, Denis worked with Jean-Pol Fargeau and with writer Emmanuèle Bernheim. She continued the collaboration with the latter for her next film, adapting a novel by Bernheim, and co-writing the script of *Vendredi soir* with her. As a book adaptation, *Vendredi soir* may have been expected to mark a return to more traditional, novelistic paradigm. In effect, not only did Denis choose to stay very close to the text of Bernheim's eponymous novel, but she also cast two known actors as the two central protagonists.[59] *Vendredi soir* could have resembled 'a regular movie with showbiz stars (Valérie Lemercier and Vincent Lindon) and a bourgeois subject (a Parisian woman has a one-night affair with a stranger)' remarks Didier Péron (Péron 2002). Serge Kaganski even compared the project's initial challenge to a kind of exercise combining all manner of obstacles:

> Argument très mince (brève rencontre), unités très réduites de lieu et de temps (un embouteillage, une nuit), seulement deux personnages principaux, des dialogues minimaux, et deux acteurs ultracélèbres, qui doivent justement faire oublier leur image et baisser leur taux d'identifiabilité. Bref, une somme de paris narratifs, formels et techniques.[60] (Kaganski 2002: 36)

Rather than being limited by these apparent hindrances, Denis appears to thrive on them, the minimal framework allowing her to pursue her 'exploration de territoires vierges en quête d'une énigmatique chimie ... et poursuit son travail sur la dissolution du récit' ('exploration of uncharted territories in search of an enigmatic chemistry ... and continue work on the dissolution of the *récit*.' (Chauvin 2002: 80).

Laure (Valérie Lemercier) is a thirty-something Parisian woman at a turning point in her life: she is leaving her flat to move in with her

---

59 Valérie Lemercier has worked in theatre as well as for the cinema, as an actress and as a director (*Quadrille*, 1996; *Le Derrière*, 1998). Abroad, she is best known for her role as the upper-class housewife in Jean-Marie Poiré's *Les Visiteurs* (1993). Vincent Lindon has acted in the films of Claude Lelouch, Diane Kurys, Benoît Jacquot and Coline Serreau amongst others.

60 'A very thin premise (a brief encounter), extremely limited units of time and space (a traffic jam, one night), only two main characters, scarce dialogue, and two very famous actors whose image and fame must in fact be forgotten. In short, a sum of narrative, formal and technical challenges.'

boyfriend or fiancé. At the beginning of the film, we see her finishing packing before leaving for dinner with friends of hers. On the way, however, she becomes caught in a massive traffic jam: Paris is paralysed by a general transport strike. Following the advice of a radio announcer advocating drivers to show solidarity on this very cold winter evening, Laure agrees to let a passer-by (Vincent Lindon) climb into her car. Almost without dialogue, a mutual attraction develops, and the pair end up spending the night together.

The style of Bernheim's short novel could be described as cinematic: she depicts her characters' surroundings and their experiences in factual, phenomenological terms. Her attention to detail and her ability to defamiliarise the ordinary by drawing attention to fragments of reality, objects, and parts of the body, appears close to Denis and Godard's approach to camerawork. In addition, the novel's minimalist outline, strictly followed by the film, is a variation on a motif that was already central to *US Go Home*: a brief encounter between two strangers who are drawn to each other by an unspoken attraction. One of the main difficulties in the transposition from word to image, however, was the subjectivity built into the text. Although it is written in the third person and dispenses with psychological explanations, the novel still describes the heroine's sensations and inner feelings, her unspoken doubts and fears. Too close to the psychological or explanatory mode, and too deterministic in terms of spectator position and identification, the voiceover was not an option for Denis. First and foremost, as Yann Tobin underlines, *Vendredi soir* 'est une démonstration du pouvoir du cinéma ... Si on le confronte à son œuvre source, le film accuse la différence fondamentale entre le roman qui *raconte* et le cinéma qui *montre*' ('is a demonstration of the power of cinema ... when confronted with its source text, the film emphasises the fundamental difference between a novel that *tells* and a cinema that *shows*.') (Tobin 2002: 38). It is in the singular and evocative description of space and time, and in the way it inscribes the characters within their environment both as physical presence and as observers/perceivers that the film recreates the subjective dimension.

The enchanted parenthesis

Described as a 'balade du temps suspendu' (Loiseau 2002: 73) ('wander in suspended time'), *Vendredi soir* certainly takes its place amongst

Denis' most 'Deleuzian' (Chapter 1) of projects. Built around the spare outline provided by the novel, the film is not constructed as plot development, but as an exploration of time as subjective and changing. In the course of a 130 minute film depicting one night in the life of two characters, time alternatively dilates or retracts, carried by a narrative that seems always on the brink of branching off.

Vendredi soir starts with a series of stills of Parisian rooftops, then a 360 degree panoramic shot that records night falling on the city's varied skyline. As the sun goes down, windows light up and the camera scrutinises the facades as if in search of a subject. It seems to find the film's central protagonist almost by chance, settling on Laure's window only after having hinted at the vertiginous choice of stories that the city contains. The repository of an endless number of tales, the city also provides both the space and the temporal vacuum in which the fiction grows: a transport strike that generates a gigantic traffic jam. Bernheim was inspired by a real event, the strike of 1995, which provoked a transport paralysis of almost mythical dimensions and completely disrupted the lives of Parisians:

> La grève des transports qui a paralysé Paris en 1995 m'a donné le maillon qui manquait pour lancer l'histoire. Et je me suis mise à l'écrire, comme ça, 'librement', sans intrigue, sans filet ... C'était la première fois qu'il m'arrivait d'être dans le même état de liberté qu'un personnage, de ne pas savoir où j'allais, ni où tout cela allait me mener. Je pouvais, comme elle, à chaque carrefour, emprunter une voie ou une autre. [61] (Bernheim 2002)

The multiplication of potential stories evoked by the opening sequences thus reverberates in Laure's trajectory. The character, having taken a life-changing decision, is left momentarily in a kind of limbo, in between two spaces (her flat and that of her boyfriend) and two lives (the single woman's life and the established life of the couple). The banality of the situation is offset by the lyrical portrayal of an evening that turns out to be a leap into the unknown. As Laure gets stuck into the traffic jam, the standstill becomes metaphorical as well

---

61 'The transport strike, which brought Paris to a standstill in 1995, provided me with the link that had been missing in order to launch the story. I started to write, like that, "freely", without a plot, without safeguards ... It was the first time that I was in the same state of freedom as the character, not knowing where I was going and where I would end up. At each crossroads I could, like her, choose this or that direction.'

as practical and suddenly expands into a time and space of unforeseen potentials – a suspended interval, a parenthesis in which the character finds an unexpected moment of reprieve and freedom.

An alternation of tempos and a series of 'false starts' thus punctuate the beginning of the film. The camera documents the traffic jam in long still takes joined by dissolves and slow travelling shots. From behind car windows, faces appear, move past and reappear, by virtue of the cars' sporadic and almost imperceptible progression. Frustrated expressions, vacant gazes, and the faces of sleeping passengers are collated or superimposed with images of a strangely deserted metro station or of the light refracted on the drops of water on a windscreen. These shots may evoke the opening sequence of Fellini's *8 1/2* (1963) but remain devoid of its nightmarish connotations: Laure's car is not a trap but a shelter. Within its exiguous space, the camera catches the young woman's gestures in close-up as she switches on the heat, then uses the fan to dry her hair still wet from the bath, and is gradually overcome by the warmth and drowsiness. Disrupting the slow, dream-like atmosphere of this opening, the first acceleration and 'false start' occurs when a hand suddenly knocks on Laure's car window. Of this man we only see a subjective glimpse, a fragmented and obscure silhouette whose intrusive and impromptu presence frightens Laure. She locks all her doors and only realises her mistake once she has switched on the radio: because of the cold, commuters deprived of means of transport may have to seek refuge with unknown drivers. The camera then catches the silhouette of a young man crossing the street in amongst the mass of cars. The viewer who recognises Grégoire Colin may pre-empt the beginning of a fiction from the presence of an actor and type of character familiar in Denis' story worlds. But the young man declines Laure's offer of a temporary shelter and disappears in the dark. The third false start occurs when Jean first comes into sight, preceded by a humorous shot of a neon shop sign in the shape of glasses. Caught in a medium shot as he progresses between the vehicles, Jean seems to be looking at the cars in search of something or someone. A series of images linked by dissolves then depicts one of the drivers, a beautiful young woman with blond hair and a mysterious smile. But the blond archetype belongs to a different story: it is to Laure's window that the man stoops to ask if he can come in.

Dès lors s'installe cette 'hâte lente' (dixit Claire Denis) qui est le tempo
de Jean et Laure et qui devient celui, fascinant, de *Vendredi soir*. Il y a
toujours une part d'expérimentation dans les films de Claire Denis.
Ici: jusqu'où aller trop loin dans le presque rien romanesque.[62]
(Loiseau 2002: 73)

The camera rarely leaves the main characters and since the film fits
within a restricted stretch of time, it generates an overall feeling of
real time. Yet the ruling temporal principle is that of a city that evokes
a gigantic body temporarily fallen into paralysis. The filmmaking
activates an array of techniques – slow motion, travelling shots, depth
or absence of depth of field, dissolves – that imbue its atmosphere
with an impression of timelessness and a dream-like feel. The music
written by Tindesticks' Dickon Hinchliffe, alternating between the
minimal and lyrical, stresses the fragile and otherworldly quality of
the moment and fills the space with expectation. Against this background, the filmmaking playfully sets out to explore the more circum-
scribed variations of rhythm and moods that reflect the characters'
own momentum and hesitations. Denis combined Hinchliffe's compositions with an array of highly contrasting musical pieces in order
to mark these changes, to outline the narrative's leaps forward or
slow-downs as the characters give in to the pull of desire, or, on the
contrary, resist the attraction of the unknown. Before Laure chooses
to follow her desire, for instance, a brutal change of rhythm vividly
evokes the irruption of a feeling of panic. Once Jean has taken his
place in Laure's car, a series of impressions and brief exchanges, and
an insert with a short fantasy scenario introduced by an iris, are
woven together to suggest a developing attraction between the two
characters. Laure decides to phone her friends to cancel dinner and
leaves the car in search of a phone box. When she joins him again,
Jean has moved into the driver's seat and taken the wheel. The tempo
suddenly increases, reflecting Laure's feeling of losing control.
Accompanied by the strident sound of violins, the flow of image
accelerates to the point where, through fast-paced travelling shots
punctuated by abrupt cuts, glimpsed images of facades and neon
signs seem to merge and become abstract. Jean eventually stops the

62 'From then on rules this 'slow haste' that is Jean and Laure's tempo, and also
becomes *Vendredi soir*'s enthralling tempo. There is always something of the
experiment in Denis' films. In this case: how to go too far in this almost non-
existent story.'

car and leaves. The following sequence is like the eye of the storm, a temporary slow-down of rhythm before the tempo picks up again, as Laure goes in search of her mysterious passenger. From then on, the rhythm follows the rule of an assumed desire: the time before and between each embrace is a time of expectation, made up of minute rituals and preparations to while away the wait.

With their dream-like music and sweeping long shots, the opening sequences recall the lyricism of the city symphonies (Chapter 1). They form a distant echo of Wim Wenders' *Wings of Desire* or even of Dziga Vertov's *Man with a camera* (1929), which *Vendredi soir*'s play on optical devices and brief animation sequence also brings to mind. Like *J'ai pas Sommeil* and *Trouble Every Day*, *Vendredi soir* is partly a homage to and a poetic variation on Paris, taking up anew the challenge that such a worn subject, 'ce déjà-vu de la poésie urbaine' ('this *déjà-vu* of urban poetry) (Péron 2002), nocturnal Paris, represents. Rekindling a long-lasting cinematic tradition that generated classic images of the capital as well as a number of enduring stereotypes, Denis combines this with a strategy already explored in her previous films. She superimposes the banal and the dream-like, the physical reality of the context and the de-familiarising effect of the filmmaking process itself: 'J'ai besoin de comprendre la réalité de l'espace que nous allons filmer. Je tenais à filmer des embouteillages, dans les rues, la nuit, par le froid de l'hiver' ('I need to understand the reality of the space we are going to film. I was determined to film traffic jams, in the streets, at night, in the winter cold') (Guilloux 2002). After Laure and Jean's first kiss – an extended sequence filmed in close-up by a camera that seems to wrap itself around the couple – the city seems to shape itself in the image of the lovers' perception. 'La ville disparaît autour du baiser. Il ne reste plus qu'un lampadaire, un bout d'asphalte, un néon' (Péron 2002) ('The city disappears around the couple kissing. Only a street lamp, a fragment of asphalt, a neon light remain.').

Giles Deleuze repeatedly stressed the important role of everyday banality in cinema's ability to superimpose the real and the imaginary. Paradoxically, because of the almost automatic acceptance of the familiar, only the slightest disturbance is necessary for the dream or nightmare dimension that lies just beneath its surface to emerge (Deleuze 1994: 3). Each of the spaces involved in *Vendredi soir*, from the city and its streets to the interior of the car, the hotel rooms, and the restaurant has a concrete presence and corresponds to an often perfectly mundane reality. But they are also metaphorical spaces that the *mise en scène* and camerawork imbue, sometimes almost imperceptibly, with a specific significance and a certain strangeness. Here, the strategies of image composition discussed earlier – the habit of de-centering the subject to leave empty spaces or focus on the unexpected – applies simultaneously to the visual treatment and to the narrative process itself:

> L'art de Claire Denis, dans sa précision digressive, fait glisser le centre du sujet (un coup de foudre) vers le bas du cadre et remplit l'espace libéré d'une profusion de détails d'ambiances, de signes mystérieux, de sons. Les images glissent idéalement les unes sur les autres, la musique les traverse de part en part.[63] (Péron 2002)

Even the quietest of streets appears full of signs at once enigmatic and imperative. Letters and numbers come to life, the giant neon spectacles of the opticians' window seems to blink ominously in the night, shop signs switch on and off. Strange apparitions also punctuate the film, as when a tall woman in red coat and glasses walking in the middle of a deserted road is caught by the beam of the car's headlights like a moth. The series of hotel rooms that Laure explores while Jean is asleep appear all alike in the unremarkable ugliness of their decoration, their cheap furniture, lurid bed covers and grim wallpaper. Yet in their silence, emptiness and interchangeability they become so many spaces for other stories. The restaurant, with its mock Italian ornamentation, turns into a small theatre, where brief scenarios of jealousy are played out and abandoned. Even Laure's automobile, caught in the midst of an immobilised sea of stranded cars like a small island, becomes a changeable microcosm that transforms into a beauty parlour or a reading room. After using the car heating system as a hair drier, the young woman switches on the radio and like a spectator at a drive-in, contemplates the number plate of the car in front of her. Resigned to a long wait, she finally switches on the interior light and turns around to inspect the pile of unwanted items that she took out of her flat to dispose of. She opens one of the boxes, and a series of books with worn covers start to clutter the inside of the car.

63 'Claire Denis' art, in its digressive precision, lets the subject (love at first sight) slide towards the bottom of the frame, and fills the free space with a profusion of atmospheric details, mysterious signs, and sounds. The images glide over each other perfectly and the music passes right through.'

At the end of the film, Laure emerges from the night as from an enchanted realm to be pulled back to the space and time of normality. Her first gesture is to look for her watch. Earlier, while he was asleep, she had put on Jean's coat and socks, but she now slips on her own clothes as if slipping back into her usual skin. As she leaves the hotel in the low light of the winter morning, the soundtrack remains completely silent. A series of backtracking travelling shots show her running in different directions. It is the reappearance of the neon spectacles which, like a visual punctuation, provides the first familiar sign, leading back to the Paris that she knows. The diegetic sound then returns, and Laure continues to run, but in slow motion, as if progressively reinscribing her body within the familiar logic of a known reality. Yet, as the young woman's wistful smile suggests, she does not so much leave behind her as carry away the experience of the past night.

Bodies, sensations and subjectivity

As is customary in Denis' approach, with its sparse dialogue and its rejection of the voiceover, this film abandons the kind of conventional sociological and psychological definition associated with the traditional characters of literature and film (Chapter 1). We know virtually nothing about *Vendredi soir*'s protagonists. Jean and Laure share little information with the viewer and with each other: they merely exchange their first names. A few signs dotted around the flat allow us to guess that Laure is a middle-class, educated woman with a regular life and maybe a few idiosyncrasies. Some of her well-packed boxes have been marked out to be given away to her mother. A note accompanying a set of keys suggests the existence of a boyfriend, and a later phone call confirms that Laure will move in with him. The young woman also seems to have a liking for books and for quaint lampshades. The casting of Valérie Lemercier further confuses expectations. Denis chose an actress who built her fame primarily in the comedy genre. Lemercier is known for her wordy performances, and for impersonations that occasionally hinge on the caricature. In *Vendredi soir*, however, she gives an understated, impressionistic performance, portraying a discreet and predominantly silent character. Of Jean, we know even less, and the mystery that shrouds him allows the character to become an object of fantasy. It is this aspect, and the reversal it implies – since the fantasy figure usually associated with femininity is this time grounded in the male character – that first attracted Vincent Lindon:

> Ce qui m'a intéressé, c'est d'être l'objet du désir d'une femme, d'incarner le fantasme, d'être l'instrument de ce film, rien de plus. C'est très intéressant de travailler un personnage en évacuant toutes les questions du genre 'd'où vient-il? A-t-il des enfants? Est-il marié?' etc.[64] (Campion: 2002)

Released from those preconceptions that conventionally aim to inflect the appraisal of a potential viewer, *Vendredi soir*'s characters fit in the modernist tradition. They are never reduced, however, to a disincarnated or objectified presence. On the one hand, the tactile gaze of the camera establishes an intimacy with them as physical beings. On the other hand, the film weaves around them a subjective world of sensory affects with which the viewer can identify or empathise.

In conventional film language, fragmented images of the body tend to be used to (sexually) objectify a character or to stress a gesture that is crucial to the progression of the plot.[65] But in *Vendredi soir*, this fragmentation, often dictated by the configuration of the space, participates essentially in the progressive invocation of the bodies. The camera tends to focus on unexpected details. In close-up, it follows the outline of a neck, the shape of a thigh under a tight skirt, the movement of a mass of hair in front of a fan. In turn, the fragment becomes a sensory extension, the close-up a focalisation on a particular sensation. The rough texture of the hotel room carpeted floor is evoked by the sight of Laure's bare feet. Similarly, the shyness and impatience of the first embrace, like the contrast between cold air and warm skin, is encapsulated in the images of hands slipping under the thick layers of winter clothes.

Not only does the camerawork render the bodily presence of the characters close and familiar, but it reinscribes them in the specific spatiality of the film. In effect, the characters' and spectators' restricted visual field is also that of the gaze of the camera determined by the

64 'I was interested in being the object of a woman's desire, to incarnate a fantasy, to be the tool of the fiction, and nothing more. It is very interesting to work on a character when questions like 'Where does he come from? Does he have children? Is he married?', etc., have been disposed of.'

65 In the first case, a female body reduced to close-up shots of breasts or legs for instance. An example of the second case would be a close-up on a hand grabbing a gun just before a murder scene.

conditions of filming. Denis recounts that, at times, Godard and herself 'avaient aussi l'impression de vivre une histoire d'amour. A la fin, nous connaissions même le grain de leur peau' ('also had the impression of living through a love story. In the end, we knew the very texture of their skin') (Denis 2002). The exiguity of the car space for instance, dictates the characters' perception as well as the *mise en scène* of their mutual attraction:

> Je ne voulais pas qu'on découpe une voiture pour mieux en filmer l'intérieur. Nous nous sommes donc retrouvés à quatre, Valérie, Vincent, Agnès Godard et moi, dans cet espace exigu. La question de changer de style ne s'est pas posée: nous étions contraints par cet espace qui amène de lui-même à cette chose bizarre de s'épier du coin de l'œil, comme quand on ne connaît pas quelqu'un. On n'ose pas le regarder en face. Il faut attendre la moitié du film pour qu'ils se voient de front pour la première fois.[66] (Guilloux 2002)

Like the characters, the viewer thus builds up an impression based on visual fragments, but also on sensations vividly evoked through the process of correspondences and de-positioning already described in relation to *Nénette et Boni*. When Jean slips into Laure's car for example, since the gaze of the camera originates from the back seat, the point of view is not that of the young woman. The spectator is thus offered an ambiguous position. Part voyeur – observing the characters as if hidden behind them – through the evocative sensations that the images generate, the viewer is nevertheless invited to sense or identify with the young woman's subjective perception, and with the instant attraction that the man's presence creates. The camera films Jean at close range, capturing images and sounds[67] that are evocative of smells, of textures, volumes, and even densities – the outline of his profile, his ear, his sturdy hands as he lights a cigarette, but also the open neck of his shirt under a leather jacket that makes rich creaking

66 'I did not want to cut up a car in order to film its interior more easily. The four of us, Valérie, Vincent, Agnès Godard, and myself, thus found ourselves in this exiguous space. The question of changing the style was never considered. It was determined by this space that by itself generates this strange behaviour where you spy on each other from the corner of your eye as if you did not know each other, did not dare to look at each other frontally. You have to wait till the middle of the film before they look at each other face to face.'

67 Denis had the opportunity to mix the sound with a SR surround system that recreates a rich and textured sound and generates a heightened feeling of being enveloped in it (Péron, 2002).

noises as he settles in the seat. Denis stressed the importance of transla-
ting these sensations as vividly as in Bernheim's writing: 'Emmanuèle
Bernheim a bien décrit ce poids, cet espace occupé par l'homme qui
entre dans la voiture. Alors, il fallait qu'on le sente dans le film, ce
n'était pas une idée d'homme, c'est un homme qui a du poids'
('Emmanuèle Bernheim has described this well, the weight, the space
occupied by the man who enters the car. So it needed to be felt in the
film that it was not an idea of man, but a physical presence with a
weight') (Denis 2002). Similarly, Bernheim acknowledged Denis'
ability to activate cinema's power of evocation: 'A la première seconde
où il rentre dans la voiture, il sent bon. On a quasiment l'impression
de sentir son odeur, c'est exactement ce que j'avais essayé de décrire
dans le livre' ('As soon as he enters the car, he smells good. You
almost feel like you are smelling him, exactly as I tried to describe it in
my book') (Bernheim: 2002). In effect, as in *Nénette et Boni* and
Trouble Every Day, in *Vendredi soir* the characters' physical presence
imprints itself in the reality around them and seems to linger on after
they depart. Laure's body leaves a dent on the mattress in which she
playfully bounces at the beginning of the film. Jean leaves the smell of
his body, of his aftershave and cigarettes in Laure's car. She touches
the wheel to feel the warmth of his hands, sits in the seat shaped by
the weight of his body. But the memory and imprint of the Other's
body carries an element of threat. Laure suddenly withdraws when
she feels Jean's teeth closing on the skin of her shoulder. This
instinctive reaction of defence recalls *Trouble Every Day*'s evocation of
desire's darker dimension. In Laure's case, however, it is also a
reminder of the proximity of her 'other' life, a reality where she
cannot afford to carry the visible memory of the embrace.

Without recourse to a voiceover and with hardly any dialogue, the
film thus constructs a vivid sensory world and a web of mental
representations where the female character's subjective experience is
evoked in all its variations – her attraction towards the unknown, her
hesitations and determination, then her pleasure and renewed desire.
Yann Tobin stressed this subjective dimension of the film which calls
to mind 'l'émerveillement des premiers théoriciens du septième art,
se rendant compte à quel point le cinéma était une "machine à lire les
pensées"' ('the wonder of the early theoreticians of the seventh art,
who realised the extent to which cinema was a "thought-reading
machine"') (Tobin 2002: 39).

The exploration of the thematic of desire and sexuality, initiated with *US Go Home* and *Nénette et Boni*, and pursued in *Trouble Every Day*, drove Denis further away from conventional models, towards the reinvention of a cinema of the senses most explicitly celebrated in *Vendredi soir*. *Vendredi soir* thus draws on an alternative and curiously hybrid cinematic lineage. Although it is a book adaptation, it is one that draws on the principles of modern fiction. Hence, in spite of its literary source, *Vendredi soir* relates back to the early avant-garde's claim for a cinema freed from the weight of the nineteenth-century novelistic models with their narrative conventions, their moral determinism, their psychological approach to characterisation. A film like *Vendredi soir* seems to revive an original drive towards a film-making that would rely on the wide range of cinematic techniques to explore hidden dimensions of reality. As Tobin's mention of a 'thought-reading machine' reminds us, Denis' filmmaking implies a return to the sources of cinema's specific powers of evocation. The film also summons forth a mixture of significant connections in the context of contemporary cinema, however. Formally and thematically it spurred comparisons with recent trends in Asian cinema. Indeed, its topic, minimal plot line and stylisation bear similarities to those of a film like Wong Kar-Wai's *In The Mood For Love* (2000). More generally, the loosening of the film's structure (of its overall organisation in shots, scenes and sequences) in favour of an impressionistic approach is the mark of a cinema born after the emergence of the small D.V. cameras, and imbued with the freedom generated by these devices. Frodon, however, links *Vendredi soir*'s stylistic inventiveness with the influential aesthetics of kung-fu cinema. At the same time, his analysis of Denis' reworking of the status of the shot calls to mind a familiar theoretical framework: his remarks echo both Deleuze's contrasting of a 'time cinema' to a 'movement cinema' (Chapter 1), and Eisenstein's theories on the combination of images.[68] Denis' filmmaking, Frodon argues,

68 Frodon talks of the *mise en scène* of the shots rather than of their editing together, yet his description of the effect of combining the images recalls Sergei Eisenstein's reflections on the subject. In a seminal series of studies, the Soviet avant-garde director compared cinema's production of meaning to ideograms, where combinations of images create a meaning that exceeds the images' individual content. Eisenstein's argument was inspired by Japanese writing where, for instance, the association of the ideogram (a graphic sign, not a word)

offre l'un des plus beaux exemples de cette esthétique nouvelle qui, inspirée surtout des films de kung-fu, travaille le cinéma contemporain en modifiant radicalement le statut du plan. Celui-ci n'est plus l'unité narrative et plastique avec laquelle se construisent les séquences qui composent l'ensemble du film. Du plan bloc on passe au plan touche, ou au plan trait, signe visuel dont seul l'assemblage à d'autres signes suscitera une recomposition mentale, productrice d'émotion et de sens.[69] (Frodon 2002)

Some of the images in the film are almost abstract, depicting a movement, a gesture, a colour and a texture – they capture the variation of intensity of a light, a fragment of reality. The film, however, weaves them together to construct a rhythm and an atmosphere, a 'state of mind'. The practice of establishing correspondences – where the visual and the aural evoke taste, smell, touch and emotions – is inscribed in this approach where the process of composition applies not so much to individual shots as to the film as a whole. While he celebrates the originality of the stylistic approach, Frodon, however, makes a crucial distinction between Denis' films and experimental cinema proper. Part of the openness of Denis' cinema comes from the ability not to reduce 'people and their lives to graphic elements amongst others' but to invoke fully-fledged characters that inhabit a complex and sensual reality: 'ce qui différencie *Vendredi soir* du cinéma expérimental, même le plus beau et le plus inventif: son humanité' ('the difference between *Vendredi soir* and even the most beautiful and inventive of experimental cinema: its humanity') (Frodon 2002).

---

for 'eye' with the sign for 'water' created the additional meaning 'to cry'. (*Film Form*, reprinted in G. Mast, M. Cohen and L Braudy (eds), *Film Theory and Criticism: Introductory Readings*, Oxford, Oxford University Press, 1992, pp. 127–38.

69 'provides one of the best examples of this new aesthetics, which is inspired in particular by kung-fu films, and impregnates contemporary cinema by radically modifying the status of the shot. The shot ceases to be the narrative and plastic unit with which the sequences that compose the film as a whole are built. The shot as unit becomes the shot as stroke or line, a visual sign that, only through its combination with other signs, will call forth a mental recomposition producing emotions and meaning.'

References

Ariès Philippe (1983), *The Horror of Our Death*, trans. Helen Weaver, Harmondsworth, Penguin.

Baudelaire, Charles (1976), 'Richard Wagner and Tannhauser in Paris', *La Revue Européenne*, Paris, E. Dentu, 1861, reprinted in *Charles Baudelaire, Œuvres complètes*, Paris, Gallimard.

Bernheim Emmanuèle (2002), Interview, *Dossier de presse du film 'Vendredi soir'*, Paris, Bac distribution.

Barthes, Roland (1957), *Mythologies*, Paris, Editions du Seuil.

Bataille, Georges (1957), *Erotisme*, Paris, 10/18.

Bataille, Georges (1961), *Les Larmes d'Eros*, Paris, Pauvert.

Baudelaire, Charles (1976), *Œuvres complètes*, Paris, Gallimard.

Beugnet, Martine (2000), *Sexualité, marginalité, contrôle – cinéma français contemporain*, Paris, L'Harmattan.

Beugnet, Martine (2001), 'Le Souci de l'Autre – Nouveau réalisme et critique sociale dans le cinéma français contemporain', *Iris* 29, 53–7.

Beugnet, Martine (2003), 'French Cinema of the Margins', in Elizabeth Ezra (ed.), *European Cinema*, Oxford, Oxford University Press.

Blüher Dominique (2001), 'Histoire de raconter: décentrement élision et fragmentation dans *Nénette et Boni, La Vie de Jésus, Fin août début septembre* et *Peau Neuve, Iris* 29, 11–24.

Bonitzer, Pascal (2001), 'Décadrages', first published in *Cahiers du cinéma*, 284, 1978, reprinted in *Théories du cinéma*, Paris, Cahiers du cinéma, 123–33.

Bonnaud, Frédéric (2001), 'Tendre est la nuit', *Les Inrockuptibles*, 3 July, 38–9.

Boss, Pete (1986), 'Vile Bodies and Bad Medicine', *Screen* 27:1, 14–26.

Cadé, Michel (1999), 'Du Côté des banlieues', *CinémAction* 91, 172–80.

Campion, Alexis (2002), 'Vendredi soir', *Le Journal du Dimanche*, 8 September.

Chauvin, Jean-Sébastien (2001), 'Au-delà des genres', *Cahiers du cinéma* 559, 77–8.

Chauvin Jean-Sébastien (2002), 'Panne des sens', *Cahiers du cinéma* 571, 80–1.

Creed, Barbara (1986), 'Horror and the Monstruous-Feminine: An Imaginary Abjection', *Screen* 27:1, 44–70.

Deleuze, Gilles (1994), *Cinema 2: L'Image-temps*, Paris, Editions de Minuit, 1985, reprinted as *Cinema 2: The Time-Image*, trans. H. Tomlinson and R. Galeta, London, The Athlone Press.

Denis, Claire (2002), *Dossier de presse du film 'Vendredi soir'*, Paris, Bac distribution.

Denorme, Vincent and Douin, Emmanuel (2001), 'Travelling Light', *Modam* 1, 20–7.

Fanon, Frantz (1986), *Black Skin, White Masks*, trans. Lam Markmann, London, Pluto Press.

Fisher, Lucy (1991), 'Sometimes I Feel like a Motherless Child: Comedy and Matricide', in Andrew Horton (ed.), *Comedy/Cinema/Theory*, Berkeley and Los Angeles, University of California Press, pp. 60–78.

Foucault, Michel (1982), *Discipline and Punish*, trans. Alan Sheridan, Harmondsworth, Peregrine.

Frodon, Jean-Michel (2001), 'Trouble Every Day', *Le Monde*, 11 July.

Frodon, Jean-Michel (2002), 'Songe érotique d'une nuit de grève des transports', *Le Monde* 11 September 2002.

Frois, Emmanuelle (2001), 'Trouble Every Day', *Le Figaro*, 11 July.

Garbarz, Franck (1997), 'Mère, pourquoi nous as-tu abandonnés?', *Positif* 432, 38–9.

Godin, Marc (1999), *Gore, autopsie d'un cinéma*, Paris, Editions du collectionneur.

Guichard, Louis (2001), 'Trouble Every Day', *Télérama*, 11 July, 36.

Guilloux, Michel (1997), 'Claire Denis: de l'amour est passé', *L'Humanité*, 29 January.

Guilloux, Michel (2002), 'Entretien avec Claire Denis', *L'Humanité*, 14 September.

Kaganski, Serge (2002), 'Toute une nuit', *Les Inrockuptibles*, 10 September.

Kaganski, Serge and Bonnaud, Frédéric (2001), *Les Inrockuptibles*, 3 July, 32–5.

Kristeva, Julia (1982), *The Powers of Horror: An essay on Abjection*, trans. Léon S. Roudiez, New York, Columbia University Press.

Lacan, Jacques (1953) 'Some Reflections on the Ego', *The International Journal of Psychoanalysis* 24, 11–17.

Lalanne, Jean-Marc (2001), 'Trouble Every Day', *Libération*, 11 July.

Loiseau, Jean-Claude (2002), 'Vendredi soir', *Télérama*, 11 Septembre, 72–3.

Modleski, Tania (1988), 'Three Men and Baby M', *Camera Obscura* 17, 69–81.

Morice, Jacques (2001), 'Trouble Every Day', *Télérama*, 11 July.

Péron, Didier (2001), 'Trouble Every Day', *Libération*, 11 July.

Péron, Didier (2002), 'Dans de beaux draps', *Libération*, 11 September.

Powrie, Phil (1997), *French Cinema in the 1980s*, Oxford: Oxford University Press.

Strauss, Frédéric (1997), 'Miam-miam', *Cahiers du cinéma*, 510, 64–5.

Tinazzi, Noël (2001), 'Trouble Every Day', *La Tribune*, 11 July.

Tobin, Yann (2002), 'Vendredi soir: redécouvertes', *Positif*, 499, 38–9.

Vincendeau, Ginette (1988), 'Daddy's Girl: Oedipal Narratives in 1930s French Films', *Iris* 8, 70–81.

Wilson, Emma (2001), 'Deforming Femininity: Catherine Breillat's *Romance*', in Lucy Mazdon (ed.), *France on Film*, London, Wallfower Press, pp. 145–58.

Conclusion

While most directors blessed by a successful début choose to follow the safe path and to attempt to meet their audiences' expectations, Claire Denis' work has remained in constant mutation, offering, within a coherent thematic framework, a renewed exploration of film's less charted territories. The examination of the issues that are at the centre of her concerns – exile and alienation, desire and transgression – have become an intrinsic part of a specific stylistic approach, unrestricted by categorisations, genres and established conventions. Working in a team with a set of long-standing collaborators, technicians and actors, Denis creates hybrid works that draw on literature as well as dance, music, photography and painting – films that rely on the power of images and sound in themselves rather than on tightly scripted narratives. Hence, paradoxically, crossing over to other art forms is one means to rediscover and reactivate forgotten powers of evocation that are unique to cinema. Whether they are concerned with racial tensions, with teenage angst, or with brief encounters between strangers, her films never take the form of demonstrations and never privilege a pre-existing screenplay over the actual act of filming. In place of plot-driven narratives and explanatory discourses, they strive to offer a vision specific to film, interpretative and analytical, but also eminently sensual. As a result, Denis' work stands apart from a tradition of screenplay and dialogue-based cinema that defines much of France's *auteur* as well as of its popular production.

Denis' career developed in the context of a French cinema increasingly dominated by a mainstream production of historical dramas, comedies and action films *à la française* that tend to overlay stereotypical national traits onto the international conventions of established genres. In contrast, such a body of work as Denis' testifies to a rare ability to go beyond pastiche, nostalgia and repetition to embrace pluralism and fragmentation and the thematic and stylistic potentials of a cinema of differences. In this way, Denis also distances herself from the dominant American models. Her choice of characters and themes as well as her *mise en scène* always privilege ambiguity and mystery over simplistic moral and genre precepts. In effect, in its denial of a clear-cut distinction between good and evil (where evil is always an Other), her work reveals a strong sense of ethics as well as an acute sensitivity to the fluctuations that affect the world around her. Her films may not fit in with the established trends of today's Western cinema, but they are nonetheless always engaged and abreast of their time.

One finds, in Denis' work, the echo of a wide range of contemporary thought and the traces of influential aesthetic and genre models, but also a vivid awareness of the physical and historical environment in which they are shot. In effect, the director has repeatedly dismissed comparisons of her filmmaking to stylistic exercises, insisting that for her formal experimentation is neither a means to draw attention to the surface of things, nor a strategy to restrict the process of representation to a play of signifiers. In her own words, to make a film is 'une plongée à travers une construction esthétique, vers un domaine plus profond, plus mystérieux' ('to plunge through an aesthetic construct, towards a more profound, more mysterious dimension') (Frodon, 2001). Hence, another paradox of Denis' work lies with its ability to hold in tension the modernity of cinema with the lyricism of the romantic and novelistic traditions: no matter how stylised the approach, her story worlds and characters never take the form of disembodied entities. On the contrary, drawing their appeal precisely from that irreducible element of mystery that they evoke, her stories offer a deeply affecting and sensual viewing experience. Jean-Sébastien Chauvin thus outlines the way in which Denis summons a variety of representational strategies in order to infer the part of the unknown that is hidden behind the surface of things:

> Ces logiques (infiltration des genres, union des contraires, répercussions invisibles de traces anciennes) concourent au sentiment de choses derrière les choses et d'une ténuité du réel.[1] (Chauvin, 2001: 78)

Denis' films are open to controversy. On occasion, critics have described her cinema as contrived and demanding. Yet few would deny the haunting quality of her images. To watch one of Denis' films and let oneself be drawn and bewitched by the rhythm, the atmosphere, and the sensuality of her filmmaking is to rediscover cinema's most essential prerogative: the capacity to infuse even the most banal of situations with magic, the power to re-enchant reality.

References

Chauvin, Jean-Sébastien (2001), 'Au-delà des genres', *Cahiers du cinéma* 559, 77–8.
Frodon, Jean-Michel (2001), 'Il s'agit de s'aventurer au-devant d'une forme', *Le Monde*, 11 July.

1 'This logic (genre infiltration, union of opposites, invisible repercussions of ancient traces) contributes to creating a feeling for that which lies behind, and for the tenuous nature of the real.'

Filmography

Chocolat (1988) 105 min., 35 mm, col.

Production: Cinémanuel, MK2 Production
Screenplay: Claire Denis, Jean-Pol Fargeau
Camera: Robert Alazraki
Editing: Claudine Merlin
Sound: Jean-Louis Ughetto, Dominique Hennequin
Music: Abdullah Ibrahim
Cast: Isaach de Bankolé, Giulia Boschi, François Cluzet, Mireille Perrier, Cécile Ducasse

Man No Run (1989) 90 min., 35 mm, col.

Production: Casa Films
Camera: Pascal Marti, Jean-Bernard Menoud
Editing: Dominique Auvray
Sound: Daniel Ollivier, Georges Prat
Music: Les Têtes Brûlées

S'en fout la mort (1990) 91 min., 35 mm, col.

Production: Cinéa, Pyramide, Les Films du Mindif, Caméra One, La Sept
Screenplay: Claire Denis, Jean-Pol Fargeau
Camera: Pascal Marti
Editing: Dominique Auvray
Sound: Jean-Pol Mugel, Alix Comte
Music: Abdulah Ibrahim
Cast: Isaach de Bankolé, Alex Descas, Jean-Claude Brialy, Solveig Dommartin, Christopher Buchholz

Jacques Rivette, le veilleur (1990) 124 min., video, col.

Production: La Sept, Amip, Art Production
Camera: Agnès Godard
Editing: Dominique Auvray, Jean Dubreil
Sound: Jean-Pierre Laforce, Henry Malkoff

Keep It For Yourself (1991) 40 min., 35 mm, b/w.

Production: Allarts, Good Machine Inc
Screenplay: Claire Denis
Camera: Agnès Godard
Editing: Dominique Auvray
Music: John Lurie
Cast: Sophie Simon, E. J. Rodriguez, Jim Stark, Vincent Gallo

Contre l'oubli (Ushari Ahmed Mahmood) (1991) 4 min., 35 mm, col.

Production: Amnesty International, Films du Paradoxe, PRV
Music: Alain Soùchon

La Robe à cerceau (1992) 24 min., vidéo, b/w.

Production: Sophie Goupil, Le Poisson Volant
Screenplay: Jacques Nolot
Camera: Agnès Godard
Editing: Nelly Quettier
Sound: Jean-Louis Ughetto
Music: Brice Leboucq
Cast: Dani, Jacques Nolot

J'ai pas sommeil (1993) 110 min., 35 mm, col.

Production: Arena Films, Orsans Productions, Pyramide, Vega Films, Les
Films du Mindif , France 3 cinéma, M6 Films
Screenplay: Claire Denis, Jean-Pol Fargeau
Camera: Agnès Godard
Editing: Nelly Quettier
Sound: Jean-Louis Hughetto, Vincent Arnadi, Thierry Labon
Cast: Katerina Golubeva, Richard Courcet, Alex Descas, Line Renaud,
Vincent Dupont, Laurent Grévill

Us Go Home (1994) 68 min., 35 mm, col.

Production: IMA productions, SFP
Screenplay: Claire Denis, Anne Wiazemsky
Camera: Agnès Godard
Editing: Dominique Auvray

Sound: Hervé Chauvel, William Flageollet
Cast: Alice Houri, Grégoire Colin, Jessica Tharaud, Martine Gautier

Nice, Very Nice (1995) 10 min., 35 mm, col.

Production: François Margolin, Margo Films, La Sept Cinéma
Screenplay: Claire Denis
Camera: Agnès Godard
Editing: Nelly Quettier
Sound: Guillaume Sclama
Cast: Grégoire Colin, François Voisin, Thierry Saïd Boulbil, Jérôme
Chabreyrie

A propos d'une déclaration (1995) 2 min., video, col.

Production: Fondation Cartier pour l'art contemporain
Screenplay: Claire Denis

Duo (1995) 2 min., 35 mm, col.

Production: Konick, BBC
Screenplay: Claire Denis

Nénette et Boni (1996) 103 min., 35 mm, col.

Production: Dacia Films, La Sept Cinéma
Screenplay: Claire Denis, Jean-Pol Fargeau
Camera: Agnès Godard
Editing: Yann Dédet
Sound: Jean-Louis Ughetto
Music: Tindersticks
Cast: Grégoire Colin, Alice Houri, Valéria Bruni-Tredeschi, Vincent
Gallo

Beau travail (2000) 90 min., 35 mm, col.

Production: Tanais, SM Film, La Sept Arte
Screenplay: Claire Denis, Jean-Pol Fargeau
Camera: Agnès Godard
Editing: Nelly Quettier
Music: Eran Tzur
Sound: Jean-Paul Mugel
Cast: Denis Lavant, Grégoire Colin, Michel Subor

Trouble Every Day (2001) 102 min., 35 mm, col.

Production: Xavier Amblard, Arte, Canal+, Dacia, A Films, Kinétique, Rezo
Screenplay: Jean-Pol Fargeau, Claire Denis

Camera: Agnès Godard
Editing: Nelly Quettier
Sound: Jean-Louis Ughetto
Music: Tindersticks
Cast: Vincent Gallo, Béatrice Dalle, Tricia Vessey, Alex Descas

Vendredi soir (2002) 90 min., 35 mm, col.

Production: Bruno Pesery, Arena Films and France 2 cinéma
Screenplay: Emmanuèle Bernheim, Claire Denis
Camera: Agnès Godard
Editing: Nelly Quettier
Music: Dickon Hinchliffe
Sound: Jean-Louis Ughetto
Cast: Valérie Lemercier, Vincent Lindon

Select bibliography

Theoretical works

Deleuze, Gilles (1994), *Cinéma 2: L'Image-temps*, Paris, Editions de minuit, 1985, reprinted as *Cinema 2: The Time-Image*, trans. H. Thomlinson and R. Galeta, London, The Athlone Press.

Dyer, Richard (1990), *Now You See It: Studies on Lesbian and Gay Films*, London and New York, Routledge.

Dyer, Richard (1997), *White*, London and New York, Routledge.

Fanon, Frantz (1986), *Peau noire, masques blancs*, Paris, Editions du Seuil, 1952, reprinted as *Black Skin, White Masks*, London, Pluto Press.

Kristeva, Julia (1982), *The Powers of Horror: An Essay on Abjection*, trans. L. S. Roudiez, New York, Columbia University Press.

Kristeva, Julia (1994) *Strangers to Ourselves*, trans. L. S. Roudiez, New York, Columbia University Press.

Silverman, Max (1999), *Facing Postmodernity: Contemporary French Thought on Culture and Society*, London and New York, Routledge.

Books on French cinema

Austin, Guy (1996), *Contemporary French Cinema*, Manchester, Manchester University Press.

Beugnet, Martine (2000), *Sexualité, marginalité, contrôle: cinéma français contemporain*, Paris, L'Harmattan.

Ezra, Elizabeth and Harris, Sue (2001) (eds), *France in Focus*, Oxford and New York, Berg.

Mazdon, Lucy (2000) (ed.), *France on Film*, London, Wallflower Press.

Powrie, Phil (1999) (ed.), *French Cinema in the 1990s*, Oxford, Oxford University Press.

Tarr, Carrie with Rollet, Brigitte (2001), *Cinema and the Second Sex: Women's Filmmaking in France in the 1980s and the 1990s*, New York and London, Continuum.

Essays and articles on Claire Denis' work

Audé, Françoise (1990), 'S'en fout la vie', *Positif* 356, 71–2.

Bonnaud, Frédéric (2001), 'Tendre est la nuit', *Les Inrockuptibles*, 3 July, 38–9.

Chauvin, Jean-Sébastien (2001), 'Au-delà des genres', *Cahiers du cinéma* 559, 77–8.

Chauvin Jean-Sébastien (2002), 'Panne des sens', *Cahiers du cinéma* 571, 80–1.

Denorme, Vincent and Douin, Emmanuel (2001), 'Travelling Light', *Modam* 1, 20–7.

Hayward, Susan (2001), 'Claire Denis's Films and the Post-colonial Body', *Studies in French Cinema* 1:3, 159–65.

Lemarié, Yannick (2000), 'A Propos d'Agnès Godard', *Positif* 471, 128–30.

Lifshitz, Sébastien (1995), *Claire Denis, la Vagabonde*, 48 minute documentary, colour, prod. La Fémis.

Garbarz, Franck (1997), 'Mère, pourquoi nous as-tu abandonnés?', *Positif* 432, 38–9.

Jousse, Thierry (1994), 'Les Insomniaques', *Cahiers du cinéma* 479, 22–6

Jousse, Thierry (1988), 'Jeux Africains', *Cahiers du cinéma* 407–8, 132–3.

Marker, Cynthia (1999), 'Sleepless in Paris: *J'ai pas sommeil*', in *French Cinema in the 1990s*, ed. Phil Powrie, Oxford, Oxford University Press, pp. 137–47.

Romney, Jonathan (2000), The Guardian/NFT interview, www.filmunlimited .co.uk.

Sillars, Jane and Beugnet, Martine (2001), '*Beau travail*: Time, Space and Myths of Identity', *Studies in French Cinema* 1:3, 166–73.

Strauss, Frédéric (1990a), 'Féminin colonial', *Cahiers du cinéma* 434, 28–33

Strauss, Frédéric (1990b), 'Combat de nègres et de coqs', *Cahiers du cinéma* 435, 64–5.

Strauss, Frédéric (1997), 'Miam-miam', *Cahiers du cinéma*, 510, 64–5.

Tobin, Yann (2002), 'Vendredi soir: redécouvertes', *Positif* 499, 38–9.

Vassé, Claire (2000), '*Beau travail*: Liberté du corps', *Positif* 471, 30–1.

Index

Note: 'n.' after a page reference indicates a note number on that page.